To Geyserl[and]

Union Pacific-Oregon Short Line
Railroads to the Yellowstone National Park

Edward F. Colborn

Alpha Editions

This edition published in 2023

ISBN : 9789362091710

Design and Setting By
Alpha Editions
www.alphaedis.com
Email - info@alphaedis.com

Contents

CHAPTER I
IN WHICH I THROW AMBS-ACE

THE work of the day being over, I sat down upon my doorstep, pipe in hand, to rest awhile in the cool of the evening. Death is not more still than is this Virginian land in the hour when the sun has sunk away, and it is black beneath the trees, and the stars brighten slowly and softly, one by one. The birds that sing all day have hushed, and the horned owls, the monster frogs, and that strange and ominous fowl (if fowl it be, and not, as some assert, a spirit damned) which we English call the whippoorwill, are yet silent. Later the wolf will howl and the panther scream, but now there is no sound. The winds are laid, and the restless leaves droop and are quiet. The low lap of the water among the reeds is like the breathing of one who sleeps in his watch beside the dead.

I marked the light die from the broad bosom of the river, leaving it a dead man's hue. Awhile ago, and for many evenings, it had been crimson,—a river of blood. A week before, a great meteor had shot through the night, blood-red and bearded, drawing a slow-fading fiery trail across the heavens; and the moon had risen that same night blood-red, and upon its disk there was drawn in shadow a thing most marvelously like a scalping knife. Wherefore, the following day being Sunday, good Mr. Stockham, our minister at Weyanoke, exhorted us to be on our guard, and in his prayer besought that no sedition or rebellion might raise its head amongst the Indian subjects of the Lord's anointed. Afterward, in the churchyard, between the services, the more timorous began to tell of divers portents which they had observed, and to recount old tales of how the savages distressed us in the Starving Time. The bolder spirits laughed them to scorn, but the women began to weep and cower, and I, though I laughed too, thought of Smith, and how he ever held the savages, and more especially that Opechancanough who was now their emperor, in a most deep distrust; telling us that the red men watched while we slept, that they might teach wiliness to a Jesuit, and how to bide its time to a cat crouched before a mousehole. I thought of the terms we now kept with these heathen; of how they came and went familiarly amongst us, spying out our weakness, and losing the salutary awe which that noblest captain had struck into their souls; of how many were employed as hunters to bring down deer for lazy masters; of how, breaking the law, and that not secretly, we gave them knives and arms, a soldier's bread, in exchange for pelts and pearls; of how their emperor was forever sending us smooth messages; of how their lips smiled and their eyes frowned. That afternoon, as I rode home through the lengthening shadows, a hunter, red-brown and naked, rose from behind a fallen tree that sprawled across my path, and made offer to bring me my meat from the moon of corn to the moon of stags in exchange for a gun. There was scant love between the savages and myself,—it was answer enough when I told him my name. I left the dark figure standing, still as a carved stone, in the heavy shadow of the trees, and, spurring my horse (sent me from home, the year before, by my cousin Percy), was soon at my house,—a poor and rude one, but pleasantly set upon a slope of green turf, and girt with maize and the broad leaves of the tobacco. When I had had my supper, I called from their hut the two Paspahegh lads bought by me from their tribe the Michaelmas before, and soundly flogged them both, having in my mind a saying of my ancient captain's, namely, "He who strikes first oft-times strikes last."

Upon the afternoon of which I now speak, in the midsummer of the year of grace 1621, as I sat upon my doorstep, my long pipe between my teeth and my eyes upon the pallid stream below, my thoughts were busy with these matters,—so busy that I did not see a horse and rider emerge from the dimness of the forest into the cleared space before my palisade, nor knew, until his voice came up the bank, that my good friend, Master John Rolfe, was without and would speak to me.

I went down to the gate, and, unbarring it, gave him my hand and led the horse within the inclosure.

"Thou careful man!" he said, with a laugh, as he dismounted. "Who else, think you, in this or any other hundred, now bars his gate when the sun goes down?"

"It is my sunset gun," I answered briefly, fastening his horse as I spoke.

He put his arm about my shoulder, for we were old friends, and together we went up the green bank to the house, and, when I had brought him a pipe, sat down side by side upon the doorstep.

"Of what were you dreaming?" he asked presently, when we had made for ourselves a great cloud of smoke. "I called you twice."

"I was wishing for Dale's times and Dale's laws."

He laughed, and touched my knee with his hand, white and smooth as a woman's, and with a green jewel upon the forefinger.

"Thou Mars incarnate!" he cried. "Thou first, last, and in the meantime soldier! Why, what wilt thou do when thou gettest to heaven? Make it too hot to hold thee? Or take out letters of marque against the Enemy?"

"I am not there yet," I said dryly. "In the meantime I would like a commission against—your relatives."

He laughed, then sighed, and, sinking his chin into his hand and softly tapping his foot against the ground, fell into a reverie.

"I would your princess were alive," I said presently.

"So do I," he answered softly. "So do I." Locking his hands behind his head, he raised his quiet face to the evening star. "Brave and wise and gentle," he mused. "If I did not think to meet her again, beyond that star, I could not smile and speak calmly, Ralph, as I do now."

"'T is a strange thing," I said, as I refilled my pipe. "Love for your brother-in-arms, love for your commander if he be a commander worth having, love for your horse and dog, I understand. But wedded love! to tie a burden around one's neck because 't is pink and white, or clear bronze, and shaped with elegance! Faugh!"

"Yet I came with half a mind to persuade thee to that very burden!" he cried, with another laugh.

"Thanks for thy pains," I said, blowing blue rings into the air.

"I have ridden to-day from Jamestown," he went on. "I was the only man, i' faith, that cared to leave its gates; and I met the world—the bachelor world—flocking to them. Not a mile of the way but I encountered Tom, Dick, and Harry, dressed in their Sunday bravery and making full tilt for the city. And the boats upon the river! I have seen the Thames less crowded."

"There was more passing than usual," I said; "but I was busy in the fields, and did not attend. What's the lodestar?"

"The star that draws us all,—some to ruin, some to bliss ineffable, woman."

"Humph! The maids have come, then?"

He nodded. "There's a goodly ship down there, with a goodly lading."

"Videlicet, some fourscore waiting damsels and milkmaids, warranted honest by my Lord Warwick," I muttered.

"This business hath been of Edwyn Sandys' management, as you very well know," he rejoined, with some heat. "His word is good: therefore I hold them chaste. That they are fair I can testify, having seen them leave the ship."

"Fair and chaste," I said, "but meanly born."

"I grant you that," he answered. "But after all, what of it? Beggars must not be choosers. The land is new and must be peopled, nor will those who come after us look too curiously into the lineage of those to whom a nation owes its birth. What we in these plantations need is a loosening of the bonds which tie us to home, to England, and a tightening of those which bind us to this land in which we have cast our lot. We put our hand to the plough, but we turn our heads and look to our Egypt and its fleshpots. 'T is children and wife—be that wife princess or peasant—that make home of a desert, that bind a man with chains of gold to the country where they abide. Wherefore, when at midday I met good Master Wickham rowing down from Henricus to Jamestown, to offer his aid to Master Bucke in his press of business to-morrow, I gave the good man Godspeed, and thought his a fruitful errand and one pleasing to the Lord."

"Amen," I yawned. "I love the land, and call it home. My withers are unwrung."

He rose to his feet, and began to pace the greensward before the door. My eyes followed his trim figure, richly though sombrely clad, then fell with a sudden dissatisfaction upon my own stained and frayed apparel.

"Ralph," he said presently, coming to a stand before me, "have you ever an hundred and twenty pounds of tobacco in hand? If not, I"—

"I have the weed," I replied. "What then?"

"Then at dawn drop down with the tide to the city, and secure for thyself one of these same errant damsels."

I stared at him, and then broke into laughter, in which, after a space and unwillingly, he himself joined. When at length I wiped the water from my eyes it was quite dark, the whippoorwills had begun to call, and Rolfe must needs hasten on. I went with him down to the gate.

"Take my advice,—it is that of your friend," he said, as he swung himself into the saddle. He gathered up the reins and struck spurs into his horse, then turned to call back to me: "Sleep upon my words, Ralph, and the next time I come I look to see a farthingale behind thee!"

"Thou art as like to see one upon me," I answered.

Nevertheless, when he had gone, and I climbed the bank and reentered the house, it was with a strange pang at the cheerlessness of my hearth, and an angry and unreasoning impatience at the lack of welcoming face or voice. In God's name, who was there to welcome me? None but my hounds, and the flying squirrel I had caught and tamed. Groping my way to the corner, I took from my store two torches, lit them, and stuck them into the holes pierced in the mantel shelf; then stood beneath the clear flame, and looked with a sudden sick distaste upon the disorder which the light betrayed. The fire was dead, and ashes and embers were scattered upon the hearth; fragments of my last meal littered the table, and upon the unwashed floor lay the bones I had thrown my dogs. Dirt and confusion reigned; only upon my armor, my sword and gun, my hunting knife and dagger, there was no spot or stain. I turned to gaze upon them where they hung against the wall, and in my soul I hated the piping times of peace, and longed for the camp fire and the call to arms.

With an impatient sigh, I swept the litter from the table, and, taking from the shelf that held my meagre library a bundle of Master Shakespeare's plays (gathered for me by Rolfe when he was last in London), I began to read; but my thoughts wandered, and the tale seemed dull and oft told. I tossed it aside, and, taking dice from my pocket, began to throw. As I cast the bits of bone, idly, and scarce caring to observe what numbers came uppermost, I had a vision of the forester's hut at home, where, when I was a boy, in the days before I ran away to the wars in the Low Countries, I had spent many a happy hour. Again I saw the bright light of the fire reflected in each well-scrubbed crock and pannikin; again I heard the cheerful hum of the wheel; again the face of the forester's daughter smiled upon me. The old gray manor house, where my mother, a stately dame, sat ever at her tapestry, and an imperious elder brother strode to and fro among his hounds, seemed less of home to me than did that tiny, friendly hut. To-morrow would be my thirty-sixth birthday. All the numbers that I cast were high. "If I throw ambs-ace," I said, with a smile for my own caprice, "curse me if I do not take Rolfe's advice!"

I shook the box and clapped it down upon the table, then lifted it, and stared with a lengthening face at what it had hidden; which done, I diced no more, but put out my lights and went soberly to bed.

CHAPTER II
IN WHICH I MEET MASTER JEREMY SPARROW

MINE are not dicers' oaths. The stars were yet shining when I left the house, and, after a word with my man Diccon, at the servants' huts, strode down the bank and through the gate of the palisade to the wharf, where I loosed my boat, put up her sail, and turned her head down the broad stream. The wind was fresh and favorable, and we went swiftly down the river through the silver mist toward the sunrise. The sky grew pale pink to the zenith; then the sun rose and drank up the mist. The river sparkled and shone; from the fresh green banks came the smell of the woods and the song of birds; above rose the sky, bright blue, with a few fleecy clouds drifting across it. I thought of the day, thirteen years before, when for the first time white men sailed up this same river, and of how noble its width, how enchanting its shores, how gay and sweet their blooms and odors, how vast their trees, how strange the painted savages, had seemed to us, storm-tossed adventurers, who thought we had found a very paradise, the Fortunate Isles at least. How quickly were we undeceived! As I lay back in the stern with half-shut eyes and tiller idle in my hand, our many tribulations and our few joys passed in review before me. Indian attacks; dissension and strife amongst our rulers; true men persecuted, false knaves elevated; the weary search for gold and the South Sea; the horror of the pestilence and the blacker horror of the Starving Time; the arrival of the Patience and Deliverance, whereat we wept like children; that most joyful Sunday morning when we followed my Lord de la Warre to church; the coming of Dale with that stern but wholesome martial code which was no stranger to me who had fought under Maurice of Nassau; the good times that followed, when bowl-playing gallants were put down, cities founded, forts built, and the gospel preached; the marriage of Rolfe and his dusky princess; Argall's expedition, in which I played a part, and Argall's iniquitous rule; the return of Yeardley as Sir George, and the priceless gift he brought us,—all this and much else, old friends, old enemies, old toils and strifes and pleasures, ran, bitter-sweet, through my memory, as the wind and flood bore me on. Of what was before me I did not choose to think, sufficient unto the hour being the evil thereof.

The river seemed deserted: no horsemen spurred Along the bridle path on the shore; the boats were few and far between, and held only servants or Indians or very old men. It was as Rolfe had said, and the free and able-bodied of the plantations had put out, posthaste, for matrimony. Chaplain's Choice appeared unpeopled; Piersey's Hundred slept in the sunshine, its wharf deserted, and but few, slow-moving figures in the tobacco fields; even the Indian villages looked scant of all but squaws and children, for the braves were gone to see the palefaces buy their wives. Below Paspahegh a cockleshell of a boat carrying a great white sail overtook me, and I was hailed by young Hamor.

"The maids are come!" he cried. "Hurrah!" and stood up to wave his hat.

"Humph!" I said. "I guess thy destination by thy hose. Are they not 'those that were thy peach-colored ones'?"

"Oons! yes!" he answered, looking down with complacency upon his tarnished finery. "Wedding garments, Captain Percy, wedding garments!"

I laughed. "Thou art a tardy bridegroom. I thought that the bachelors of this quarter of the globe slept last night in Jamestown."

His face fell. "I know it," he said ruefully; "but my doublet had more rents than slashes in it, and Martin Tailor kept it until cockcrow. That fellow rolls in tobacco; he hath grown rich off our impoverished wardrobes since the ship down yonder passed the capes. After all," he brightened, "the bargaining takes not place until toward midday, after solemn service and thanksgiving. There's time enough!" He waved me a farewell, as his great sail and narrow craft carried him past me.

I looked at the sun, which truly was not very high, with a secret disquietude; for I had had a scurvy hope that after all I should be too late, and so the noose which I felt tightening about my neck might unknot itself. Wind and tide were against me, and an hour later saw me nearing the peninsula and marveling at the shipping which crowded its waters. It was as if every sloop, barge, canoe, and dugout between Point Comfort and Henricus were anchored off its shores, while above them towered the masts of the Marmaduke and Furtherance, then in port, and of the tall ship which had brought in those doves for sale. The river with its dancing freight, the blue heavens and bright sunshine, the green trees waving in the wind, the stir and bustle in the street and market place thronged with gayly dressed gallants, made a fair and pleasant scene. As I drove my boat in between the sloop of the commander of Shirley Hundred and the canoe of the Nansemond werowance, the two bells then newly hung in the church began to peal and the drum to beat. Stepping ashore, I had a rear view only of the folk who had clustered along the banks and in the street, their faces and footsteps being with one accord directed toward the market place. I went with the throng, jostled alike by velvet and dowlas, by youths with their estates upon their backs and naked fantastically painted savages, and trampling the tobacco with which the greedy citizens had planted the very street. In the square I brought up before the Governor's house, and found myself cheek by jowl with Master Pory, our Secretary, and Speaker of the Assembly.

"Ha, Ralph Percy!" he cried, wagging his gray head, "we two be the only sane younkers in the plantations! All the others are horn-mad!"

"I have caught the infection," I said, "and am one of the bedlamites."

He stared, then broke into a roar of laughter. "Art in earnest?" he asked, holding his fat sides. "Is Saul among the prophets?"

"Yes," I answered. "I diced last night,—yea or no; and the 'yea'—plague on 't—had it."

He broke into another roar. "And thou callest that bridal attire, man! Why, our cow-keeper goes in flaming silk to-day!"

I looked down upon my suit of buff, which had in truth seen some service, and at my great boots, which I had not thought to clean since I mired in a swamp, coming from Henricus the week before; then shrugged my shoulders.

"You will go begging," he continued, wiping his eyes. "Not a one of them will so much as look at you."

"Then will they miss seeing a man, and not a popinjay," I retorted. "I shall not break my heart."

A cheer arose from the crowd, followed by a crashing peal of the bells and a louder roll of the drum. The doors of the houses around and to right and left of the square swung open, and the company which had been quartered overnight upon the citizens began to emerge. By twos and threes, some with hurried steps and downcast eyes, others more slowly and with free glances at the staring men, they gathered to the centre of the square, where, in surplice and band, there awaited them godly Master Bucke and Master Wickham of Henricus. I stared with the rest, though I did not add my voice to theirs.

Before the arrival of yesterday's ship there had been in this natural Eden (leaving the savages out of the reckoning) several thousand Adams, and but some threescore Eves. And for the most part, the Eves were either portly and bustling or withered and shrewish housewives, of age and experience to defy the serpent. These were different. Ninety slender figures decked in all the bravery they could assume; ninety comely faces, pink and white, or clear brown with the rich blood showing through; ninety pair of eyes, laughing and alluring, or downcast with long fringes sweeping rounded cheeks; ninety pair of ripe red lips,—the crowd shouted itself hoarse and would not be restrained, brushing aside like straws the staves of the marshal and his men, and surging in upon the line of adventurous damsels. I saw young men, panting, seize hand or arm and strive to pull toward them some reluctant fair; others snatched kisses, or fell on their knees and began speeches out of Euphues; others commenced an inventory of their possessions,—acres, tobacco, servants, household plenishing. All was hubbub, protestation, frightened cries, and hysterical laughter. The officers ran to and fro, threatening and commanding; Master Pory alternately cried "Shame!" and laughed his loudest; and I plucked away a jackanapes of sixteen who had his hand upon a girl's ruff, and shook him until the breath was well-nigh out of him. The clamor did but increase.

"Way for the Governor!" cried the marshal. "Shame on you, my masters! Way for his Honor and the worshipful Council!"

The three wooden steps leading down from the door of the Governor's house suddenly blossomed into crimson and gold, as his Honor with the attendant Councilors emerged from the hall and stood staring at the mob below.

The Governor's honest moon face was quite pale with passion. "What a devil is this?" he cried wrathfully. "Did you never see a woman before? Where's the marshal? I'll imprison the last one of you for rioters!"

Upon the platform of the pillory, which stood in the centre of the market place, suddenly appeared a man of a gigantic frame, with a strong face deeply lined and a great shock of grizzled hair,—a strange thing, for he was not old. I knew him to be one Master Jeremy Sparrow, a minister brought by the Southampton a month before, and as yet without a charge, but at that time I had not spoken with him. Without word of warning he thundered into a psalm of thanksgiving, singing it at the top of a powerful and yet sweet and tender voice, and with a fervor and exaltation that caught the heart of the riotous crowd. The two ministers in the throng beneath took up the strain; Master Pory added a husky tenor, eloquent of much sack; presently we were all singing. The audacious suitors, charmed into rationality, fell back, and the broken line re-formed. The Governor and the Council descended, and with pomp and solemnity took their places between the maids and the two ministers who were to head the column. The psalm ended, the drum beat a thundering roll, and the procession moved forward in the direction of the church.

Master Pory having left me, to take his place among his brethren of the Council, and the mob of those who had come to purchase and of the curious idle having streamed away at the heels of the marshal and his officers, I found myself alone in the square, save for the singer, who now descended from the pillory and came up to me.

"Captain Ralph Percy, if I mistake not?" he said, in a voice as deep and rich as the bass of an organ.

"The same," I answered. "And you are Master Jeremy Sparrow?"

"Yea, a silly preacher,—the poorest, meekest, and lowliest of the Lord's servitors."

His deep voice, magnificent frame, and bold and free address so gave the lie to the humility of his words that I had much ado to keep from laughing. He saw, and his face, which was of a cast most martial, flashed into a smile, like sunshine on a scarred cliff.

"You laugh in your sleeve," he said good-humoredly, "and yet I am but what I profess to be. In spirit I am a very Job, though nature hath fit to dress me as a Samson. I assure you, I am worse misfitted than is Master Yardstick yonder in those Falstaffian hose. But, good sir, will you not go to church?"

"If the church were Paul's, I might," I answered. "As it is, we could not get within fifty feet of the door."

"Of the great door, ay, but the ministers may pass through the side door. If you please, I will take you in with me. The pretty fools yonder march slowly; if we turn down this lane, we will outstrip them quite."

"Agreed," I said, and we turned into a lane thick planted with tobacco, made a detour of the Governor's house, and outflanked the procession, arriving at the small door before it had entered the churchyard. Here we found the sexton mounting guard.

"I am Master Sparrow, the minister that came in the Southampton," my new acquaintance explained. "I am to sit in the choir. Let us pass, good fellow."

The sexton squared himself before the narrow opening, and swelled with importance.

"You, reverend sir, I will admit, such being my duty. But this gentleman is no preacher; I may not allow him to pass."

"You mistake, friend," said my companion gravely. "This gentleman, my worthy colleague, has but just come from the island of St. Brandon, where he preaches on the witches' Sabbath: hence the disorder of his apparel. His admittance be on my head: wherefore let us by."

"None to enter at the west door save Councilors, commander, and ministers. Any attempting to force an entrance to be arrested and laid by the heels if they be of the generality, or, if they be of quality, to be duly fined and debarred from the purchase of any maid whatsoever," chanted the sexton.

"Then, in God's name, let's on!" I exclaimed "Here, try this!" and I drew from my purse, which was something of the leanest, a shilling.

"Try this," quoth Master Jeremy Sparrow, and knocked the sexton down.

We left the fellow sprawling in the doorway, sputtering threats to the air without, but with one covetous hand clutching at the shilling which I threw behind me, and entered the church, which we found yet empty, though through the open great door we heard the drum beat loudly and a deepening sound of footsteps.

"I have choice of position," I said. "Yonder window seems a good station. You remain here in the choir?"

"Ay," he answered, with a sigh; "the dignity of my calling must be upheld: wherefore I sit in high places, rubbing elbows with gold lace, when of the very truth the humility of my spirit is such that I would feel more at home in the servants' seats or among the negars that we bought last year."

Had we not been in church I would have laughed, though indeed I saw that he devoutly believed his own words. He took his seat in the largest and finest of the chairs behind the great velvet one reserved for the Governor, while I went and leaned against my window, and we stared at each other across the flower-decked building in profound silence, until, with one great final crash, the bells ceased, the drum stopped beating, and the procession entered.

CHAPTER III
IN WHICH I MARRY IN HASTE

THE long service of praise and thanksgiving was well-nigh over when I first saw her.

She sat some ten feet from me, in the corner, and so in the shadow of a tall pew. Beyond her was a row of milkmaid beauties, red of cheek, free of eye, deep-bosomed, and beribboned like Maypoles. I looked again, and saw—and see—a rose amongst blowzed poppies and peonies, a pearl amidst glass beads, a Perdita in a ring of rustics, a nonparella of all grace and beauty! As I gazed with all my eyes, I found more than grace and beauty in that wonderful face,—found pride, wit, fire, determination, finally shame and anger. For, feeling my eyes upon her, she looked up and met what she must have thought the impudent stare of an appraiser. Her face, which had been without color, pale and clear like the sky about the evening star, went crimson in a moment. She bit her lip and shot at me one withering glance, then dropped her eyelids and hid the lightning. When I looked at her again, covertly, and from under my hand raised as though to push back my hair, she was pale once more, and her dark eyes were fixed upon the water and the green trees without the window.

The congregation rose, and she stood up with the other maids. Her dress of dark woolen, severe and unadorned, her close ruff and prim white coif, would have cried "Puritan," had ever Puritan looked like this woman, upon whom the poor apparel had the seeming of purple and ermine.

Anon came the benediction. Governor, Councilors, commanders, and ministers left the choir and paced solemnly down the aisle; the maids closed in behind; and we who had lined the walls, shifting from one heel to the other for a long two hours, brought up the rear, and so passed from the church to a fair green meadow adjacent thereto. Here the company disbanded; the wearers of gold lace betaking themselves to seats erected in the shadow of a mighty oak, and the ministers, of whom there were four, bestowing themselves within pulpits of turf. For one altar and one clergyman could not hope to dispatch that day's business.

As for the maids, for a minute or more they made one cluster; then, shyly or with laughter, they drifted apart like the petals of a wind-blown rose, and silk doublet and hose gave chase. Five minutes saw the goodly company of damsels errant and would-be bridegrooms scattered far and near over the smiling meadow. For the most part they went man and maid, but the fairer of the feminine cohort had rings of clamorous suitors from whom to choose. As for me, I walked alone; for if by chance I neared a maid, she looked (womanlike) at my apparel first, and never reached my face, but squarely turned her back. So disengaged, I felt like a guest at a mask, and in some measure enjoyed the show, though with an uneasy consciousness that I was pledged to become, sooner or later, a part of the spectacle. I saw a shepherdess fresh from Arcadia wave back a dozen importunate gallants, then throw a knot of blue ribbon into their midst, laugh with glee at the scramble that ensued, and finally march off with the wearer of the favor. I saw a neighbor of mine, tall Jack Pride, who lived twelve miles above me, blush and stammer, and bow again and again to a milliner's apprentice of a girl, not five feet high and all eyes, who dropped a curtsy at each bow. When I had passed them fifty yards or more, and looked back, they were still bobbing and bowing. And I heard a dialogue between Phyllis and Corydon. Says Phyllis, "Any poultry?"

Corydon. "A matter of twalve hens and twa cocks."

Phyllis. "A cow?"

Corydon. "Twa."

Phyllis. "How much tobacco?"

Corydon. "Three acres, hinny, though I dinna drink the weed mysel'. I'm a Stewart, woman, an' the King's puir cousin."

Phyllis. "What household plenishing?"

Corydon. "Ane large bed, ane flock bed, ane trundle bed, ane chest, ane trunk, ane leather cairpet, sax cawfskin chairs an' twa-three rush, five pair o' sheets an' auchteen dowlas napkins, sax alchemy spunes"—

Phyllis. "I'll take you."

At the far end of the meadow, near to the fort, I met young Hamor, alone, flushed, and hurrying back to the more populous part of the field.

"Not yet mated?" I asked. "Where are the maids' eyes?"

"By—!" he answered, with an angry laugh. "If they're all like the sample I've just left, I'll buy me a squaw from the Paspaheghs!"

I smiled. "So your wooing has not prospered?"

His vanity took fire. "I have not wooed in earnest," he said carelessly, and hitched forward his cloak of sky-blue tuftaffeta with an air. "I sheered off quickly enough, I warrant you, when I found the nature of the commodity I had to deal with."

"Ah!" I said. "When I left the crowd they were going very fast. You had best hurry, if you wish to secure a bargain."

"I'm off," he answered; then, jerking his thumb over his shoulder, "If you keep on to the river and that clump of cedars, you will find Termagaunt in ruff and farthingale."

When he was gone, I stood still for a while and watched the slow sweep of a buzzard high in the blue, after which I unsheathed my dagger, and with it tried to scrape the dried mud from my boots. Succeeding but indifferently, I put the blade up, stared again at the sky, drew a long breath, and marched upon the covert of cedars indicated by Hamor.

As I neared it, I heard at first only the wash of the river; but presently there came to my ears the sound of a man's voice, and then a woman's angry "Begone, sir!"

"Kiss and be friends," said the man.

The sound that followed being something of the loudest for even the most hearty salutation, I was not surprised, on parting the bushes, to find the man nursing his cheek, and the maid her hand.

"You shall pay well for that, you sweet vixen!" he cried, and caught her by both wrists.

She struggled fiercely, bending her head this way and that, but his hot lips had touched her face before I could come between.

When I had knocked him down he lay where he fell, dazed by the blow, and blinking up at me with his small ferret eyes. I knew him to be one Edward Sharpless, and I knew no good of him. He had been a lawyer in England. He lay on the very brink of the stream, with one arm touching the water. Flesh and blood could not resist it, so, assisted by the toe of my boot, he took a cold bath to cool his hot blood.

When he had clambered out and had gone away, cursing, I turned to face her. She stood against the trunk of a great cedar, her head thrown back, a spot of angry crimson in each cheek, one small hand clenched at her throat. I had heard her laugh as Sharpless touched the water, but now there was only defiance in her face. As we gazed at each other, a burst of laughter came to us from the meadow behind. I looked over my shoulder, and beheld young Hamor, probably disappointed of a wife,—with Giles Allen and Wynne, returning to his abandoned quarry. She saw, too, for the crimson spread and deepened and her bosom heaved. Her dark eyes, glancing here and there like those of a hunted creature, met my own.

"Madam," I said, "will you marry me?"

She looked at me strangely. "Do you live here?" she asked at last, with a disdainful wave of her hand toward the town.

"No, madam," I answered. "I live up river, in Weyanoke Hundred, some miles from here."

"Then, in God's name, let us be gone!" she cried, with sudden passion.

I bowed low, and advanced to kiss her hand.

The finger tips which she slowly and reluctantly resigned to me were icy, and the look with which she favored me was not such an one as poets feign for like occasions. I shrugged the shoulders of my spirit, but said nothing. So, hand in hand, though at arms' length, we passed from the shade of the cedars into the open meadow, where we presently met Hamor and his party. They would have barred the way, laughing and making unsavory jests, but I drew her closer to me and laid my hand upon my sword. They stood aside, for I was the best swordsman in Virginia.

The meadow was now less thronged. The river, up and down, was white with sailboats, and across the neck of the peninsula went a line of horsemen, each with his purchase upon a pillion behind him. The Governor, the Councilors, and the commanders had betaken themselves to the Governor's house, where a great dinner was to be given. But Master Piersey, the Cape Merchant, remained to see the Company reimbursed to the last leaf, and the four ministers still found occupation, though one couple trod not upon the heels of another, as they had done an hour agone.

"I must first satisfy the treasurer," I said, coming to a halt within fifty feet of the now deserted high places.

She drew her hand from mine, and looked me up and down.

"How much is it?" she asked at last. "I will pay it."

I stared at her.

"Can't you speak?" she cried, with a stamp of her foot. "At what am I valued? Ten pounds—fifty pounds"—

"At one hundred and twenty pounds of tobacco, madam," I said dryly. "I will pay it myself. To what name upon the ship's list do you answer?"

"Patience Worth," she replied.

I left her standing there, and went upon my errand with a whirling brain. Her enrollment in that company proclaimed her meanly born, and she bore herself as of blood royal; of her own free will she had crossed an ocean to meet this day, and she held in passionate hatred this day and all that it contained; she was come to Virginia to better her condition, and the purse which she had drawn from her bosom was filled with gold pieces. To another

I would have advised caution, delay, application to the Governor, inquiry; for myself I cared not to make inquiries.

The treasurer gave me my receipt, and I procured, from the crowd around him, Humfrey Kent, a good man and true, and old Belfield, the perfumer, for witnesses. With them at my heels I went back to her, and, giving her my hand, was making for the nearest minister, when a voice at a little distance hailed me, crying out, "This way, Captain Percy!"

I turned toward the voice, and beheld the great figure of Master Jeremy Sparrow sitting, cross-legged like the Grand Turk, upon a grassy hillock, and beckoning to me from that elevation.

"Our acquaintance hath been of the shortest," he said genially, when the maid, the witnesses, and I had reached the foot of the hillock, "but I have taken a liking to you and would fain do you a service. Moreover, I lack employment. The maids take me for a hedge parson, and sheer off to my brethren, who truly are of a more clerical appearance. Whereas if they could only look upon the inner man! You have been long in choosing, but have doubtless chosen"—He glanced from me to the woman beside me, and broke off with open mouth and staring eyes. There was excuse, for her beauty was amazing. "A paragon," he ended, recovering himself.

"Marry us quickly, friend," I said. "Clouds are gathering, and we have far to go."

He came down from his mound, and we went and stood before him. I had around my neck the gold chain given me upon a certain occasion by Prince Maurice, and in lieu of other ring I now twisted off the smallest link and gave it to her.

"Your name?" asked Master Sparrow, opening his book.

"Ralph Percy, Gentleman."

"And yours?" he demanded, staring at her with a somewhat too apparent delight in her beauty.

She flushed richly and bit her lip.

He repeated the question.

She stood a minute in silence, her eyes upon the darkening sky. Then she said in a low voice, "Jocelyn Leigh."

It was not the name I had watched the Cape Merchant strike off his list. I turned upon her and made her meet my eyes. "What is your name?" I demanded. "Tell me the truth!"

"I have told it," she answered proudly. "It is Jocelyn Leigh."

I faced the minister again. "Go on," I said briefly.

"The Company commands that no constraint be put upon its poor maids. Wherefore, do you marry this man of your own free will and choice?"

"Ay," she said, "of my own free will."

Well, we were married, and Master Jeremy Sparrow wished us joy, and Kent would have kissed the bride had I not frowned him off. He and Belfield strode away, and I left her there, and went to get her bundle from the house that had sheltered her overnight. Returning, I found her seated on the turf, her chin in her hand and her dark eyes watching the distant play of lightning. Master Sparrow had left his post, and was nowhere to be seen.

I gave her my hand and led her to the shore; then loosed my boat and helped her aboard. I was pushing off when a voice hailed us from the bank, and the next instant a great bunch of red roses whirled past me and fell into her lap. "Sweets to the sweet, you know," said Master Jeremy Sparrow genially. "Goodwife Allen will never miss them."

I was in two minds whether to laugh or to swear,—for I had never given her flowers,—when she settled the question for me by raising the crimson mass and bestowing it upon the flood.

A sudden puff of wind brought the sail around, hiding his fallen countenance. The wind freshened, coming from the bay, and the boat was off like a startled deer. When I next saw him he had recovered his equanimity, and, with a smile upon his rugged features, was waving us a farewell. I looked at the beauty opposite me, and, with a sudden movement of pity for him, mateless, stood up and waved to him vigorously in turn.

CHAPTER IV
IN WHICH I AM LIKE TO REPENT AT LEISURE

WHEN we had passed the mouth of the Chickahominy, I broke the silence, now prolonged beyond reason, by pointing to the village upon its bank, and telling her something of Smith's expedition up that river, ending by asking her if she feared the savages.

When at length she succeeded in abstracting her attention from the clouds, it was to answer in the negative, in a tone of the supremest indifference, after which she relapsed into her contemplation of the weather.

Further on I tried again. "That is Kent's, yonder. He brought his wife from home last year. What a hedge of sunflowers she has planted! If you love flowers, you will find those of paradise in these woods."

No answer.

Below Martin-Brandon we met a canoe full of Paspaheghs, bound upon a friendly visit to some one of the down-river tribes; for in the bottom of the boat reposed a fat buck, and at the feet of the young men lay trenchers of maize cakes and of late mulberries. I hailed them, and when we were alongside held up the brooch from my hat, then pointed to the purple fruit. The exchange was soon made; they sped away, and I placed the mulberries upon the thwart beside her.

"I am not hungry," she said coldly. "Take them away."

I bit my lip, and returned to my place at the tiller. This rose was set with thorns, and already I felt their sting. Presently she leaned back in the nest I had made for her. "I wish to sleep," she said haughtily, and, turning her face from me, pillowed her head upon her arms.

I sat, bent forward, the tiller in my hand, and stared at my wife in some consternation. This was not the tame pigeon, the rosy, humble, domestic creature who was to make me a home and rear me children. A sea bird with broad white wings swooped down upon the water, now dark and ridged, rested there a moment, then swept away into the heart of the gathering storm. She was liker such an one. Such birds were caught at times, but never tamed and never kept.

The lightning, which had played incessantly in pale flashes across the low clouds in the south, now leaped to higher peaks and became more vivid, and the muttering of the thunder changed to long, booming peals. Thirteen years before, the Virginia storms had struck us with terror. Compared with those of the Old World we had left, they were as cannon to the whistling of arrows, as breakers on an iron coast to the dull wash of level seas. Now they were nothing to me, but as the peals changed to great crashes as of falling cities, I marveled to see my wife sleeping so quietly. The rain began to fall, slowly, in large sullen drops, and I rose to cover her with my cloak. Then I saw that the sleep was feigned, for she was gazing at the storm with wide eyes, though with no fear in their dark depths. When I moved they closed, and when I reached her the lashes still swept her cheeks, and she breathed evenly through parted lips. But, against her will, she shrank from my touch as I put the cloak about her; and when I had returned to my seat, I bent to one side and saw, as I had expected to see, that her eyes were wide open again. If she had been one whit less beautiful, I would have wished her back at Jamestown, back on the Atlantic, back at whatever outlandish place, where manners were unknown, that had owned her and cast her out. Pride and temper! I set my lips, and vowed that she should find her match.

The storm did not last. Ere we had reached Piersey's the rain had ceased and the clouds were breaking; above Chaplain's Choice hung a great rainbow; we passed Tants Weyanoke in the glory of the sunset, all shattered gold and crimson. Not a word had been spoken. I sat in a humor grim enough, and she lay there before me, wide awake, staring at the shifting banks and running water, and thinking that I thought she slept.

At last my own wharf rose before me through the gathering dusk, and beyond it shone out a light; for I had told Diccon to set my house in order, and to provide fire and torches, that my wife might see I wished to do her honor. I looked at that wife, and of a sudden the anger in my heart melted away. It was a wilderness vast and dreadful to which she had come. The mighty stream, the towering forests, the black skies and deafening thunder, the wild cries of bird and beast the savages, uncouth and terrible,—for a moment I saw my world as the woman at my feet must see it, strange, wild, and menacing, an evil land, the other side of the moon. A thing that I had forgotten came to my mind: how that, after our landing at Jamestown, years before, a boy whom we had with us did each night fill with cries and lamentations the hut where he lay with my cousin Percy, Gosnold, and myself, nor would cease though we tried both crying shame and a rope's end. It was not for homesickness, for he had no mother or kin or home; and at length Master Hunt brought him to confess that it was but pure panic terror of the land itself,—not of the Indians or of our hardships, both of which he faced bravely enough, but of the strange trees and the high and long roofs of vine, of the black sliding earth and the white mist, of the fireflies and the whippoorwills,—a sick fear of primeval Nature and her tragic mask.

This was a woman, young, alone, and friendless, unless I, who had sworn to cherish and protect her, should prove myself her friend. Wherefore, when, a few minutes later, I bent over her, it was with all gentleness that I touched and spoke to her.

"Our journey is over," I said. "This is home, my dear."

She let me help her to her feet, and up the wet and slippery steps to the level of the wharf. It was now quite dark, there being no moon, and thin clouds obscuring the stars. The touch of her hand, which I perforce held since I must guide her over the long, narrow, and unrailed trestle, chilled me, and her breathing was hurried, but she moved by my side through the gross darkness unfalteringly enough. Arrived at the gate of the palisade, I beat upon it with the hilt of my sword, and shouted to my men to open to us. A moment, and a dozen torches came flaring down the bank. Diccon shot back the bolts, and we entered. The men drew up and saluted; for I held my manor a camp, my servants soldiers, and myself their captain.

I have seen worse favored companies, but doubtless the woman beside me had not. Perhaps, too, the red light of the torches, now flaring brightly, now sunk before the wind, gave their countenances a more villainous cast than usual. They were not all bad. Diccon had the virtue of fidelity, if none other; there were a brace of Puritans, and a handful of honest fools, who, if they drilled badly, yet abhorred mutiny. But the half dozen I had taken off Argall's hands; the Dutchmen who might have been own brothers to those two Judases, Adam and Francis; the thief and the highwayman I had bought from the precious crew sent us by the King the year before; the negro and the Indians—small wonder that she shrank and cowered. It was but for a moment. I was yet seeking for words sufficiently reassuring when she was herself again. She did not deign to notice the men's awkward salute, and when Diccon, a handsome rogue enough, advancing to light us up the bank, brushed by her something too closely, she drew away her skirts as though he had been a lazar. At my own door I turned and spoke to the men, who had followed us up the ascent.

"This lady," I said, taking her hand as she stood beside me, "is my true and lawful wife, your mistress, to be honored and obeyed as such. Who fails in reverence to her I hold as mutinous to myself, and will deal with him accordingly. She gives you to-morrow for holiday, with double rations, and to each a measure of rum. Now thank her properly."

They cheered lustily, of course, and Diccon, stepping forward, gave us thanks in the name of them all, and wished us joy. After which, with another cheer, they backed from out our presence, then turned and made for their quarters, while I led my wife within the house and closed the door.

Diccon was an ingenious scoundrel. I had told him to banish the dogs, to have the house cleaned and lit, and supper upon the table; but I had not ordered the floor to be strewn with rushes, the walls draped with flowering vines, a great jar filled with sunflowers, and an illumination of a dozen torches. Nevertheless, it looked well, and I highly approved the capon and maize cakes, the venison pasty and ale, with which the table was set. Through the open doors of the two other rooms were to be seen more rushes, more flowers, and more lights.

To the larger of these rooms I now led the way, deposited her bundle upon the settle, and saw that Diccon had provided fair water for her face and hands; which done, I told her that supper waited upon her convenience, and went back to the great room.

She was long in coming, so long that I grew impatient and went to call her. The door was ajar, and so I saw her, kneeling in the middle of the floor, her head thrown back, her hands raised and clasped, on her face terror and anguish of spirit written so large that I started to see it. I stared in amazement, and, had I followed my first impulse, would have gone to her, as I would have gone to any other creature in so dire distress. On second thoughts, I went noiselessly back to my station in the great room. She had not seen me, I was sure. Nor had I long to wait. Presently she appeared, and I could have doubted the testimony of my eyes, so changed were the agonized face and figure of a few moments before. Beautiful and disdainful, she moved to the table, and took the great chair drawn before it with the air of an empress mounting a throne. I contented myself with the stool.

She ate nothing, and scarcely touched the canary I poured for her. I pressed upon her wine and viands,—in vain; I strove to make conversation,—equally in vain. Finally, tired of "yes" and "no" uttered as though she were reluctantly casting pearls before swine, I desisted, and applied myself to my supper in a silence as sullen as her own. At last we rose from table, and I went to look to the fastenings of door and windows, and returning found her standing in the centre of the room, her head up and her hands clenched at her sides. I saw that we were to have it out then and there, and I was glad of it.

"You have something to say," I said. "I am quite at your command," and I went and leaned against the chimneypiece.

The low fire upon the hearth burnt lower still before she broke the silence. When she did speak it was slowly, and with a voice which was evidently controlled only by a strong effort of a strong will. She said:—

"When—yesterday, to-day, ten thousand years ago you went from this horrible forest down to that wretched village yonder, to those huts that make your London, you went to buy you a wife?"

"Yes, madam," I answered. "I went with that intention."

"You had made your calculation? In your mind you had pitched upon such and such an article, with such and such qualities, as desirable? Doubtless you meant to get your money's worth?"

"Doubtless," I said dryly.

"Will you tell me what you were inclined to consider its equivalent?"

I stared at her, much inclined to laugh. The interview promised to be interesting.

"I went to Jamestown to get me a wife," I said at length, "because I had pledged my word that I would do so. I was not over-anxious. I did not run all the way. But, as you say, I intended to do the best I could for myself; one hundred and twenty pounds of tobacco being a considerable sum, and not to be lightly thrown away. I went to look for a mistress for my house, a companion for my idle hours, a rosy, humble, docile lass, with no aspirations beyond cleanliness and good temper, who was to order my household and make me a home. I was to be her head and her law, but also her sword and shield. That is what I went to look for."

"And you found—me!" she said, and broke into strange laughter.

I bowed.

"In God's name, why did you not go further?"

I suppose she saw in my face why I went no further, for into her own the color came flaming.

"I am not what I seem!" she cried out. "I was not in that company of choice!"

I bowed again. "You have no need to tell me that, madam," I said. "I have eyes. I desire to know why you were there at all, and why you married me."

She turned from me, until I could see nothing but the coiled wealth of her hair and the bit of white neck between it and the ruff. We stood so in silence, she with bent head and fingers clasping and unclasping, I leaning against the wall and staring at her, for what seemed a long time. At least I had time to grow impatient, when she faced me again, and all my irritation vanished in a gasp of admiration.

Oh, she was beautiful, and of a sweetness most alluring and fatal! Had Medea worn such a look, sure Jason had quite forgot the fleece, and with those eyes Circe had needed no other charm to make men what she would. Her voice, when she spoke, was no longer imperious; it was low pleading music. And she held out entreating hands.

"Have pity on me," she said. "Listen kindly, and have pity on me. You are a strong man and wear a sword. You can cut your way through trouble and peril. I am a woman, weak, friendless, helpless. I was in distress and peril, and I had no arm to save, no knight to fight my battle. I do not love deceit. Ah, do not think that I have not hated myself for the lie I have been. But these forest creatures that you take,—will they not bite against springe and snare? Are they scrupulous as to how they free themselves? I too was in the toils of the hunter, and I too was not scrupulous. There was a thing of which I stood in danger that would have been bitterer to me, a thousand times, than death. I had but one thought, to escape; how, I did not care,—only to escape. I had a waiting woman named Patience Worth. One night she came to me, weeping. She had wearied of service, and had signed to go to Virginia as one of Sir Edwyn Sandys' maids, and at the last moment her heart had failed her. There had been pressure brought to bear upon me that day,—I had been angered to the very soul. I sent her away with a heavy bribe, and in her dress and under her name I fled from—I went aboard that ship. No one guessed that I was not the Patience Worth to whose name I answered. No one knows now,—none but you, none but you."

"And why am I so far honored, madam?" I said bluntly.

She crimsoned, then went white again. She was trembling now through her whole frame. At last she broke out: "I am not of that crew that came to marry! To me you are the veriest stranger,—you are but the hand at which I caught to draw myself from a pit that had been digged for me. It was my hope that this hour would never come. When I fled, mad for escape, willing to dare anything but that which I left behind, I thought, 'I may die before that ship with its shameless cargo sets sail.' When the ship set sail, and we met with stormy weather, and there was much sickness aboard, I thought, 'I may drown or I may die of the fever.' When, this afternoon, I lay there in the boat, coming up this dreadful river through the glare of the lightning, and you thought I slept, I was thinking, 'The bolts may strike me yet, and all will be well.' I prayed for that death, but the storm passed. I am not without shame. I know that you must think all ill of me, that you must feel yourself gulled and cheated. I am sorry—that is all I can say—I am sorry. I am your wife— I was married to you to-day—but I know you not and love you not. I ask you to hold me as I hold myself, a guest in your house, nothing more. I am quite at your mercy. I am entirely friendless, entirely alone. I appeal to your generosity, to your honor"—

Before I could prevent her she was kneeling to me, and she would not rise, though I bade her do so.

I went to the door, unbarred it, and looked out into the night, for the air within the room stifled me. It was not much better outside. The clouds had gathered again, and were now hanging thick and low. From the distance came a rumble of thunder, and the whole night was dull, heavy, and breathless. Hot anger possessed me: anger against Rolfe for suggesting this thing to me; anger against myself for that unlucky throw; anger, most of all, against the woman who had so cozened me. In the servants' huts, a hundred yards away, lights were still burning, against rule, for the hour was late. Glad that there was something I could rail out against, I strode down upon the men, and caught them assembled in Diccon's cabin, dicing for to-morrow's rum. When I had struck out the light with my rapier, and had rated the rogues to their several quarters, I went back through the gathering storm to the brightly-lit, flower-decked room, and to Mistress Percy.

She was still kneeling, her hands at her breast, and her eyes, wide and dark, fixed upon the blackness without the open door. I went up to her and took her by the hand.

"I am a gentleman, madam," I said. "You need have no fear of me. I pray you to rise."

She stood up at that, and her breath came hurriedly through her parted lips, but she did not speak.

"It grows late, and you must be weary," I continued. "Your room is yonder. I trust that you will sleep well. Good-night."

I bowed low, and she curtsied to me. "Good-night," she said.

On her way to the door, she brushed against the rack wherein hung my weapons. Among them was a small dagger. Her quick eye caught its gleam, and I saw her press closer to the wall, and with her right hand strive stealthily to detach the blade from its fastening. She did not understand the trick. Her hand dropped to her side, and she was passing on, when I crossed the room, loosened the dagger, and offered it to her, with a smile and a bow. She flushed scarlet and bit her lips, but she took it.

"There are bars to the door within," I said. "Again, good-night."

"Good-night," she answered, and, entering the room, she shut the door. A moment more, and I heard the heavy bars drop into place.

CHAPTER V
IN WHICH A WOMAN HAS HER WAY

TEN days later, Rolfe, going down river in his barge, touched at my wharf, and finding me there walked with me toward the house.

"I have not seen you since you laughed my advice to scorn—and took it," he said. "Where's the farthingale, Benedick the married man?"

"In the house."

"Oh, ay!" he commented. "It's near to supper time. I trust she's a good cook?"

"She does not cook," I said dryly. "I have hired old Goody Cotton to do that."

He eyed me closely. "By all the gods! a new doublet! She is skillful with her needle, then?"

"She may be," I answered. "Having never seen her with one, I am no judge. The doublet was made by the tailor at Flowerdieu Hundred."

By this we had reached the level sward at the top of the bank. "Roses!" he exclaimed,—"a long row of them new planted! An arbor, too, and a seat beneath the big walnut! Since when hast thou turned gardner, Ralph?"

"It's Diccon's doing. He is anxious to please his mistress."

"Who neither sews, nor cooks, nor plants! What does she do?"

"She pulls the roses," I said. "Come in."

When we had entered the house he stared about him; then cried out, "Acrasia's bower! Oh, thou sometime Guyon!" and began to laugh.

It was late afternoon, and the slant sunshine streaming in at door and window striped wall and floor with gold. Floor and wall were no longer logs gnarled and stained: upon the one lay a carpet of delicate ferns and aromatic leaves, and glossy vines, purple-berried, tapestried the other. Flowers—purple and red and yellow—were everywhere. As we entered, a figure started up from the hearth.

"St. George!" exclaimed Rolfe. "You have never married a blackamoor?"

"It is the negress, Angela," I said. "I bought her from William Pierce the other day. Mistress Percy wished a waiting damsel."

The creature, one of the five females of her kind then in Virginia, looked at us with large, rolling eyes. She knew a little Spanish, and I spoke to her in that tongue, bidding her find her mistress and tell her that company waited. When she was gone I placed a jack of ale upon the table, and Rolfe and I sat down to discuss it. Had I been in a mood for laughter, I could have found reason in his puzzled face. There were flowers upon the table, and beside them a litter of small objects, one of which he now took up.

"A white glove," he said, "perfumed and silver-fringed, and of a size to fit Titania."

I spread its mate out upon my palm. "A woman's hand. Too white, too soft, and too small."

He touched lightly, one by one, the slender fingers of the glove he held. "A woman's hand,—strength in weakness, veiled power, the star in the mist, guiding, beckoning, drawing upward!"

I laughed and threw the glove from me. "The star, a will-of-the-wisp; the goal, a slough," I said.

As he sat opposite me a change came over his face, a change so great that I knew before I turned that she was in the room.

The bundle which I had carried for her from Jamestown was neither small nor light. Why, when she fled, she chose to burden herself with such toys, or whether she gave a thought to the suspicions that might be raised in Virginia if one of Sir Edwyn's maids bedecked herself in silk and lace and jewels, I do not know, but she had brought to the forest and the tobacco fields the gauds of a maid of honor. The Puritan dress in which I first saw her was a thing of the past; she clothed herself now like the parrakeets in the forest,—or liker the lilies of the field, for verily she toiled not, neither did she spin.

Rolfe and I rose from our seats. "Mistress Percy," I said, "let me present to you a right worthy gentleman and my very good friend, Master John Rolfe."

She curtsied, and he bowed low. He was a man of quick wit and had been at court, but for a time he could find no words. Then: "Mistress Percy's face is not one to be forgotten. I have surely seen it before, though where"—

Her color mounted, but she answered him indifferently enough. "Probably in London, amongst the spectators of some pageant arranged in honor of the princess, your wife, sir," she said carelessly. "I had twice the fortune to see the Lady Rebekah passing through the streets."

"Not in the streets only," he said courteously. "I remember now: 't was at my lord bishop's dinner. A very courtly company it was. You were laughing with my Lord Rich. You wore pearls in your hair"—

She met his gaze fully and boldly. "Memory plays us strange tricks at times," she told him in a clear, slightly raised voice, "and it hath been three years since Master Rolfe and his Indian princess were in London. His memory hath played him false."

She took her seat in the great chair which stood in the centre of the room, bathed in the sunlight, and the negress brought a cushion for her feet. It was not until this was done, and until she had resigned her fan to the slave, who stood behind her slowly waving the plumed toy to and fro, that she turned her lovely face upon us and bade us be seated.

An hour later a whippoorwill uttered its cry close to the window, through which now shone the crescent moon. Rolfe started up. "Beshrew me! but I had forgot that I am to sleep at Chaplain's to-night. I must hurry on."

I rose, also. "You have had no supper!" I cried. "I too have forgotten."

He shook his head. "I cannot wait. Moreover, I have feasted,—yea, and drunk deep."

His eyes were very bright, with an exaltation in them as of wine. Mine, I felt, had the same light. Indeed, we were both drunk with her laughter, her beauty, and her wit. When he had kissed her hand, and I had followed him out of the house and down the bank, he broke the silence.

"Why she came to Virginia I do not know "—

"Nor care to ask," I said.

"Nor care to ask," he repeated, meeting my gaze. "And I know neither her name nor her rank. But as I stand here, Ralph, I saw her, a guest, at that feast of which I spoke; and Edwyn Sandys picked not his maids from such assemblies."

I stopped him with my hand upon his shoulder. "She is one of Sandys' maids," I asserted, with deliberation, "a waiting damsel who wearied of service and came to Virginia to better herself. She was landed with her mates at Jamestown a week or more agone, went with them to church and thence to the courting meadow, where she and Captain Ralph Percy, a gentleman adventurer, so pleased each other that they were married forthwith. That same day he brought her to his house, where she now abides, his wife, and as such to be honored by those who call themselves his friends. And she is not to be lightly spoken of, nor comment passed upon her grace, beauty, and bearing (something too great for her station, I admit), lest idle tales should get abroad."

"Am I not thy friend, Ralph?" he asked with smiling eyes.

"I have thought so at times," I answered.

"My friend's honor is my honor," he went on. "Where his lips are sealed mine open not. Art content?"

"Content," I said, and pressed the hand he held out to me.

We reached the steps of the wharf, and descending them he entered his barge, rocking lazily with the advancing tide. His rowers cast loose from the piles, and the black water slowly widened between us. From over my shoulder came a sudden bright gleam of light from the house above, and I knew that Mistress Percy was as usual wasting good pine knots. I had a vision of the many lights within, and of the beauty whom the world called my wife, sitting erect, bathed in that rosy glow, in the great armchair, with the turbaned negress behind her. I suppose Rolfe saw the same thing, for he looked from the light to me, and I heard him draw his breath.

"Ralph Percy, thou art the very button upon the cap of Fortune," he said.

To myself my laugh sounded something of the bitterest, but to him, I presume, it vaunted my return through the darkness to the lit room and its resplendent pearl. He waved farewell, and the dusk swallowed up him and his boat. I went back to the house and to her.

She was sitting as we had left her, with her small feet crossed upon the cushion beneath them, her hands folded in her silken lap, the air from the waving fan blowing tendrils of her dark hair against her delicate standing ruff. I went and leaned against the window, facing her.

"I have been chosen Burgess for this hundred," I said abruptly. "The Assembly meets next week. I must be in Jamestown then and for some time to come."

She took the fan from the negress, and waved it lazily to and fro. "When do we go?" she asked at last.

"We!" I answered. "I had thought to go alone."

The fan dropped to the floor, and her eyes opened wide. "And leave me here!" she exclaimed. "Leave me in these woods, at the mercy of Indians, wolves, and your rabble of servants!"

I smiled. "We are at peace with the Indians; it would be a stout wolf that could leap this palisade; and the servants know their master too well to care to offend their mistress. Moreover, I would leave Diccon in charge."

"Diccon!" she cried. "The old woman in the kitchen hath told me tales of Diccon! Diccon Bravo! Diccon Gamester! Diccon Cutthroat!"

"Granted," I said. "But Diccon Faithful as well. I can trust him."

"But I do not trust him!" she retorted. "And I wish to go to Jamestown. This forest wearies me." Her tone was imperious.

"I must think it over," I said coolly. "I may take you, or I may not. I cannot tell yet."

"But I desire to go, sir!"

"And I may desire you to stay."

"You are a churl!"

I bowed. "I am the man of your choice, madam."

She rose with a stamp of her foot, and, turning her back upon me, took a flower from the table and commenced to pull from it its petals. I unsheathed my sword, and, seating myself, began to polish away a speck of rust upon the blade. Ten minutes later I looked up from the task, to receive full in my face a red rose tossed from the other side of the room. The missile was followed by an enchanting burst of laughter.

"We cannot afford to quarrel, can we?" cried Mistress Jocelyn Percy. "Life is sad enough in this solitude without that. Nothing but trees and water all day long, and not a soul to speak to! And I am horribly afraid of the Indians! What if they were to kill me while you were away? You know you swore before the minister to protect me. You won't leave me to the mercies of the savages, will you? And I may go to Jamestown, may n't I? I want to go to church. I want to go to the Governor's house. I want to buy a many things. I have gold in plenty, and but this one decent dress. You'll take me with you, won't you?"

"There's not your like in Virginia," I told her. "If you go to town clad like that and with that bearing, there will be talk enough. And ships come and go, and there are those besides Rolfe who have been to London."

For a moment the laughter died from her eyes and lips, but it returned. "Let them talk," she said. "What care I? And I do not think your ship captains, your traders and adventurers, do often dine with my lord bishop. This barbarous forest world and another world that I wot of are so far apart that the inhabitants of the one do not trouble those of the other. In that petty village down there I am safe enough. Besides, sir, you wear a sword."

"My sword is ever at your service, madam."

"Then I may go to Jamestown?"

"If you will it so."

With her bright eyes upon me, and with one hand softly striking a rose against her laughing lips, she extended the other hand.

"You may kiss it, if you wish, sir," she said demurely.

I knelt and kissed the white fingers, and four days later we went to Jamestown.

CHAPTER VI
IN WHICH WE GO TO JAMESTOWN

IT was early morning when we set out on horseback for Jamestown. I rode in front, with Mistress Percy upon a pillion behind me, and Diccon on the brown mare brought up the rear. The negress and the mails I had sent by boat.

Now, a ride through the green wood with a noble horse beneath you, and around you the freshness of the morn, is pleasant enough. Each twig had its row of diamonds, and the wet leaves that we pushed aside spilled gems upon us. The horses set their hoofs daintily upon fern and moss and lush grass. In the purple distances deer stood at gaze, the air rang with innumerable bird notes, clear and sweet, squirrels chattered, bees hummed, and through the thick leafy roof of the forest the sun showered gold dust. And Mistress Jocelyn Percy was as merry as the morning. It was now fourteen days since she and I had first met, and in that time I had found in her thrice that number of moods. She could be as gay and sweet as the morning, as dark and vengeful as the storms that came up of afternoons, pensive as the twilight, stately as the night,—in her there met a hundred minds. Also she could be childishly frank—and tell you nothing.

To-day she chose to be gracious. Ten times in an hour Diccon was off his horse to pluck this or that flower that her white forefinger pointed out. She wove the blooms into a chaplet, and placed it upon her head; she filled her lap with trailers of the vine that swayed against us, and stained her fingers and lips with the berries Diccon brought her; she laughed at the squirrels, at the scurrying partridges, at the turkeys that crossed our path, at the fish that leaped from the brooks, at old Jocomb and his sons who ferried us across the Chickahominy. She was curious concerning the musket I carried; and when, in an open space in the wood, we saw an eagle perched upon a blasted pine, she demanded my pistol. I took it from my belt and gave it to her, with a laugh. "I will eat all of your killing," I said.

She aimed the weapon. "A wager!" she declared. "There be mercers in Jamestown? If I hit, thou 'lt buy me a pearl hatband?"

"Two."

She fired, and the bird rose with a scream of wrath and sailed away. But two or three feathers came floating to the ground, and when Diccon had brought them to her she pointed triumphantly to the blood upon them. "You said two!" she cried.

The sun rose higher, and the heat of the day set in. Mistress Percy's interest in forest bloom and creature flagged. Instead of laughter, we had sighs at the length of way; the vines slid from her lap, and she took the faded flowers from her head and cast them aside. She talked no more, and by and by I felt her head droop against my shoulder.

"Madam is asleep," said Diccon's voice behind me.

"Ay," I answered. "She'll find a jack of mail but a hard pillow. And look to her that she does not fall."

"I had best walk beside you, then," he said.

I nodded, and he dismounted, and throwing the mare's bridle over his arm strode on beside us, with his hand upon the frame of the pillion. Ten minutes passed, the last five of which I rode with my face over my shoulder. "Diccon!" I cried at last, sharply.

He came to his senses with a start. "Ay, sir?" he questioned, his face dark red.

"Suppose you look at me for a change," I said. "How long since Dale came in, Diccon?"

"Ten years, sir."

"Before we enter Jamestown we'll pass through a certain field and beneath a certain tree. Do you remember what happened there, some years ago?"

"I am not like to forget, sir. You saved me from the wheel."

"Upon which you were bound, ready to be broken for drunkenness, gaming, and loose living. I begged your life from Dale for no other reason, I think, than that you had been a horse-boy in my old company in the Low Countries. God wot, the life was scarcely worth the saving!"

"I know it, sir."

"Dale would not let you go scot-free, but would sell you into slavery. At your own entreaty I bought you, since when you have served me indifferently well. You have showed small penitence for past misdeeds, and your amendment hath been of yet lesser bulk. A hardy rogue thou wast born, and a rogue thou wilt remain to the end of time. But we have lived and hunted, fought and bled together, and in our own fashion I think we bear each other good will,— even some love. I have winked at much, have shielded you in much, perhaps. In return I have demanded one thing, which if you had not given I would have found you another Dale to deal with."

"Have I ever refused it, my captain?"

"Not yet. Take your hand from that pillion and hold it up; then say after me these words: 'This lady is my mistress, my master's wife, to be by me reverenced as such. Her face is not for my eyes nor her hand for my lips. If

I keep not myself clean of all offense toward her, may God approve that which my master shall do!'"

The blood rushed to his face. I watched his fingers slowly loosening their grasp.

"Tardy obedience is of the house of mutiny," I said sternly. "Will you, sirrah, or will you not?"

He raised his hand and repeated the words.

"Now hold her as before," I ordered, and, straightening myself in the saddle, rode on, with my eyes once more on the path before me.

A mile further on, Mistress Percy stirred and raised her head from my shoulder. "Not at Jamestown yet?" she sighed, as yet but half awake. "Oh, the endless trees! I dreamed I was hawking at Windsor, and then suddenly I was here in this forest, a bird, happy because I was free; and then a falcon came swooping down upon me,—it had me in its talons, and I changed to myself again, and it changed to—What am I saying? I am talking in my sleep. Who is that singing?"

In fact, from the woods in front of us, and not a bowshot away, rang out a powerful voice:—

"In the merry month of May,

In a morn by break of day,

With a troop of damsels playing

Forth I went, forsooth, a-maying;'" and presently, the trees thinning in front of us, we came upon a little open glade and upon the singer. He lay on his back, on the soft turf beneath an oak, with his hands clasped behind his head and his eyes upturned to the blue sky showing between leaf and branch. On one knee crossed above the other sat a squirrel with a nut in its paws, and half a dozen others scampered here and there over his great body, like so many frolicsome kittens. At a little distance grazed an old horse, gray and gaunt, springhalt and spavined, with ribs like Death's own. Its saddle and bridle adorned a limb of the oak.

The song went cheerfully on:—

"Much ado there was, God wot:

would love and she would not;

said, "Never man was true."

He said, "None was false to you."""

"Give you good-day, reverend sir!" I called. "Art conning next Sunday's hymn?"

Nothing abashed, Master Jeremy Sparrow gently shook off the squirrels, and getting to his feet advanced to meet us.

"A toy," he declared, with a wave of his hand, "a trifle, a silly old song that came into my mind unawares, the leaves being so green and the sky so blue. Had you come a little earlier or a little later, you would have heard the ninetieth psalm. Give you good-day madam. I must have sung for that the very queen of May was coming by."

"Art on your way to Jamestown?" I demanded. "Come ride with us. Diccon, saddle his reverence's horse."

"Saddle him an thou wilt, friend," said Master Sparrow, "for he and I have idled long enough, but I fear I cannot keep pace with this fair company. I and the horse are footing it together."

"He is not long for this world," I remarked, eyeing his ill-favored steed, "but neither are we far from Jamestown. He'll last that far."

Master Sparrow shook his head, with a rueful countenance. "I bought him from one of the French vignerons below Westover," he said. "The fellow was astride the poor creature, beating him with a club because he could not go. I laid Monsieur Crapaud in the dust, after which we compounded, he for my purse, I for the animal; since when the poor beast and I have tramped it together, for I could not in conscience ride him. Have you read me Aesop's fables, Captain Percy?"

"I remember the man, the boy, and the ass," I replied. "The ass came to grief in the end. Put thy scruples in thy pocket, man, and mount thy pale horse."

"Not I!" he said, with a smile. "'T is a thousand pities, Captain Percy, that a small, mean, and squeamish spirit like mine should be cased like a very Guy of Warwick. Now, if I were slight of body, or even if I were no heavier than your servant there"—

"Oh!" I said. "Diccon, give his reverence the mare, and do you mount his horse and bring him slowly on to town. If he will not carry you, you can lead him in."

Sunshine revisited the countenance of Master Jeremy Sparrow; he swung his great body into the saddle, gathered up the reins, and made the mare to caracole across the path for very joy.

"Have a care of the poor brute, friend!" he cried genially to Diccon, whose looks were of the sulkiest. "Bring him gently on, and leave him at Master Bucke's, near to the church."

"What do you do at Jamestown?" I asked, as we passed from out the glade into the gloom of a pine wood. "I was told that you were gone to Henricus, to help Master Thorpe convert the Indians."

"Ay," he answered, "I did go. I had a call,—I was sure I had a call. I thought of myself as a very apostle to the Gentiles. I went from Henricus one day's journey into the wilderness, with none but an Indian lad for interpreter, and coming to an Indian village gathered its inhabitants about me, and sitting down upon a hillock read and expounded to them the Sermon on the Mount. I was much edified by the solemnity of their demeanor and the earnestness of their attention, and had conceived great hopes for their spiritual welfare, when, the reading and exhortation being finished, one of their old men arose and made me a long speech, which I could not well understand, but took to be one of grateful welcome to myself and my tidings of peace and good will. He then desired me to tarry with them, and to be present at some entertainment or other, the nature of which I could not make out. I tarried; and toward evening they conducted me with much ceremony to an open space in the midst of the village. There I found planted in the ground a thick stake, and around it a ring of flaming brushwood. To the stake was fastened an Indian warrior, captured, so my interpreter informed me, from some hostile tribe above the falls. His arms and ankles were secured to the stake by means of thongs passed through incisions in the flesh; his body was stuck over with countless pine splinters, each burning like a miniature torch; and on his shaven crown was tied a thin plate of copper heaped with red-hot coals. A little to one side appeared another stake and another circle of brushwood: the one with nothing tied to it as yet, and the other still unlit. My friend, I did not tarry to see it lit. I tore a branch from an oak, and I became as Samson with the jaw bone of the ass. I fell upon and smote those Philistines. Their wretched victim was beyond all human help, but I dearly avenged him upon his enemies. And they had their pains for naught when they planted that second stake and laid the brush for their hell fire. At last I dropped into the stream upon which their damnable village was situate, and got safely away. Next day I went to George Thorpe and resigned my ministry, telling him that we were nowhere commanded to preach to devils; when the Company was ready to send shot and steel amongst them, they might count upon me. After which I came down the river to Jamestown, where I found worthy Master Bucke well-nigh despaired of with the fever. Finally he was taken up river for change of air, and, for lack of worthier substitute, the Governor and Captain West constrained me to remain and minister to the shepherdless flock. Where will you lodge, good sir?"

"I do not know," I said. "The town will be full, and the guest house is not yet finished."

"Why not come to me?" he asked. "There are none in the minister's house but me and Goodwife Allen who keeps it. There are five fair large rooms and a goodly garden, though the trees do too much shadow the house. If you will come and let the sunshine in,"—a bow and smile for madam,—"I shall be your debtor."

His plea pleased me well. Except the Governor's and Captain West's, the minister's house was the best in the town. It was retired, too, being set in its own grounds, and not upon the street, and I desired privacy. Goodwife Allen was stolid and incurious. Moreover, I liked Master Jeremy Sparrow.

I accepted his hospitality and gave him thanks. He waved them away, and fell to complimenting Mistress Percy, who was pleased to be gracious to us both. Well content for the moment with the world and ourselves, we fared on through the alternating sunshine and shade, and were happy with the careless inhabitants of the forest. Oversoon we came to the peninsula, and crossed the neck of land. Before us lay the town: to the outer eye a poor and mean village, indeed, but to the inner the stronghold and capital of our race in the western world, the germ from which might spring stately cities, the newborn babe which might in time equal its parent in stature, strength, and comeliness. So I and a few besides, both in Virginia and at home, viewed the mean houses, the poor church and rude fort, and loved the spot which had witnessed much suffering and small joy, but which held within it the future, which was even now a bit in the mouth of Spain, a thing in itself outweighing all the toil and anguish of our planting. But there were others who saw only the meanness of the place, its almost defenselessness, its fluxes and fevers, the fewness of its inhabitants and the number of its graves. Finding no gold and no earthly paradise, and that in the sweat of their brow they must eat their bread, they straightway fell into the dumps, and either died out of sheer perversity, or went yelping home to the Company with all manner of dismal tales,—which tales, through my Lord Warwick's good offices, never failed to reach the sacred ears of his Majesty, and to bring the colony and the Company into disfavor.

We came to the palisade, and found the gates wide open and the warder gone.

"Where be the people?" marveled Master Sparrow, as we rode through into the street. In truth, where were the people? On either side of the street the doors of the houses stood open, but no person looked out from them or loitered on the doorsteps; the square was empty; there were no women at the well, no children underfoot, no gaping crowd before gaol and pillory, no guard before the Governor's house,—not a soul, high or low, to be seen.

"Have they all migrated?" cried Sparrow. "Are they gone to Croatan?"

"They have left one to tell the tale, then," I said, "for here he comes running."

CHAPTER VII
IN WHICH WE PREPARE TO FIGHT THE SPANIARD

A MAN came panting down the street. "Captain Ralph Percy!" he cried. "My master said it was your horse coming across the neck. The Governor commands your attendance at once, sir."

"Where is the Governor? Where are all the people?" I demanded.

"At the fort. They are all at the fort or on the bank below. Oh, sirs, a woeful day for us all!"

"A woeful day!" I exclaimed. "What's the matter?"

The man, whom I recognized as one of the commander's servants, a fellow with the soul of a French valet de chambre, was wild with terror.

"They are at the guns!" he quavered. "Alackaday! what can a few sakers and demiculverins do against them?"

"Against whom?" I cried.

"They are giving out pikes and cutlasses! Woe's me, the sight of naked steel hath ever made me sick!"

I drew my dagger, and flashed it before him. "Does 't make you sick?" I asked. "You shall be sicker yet, if you do not speak to some purpose."

The fellow shrank back, his eyeballs starting from his head.

"It's a tall ship," he gasped, "a very big ship! It hath ten culverins, beside fowlers and murderers, sabers, falcons, and bases!"

I took him by the collar and shook him off his feet.

"There are priests on board!" he managed to say as I set him down. "This time to-morrow we'll all be on the rack! And next week the galleys will have us!"

"It's the Spaniard at last," I said. "Come on!"

When we reached the river bank before the fort, it was to find confusion worse confounded. The gates of the palisade were open, and through them streamed Councilors, Burgesses, and officers, while the bank itself was thronged with the generality. Ancient planters, Smith's men, Dale's men, tenants and servants, women and children, including the little eyases we imported the year before, negroes, Paspaheghs, French vignerons, Dutch sawmill men, Italian glassworkers,—all seethed to and fro, all talked at once, and all looked down the river. Out of the babel of voices these words came to us over and over: "The Spaniard!" "The Inquisition!" "The galleys!" They were the words oftenest heard at that time, when strange sails hove in sight.

But where was the Spaniard? On the river, hugging the shore, were many small craft, barges, shallops, sloops, and pinnaces, and beyond them the masts of the Truelove, the Due Return, and the Tiger, then in port; on these three, of which the largest, the Due Return, was of but eighty tons burthen, the mariners were running about and the masters bawling orders. But there was no other ship, no bark, galleon, or man-of-war, with three tiers of grinning ordnance, and the hated yellow flag flaunting above.

I sprang from my horse, and, leaving it and Mistress Percy in Sparrow's charge, hastened up to the fort. As I passed through the palisade I heard my name called, and turning waited for Master Pory to come up. He was panting and puffing, his jovial face very red.

"I was across the neck of land when I heard the news," he said. "I ran all the way, and am somewhat scant of breath. Here's the devil to pay!"

"It looks another mare's-nest," I replied. "We have cried 'Spaniard!' pretty often."

"But this time the wolf's here," he answered. "Davies sent a horseman at a gallop from Algernon with the tidings. He passed the ship, and it was a very great one. We may thank this dead calm that it did not catch us unawares."

Within the palisade was noise enough, but more order than without. On the half-moons commanding the river, gunners were busy about our sakers, falcons, and three culverins. In one place, West, the commander, was giving out brigandines, jacks, skulls, muskets, halberds, swords, and longbows; in another, his wife, who was a very Mary Ambree, supervised the boiling of a great caldron of pitch. Each loophole in palisade and fort had already its marksman. Through the west port came a horde of reluctant invaders,—cattle, swine, and poultry,—driven in by yelling boys.

I made my way through the press to where I saw the Governor, surrounded by Councilors and Burgesses, sitting on a keg of powder, and issuing orders at the top of his voice. "Ha, Captain Percy!" he cried, as I came up. "You are in good time, man! You've served your apprenticeship at the wars. You must teach us how to beat the dons."

"To Englishmen, that comes by nature, sir," I said. "Art sure we are to have the pleasure?"

"Not a doubt of it this time," he answered. "The ship slipped in past the Point last night. Davies signaled her to stop, and then sent a ball over her; but she kept on. True, it was too dark to make out much; but if she were friendly, why did she not stop for castle duties? Moreover, they say she was of at least five hundred tons, and no ship of that size hath ever visited these waters. There was no wind, and they sent a man on at once, hoping to outstrip the enemy and warn us. The man changed horses at Basse's Choice, and passed the ship about dawn. All he could tell for the mist was that it was a very great ship, with three tiers of guns."

"The flag?"

"She carried none."

"Humph!" I said. "It hath a suspicious look. At least we do well to be ready. We'll give them a warm welcome."

"There are those here who counsel surrender," continued the Governor. "There's one, at least, who wants the Tiger sent downstream with a white flag and my sword."

"Where?" I cried. "He's no Englishman, I warrant!"

"As much an Englishman as thou, sir!" called out a gentleman whom I had encountered before, to wit, Master Edward Sharpless. "It's well enough for swingebuckler captains, Low Country fire-eaters, to talk of holding out againt a Spanish man-of-war with twice our number of fighting men, and enough ordnance to batter the town out of existence. Wise men know when the odds are too heavy!"

"It's well enough for lily-livered, goose-fleshed lawyers to hold their tongues when men and soldiers talk," I retorted. "We are not making indentures to the devil, and so have no need of such gentry."

There was a roar of laughter from the captains and gunners, but terror of the Spaniard had made Master Edward Sharpless bold to all besides.

"They will wipe us off the face of the earth!" he lamented. "There won't be an Englishman left in America! they'll come close in upon us! they'll batter down the fort with their culverins; they'll turn all their swivels, sakers, and falcons upon us; they'll throw into our midst stinkpots and grenades; they'll mow us down with chain shot! Their gunners never miss!" His voice rose to a scream, and he shook as with an ague. "Are you mad? It's Spain that's to be fought! Spain the rich! Spain the powerful! Spain the lord of the New World!"

"It's England that fights!" I cried. "For very shame, hold thy tongue!"

"If we surrender at once, they'll let us go!" he whined. "We can take the small boats and get to the Bermudas, they'll let us go."

"Into the galleys," muttered West.

The craven tried another feint. "Think of the women and children!"

"We do," I said sternly. "Silence, fool!"

The Governor, a brave and honest man, rose from the keg of powder. "All this is foreign to the matter, Master Sharpless. I think our duty is clear, be the odds what they may. This is our post, and we will hold it or die beside it. We are few in number, but we are England in America, and I think we will remain here. This is the King's fifth kingdom, and we will keep it for him. We will trust in the Lord and fight it out."

"Amen," I said, and "Amen," said the ring of Councilors and Burgesses and the armed men beyond.

The hum of voices now rose into excited cries, and the watchman stationed atop the big culverin called out, "Sail ho!" With one accord we turned our faces downstream. There was the ship, undoubtedly. Moreover, a strong breeze had sprung up, blowing from the sea, filling her white sails, and rapidly lessening the distance between us. As yet we could only tell that she was indeed a large ship with all sail set.

Through the gates of the palisade now came, pellmell, the crowd without. In ten minutes' time the women were in line ready to load the muskets, the children sheltered as best they might be, the men in ranks, the gunners at their guns, and the flag up. I had run it up with my own hand, and as I stood beneath the folds Master Sparrow and my wife came to my side.

"The women are over there," I said to the latter, "where you had best betake yourself."

"I prefer to stay here," she answered. "I am not afraid." Her color was high, and she held her head up. "My father fought the Armada," she said.

"Get me a sword from that man who is giving them out."

From his coign of vantage the watch now called out: "She's a long ship,—five hundred tons, anyhow! Lord! the metal that she carries! She's rasedecked!"

"Then she's Spanish, sure enough!" cried the Governor.

From the crowd of servants, felons, and foreigners rose a great clamor, and presently we made out Sharpless perched on a cask in their midst and wildly gesticulating.

"The Tiger, the Truelove, and the Due Return have swung across channel!" announced the watch. "They 've trained their guns on the Spaniard!"

The Englishmen cheered, but the bastard crew about Sharpless groaned. Extreme fear had made the lawyer shameless. "What guns have those boats?" he screamed. "Two falcons apiece and a handful of muskets, and they go out against a man-of-war! She'll trample them underfoot! She'll sink them with a shot apiece! The Tiger is forty tons, and the Truelove is sixty. You 're all mad!"

"Sometimes quality beats quantity," said West.

"Didst ever hear of the Content?" sang out a gunner.

"Or of the Merchant Royal?" cried another.

"Or of the Revenge?" quoth Master Jeremy Sparrow. "Go hang thyself, coward, or, if you choose, swim out to the Spaniard, and shift from thy wet doublet and hose into a sanbenito. Let the don come, shoot if he can, and land if he will! We'll singe his beard in Virginia as we did at Cales!

'The great St. Philip, the pride of the Spaniards,

Was burnt to the bottom and sunk in the sea.

the St. Andrew and eke the St. Matthew

We took in fight manfully and brought away.'

And so we'll do with this one, my masters! We'll sink her, or we'll take her and send her against her own galleons and galleasses!

'Dub-a-dub, dub-a-dub, thus strike their drums,

Tantara, tantara, the Englishman comes!'"

His great voice and great presence seized and held the attention of all. Over his doublet of rusty black he had clapped a yet rustier back and breast; on his bushy hair rode a headpiece many sizes too small; by his side was an old broadsword, and over his shoulder a pike. Suddenly, from gay hardihood his countenance changed to an expression more befitting his calling. "Our cause is just, my masters!" he cried. "We stand here not for England alone; we stand for the love of law, for the love of liberty, for the fear of God, who will not desert his servants and his cause, nor give over to Anti-Christ this virgin world. This plantation is the leaven which is to leaven the whole lump, and surely he will hide it in the hollow of his hand and in the shadow of his wing. God of battles, hear us! God of England, God of America, aid the children of the one, the saviors of the other!"

He had dropped the pike to raise his clasped hands to the blue heavens, but now he lifted it again, threw back his shoulders, and flung up his head. He laid his hand on the flagstaff, and looked up to the banner streaming in the breeze. "It looks well so high against the blue, does n't it, friends?" he cried genially. "Suppose we keep it there forever and a day!"

A cheer arose, so loud that it silenced, if it did not convince, the craven few. As for Master Edward Sharpless, he disappeared behind the line of women.

The great ship came steadily on, her white sails growing larger and larger, moment by moment, her tiers of guns more distinct and menacing, her whole aspect more defiant. Her waist seemed packed with men. But no streamers, no flag.

A puff of smoke floated up from the deck of the Tiger, and a ball from one of her two tiny falcons passed through the stranger's rigging. A cheer for the brave little cockboat arose from the English. "David and his pebble!" exclaimed Master Jeremy Sparrow. "Now for Goliath's twenty-pounders!"

But no flame and thunder issued from the guns aboard the stranger. Instead, from her deck there came to us what sounded mightily like a roar of laughter. Suddenly, from each masthead and yard shot out streamers of red and blue, up from the poop rose and flaunted in the wind the crosses of St. George and St. Andrew, and with a crash trumpet, drum, and fife rushed into

"Here's to jolly good ale and old!"

"By the Lord, she's English!" shouted the Governor.

On she came, banners flying, music playing, and inextinguishable laughter rising from her decks. The Tiger, the Truelove, and the Due Return sent no more hailstones against her; they turned and resolved themselves into her consort. The watch, a grim old sea dog that had come in with Dale, swung himself down from his post, and came toward the Governor at a run. "I know her now, sir!" he shouted. "I was at the winning of Cales, and she's the Santa Teresa, that we took and sent home to the Queen. She was Spanish once, sir, but she's English now."

The gates were flung open, and the excited people poured out again upon the river bank. I found myself beside the Governor, whose honest countenance wore an expression of profound bewilderment.

"What d' ye make of her, Percy?" he said. "The Company does n't send servants, felons, 'prentices, or maids in such craft; no, nor officers or governors, either. It's the King's ship, sure enough, but what is she doing here?—that 's the question. What does she want, and whom does she bring?"

"We'll soon know," I answered, "for there goes her anchor."

Five minutes later a boat was lowered from the ship, and came swiftly toward us. The boat had four rowers, and in the stern sat a tall man, black-bearded, high-colored, and magnificently dressed. It touched the sand some two hundred feet from the spot where Governor, Councilors, officers, and a sprinkling of other sorts stood staring at it, and at the great ship beyond. The man in the stern leaped out, looked around him, and then walked toward us. As he walked slowly, we had leisure to note the richness of his doublet and cloak,—the one slashed, the other lined with scarlet taffeta,—the arrogance of his mien and gait, and the superb full-blooded beauty of his face.

"The handsomest man that ever I saw!" ejaculated the Governor.

Master Pory, standing beside him, drew in his breath, then puffed it out again. "Handsome enough, your Honor," he said, "unless handsome is as handsome does. That, gentlemen, is my Lord Carnal,—that is the King's latest favorite."

CHAPTER VIII
IN WHICH ENTERS MY LORD CARNAL

I FELT a touch upon my shoulder, and turned to find Mistress Percy beside me. Her cheeks were white, her eyes aflame, her whole frame tense. The passion that dominated her was so clearly anger at white heat that I stared at her in amazement. Her hand slid from my shoulder to the bend of my arm and rested there. "Remember that I am your wife, sir," she said in a low, fierce voice,—"your kind and loving wife. You said that your sword was mine; now bring your wit to the same service!"

There was not time to question her meaning. The man whose position in the realm had just been announced by the Secretary, and of whom we had all heard as one not unlikely to supplant even Buckingham himself, was close at hand. The Governor, headpiece in hand, stepped forward; the other swept off his Spanish hat; both bowed profoundly.

"I speak to his Honor the Governor of Virginia?" inquired the newcomer. His tone was offhand, his hat already back upon his head.

"I am George Yeardley, at my Lord Carnal's service," answered the Governor.

The favorite raised his eyebrows. "I don't need to introduce myself, it seems," he said. "You've found that I am not the devil, after all,—at least not the Spanish Apollyon. Zooks! a hawk above a poultry yard could n't have caused a greater commotion than did my poor little ship and my few poor birding pieces! Does every strange sail so put you through your paces?"

The Governor's color mounted. "We are not at home," he answered stiffly. "Here we are few and weak and surrounded by many dangers, and have need to be vigilant, being planted, as it were, in the very grasp of that Spain who holds Europe in awe, and who claims this land as her own. That we are here at all is proof enough of our courage, my lord."

The other shrugged his shoulders. "I don't doubt your mettle," he said negligently. "I dare say it matches your armor."

His glance had rested for a moment upon the battered headpiece and ancient rusty breastplate with which Master Jeremy Sparrow was bedight.

"It is something antique, truly, something out of fashion," remarked that worthy,—"almost as out of fashion as courtesy from guests, or respect for dignities from my-face-is-my-fortune minions and lords on carpet considerations."

The hush of consternation following this audacious speech was broken by a roar of laughter from the favorite himself. "Zounds!" he cried, "your courage is worn on your sleeve, good giant! I'll uphold you to face Spaniards, strappado, rack, galleys, and all!"

The bravado with which he spoke, the insolence of his bold glance and curled lip, the arrogance with which he flaunted that King's favor which should be a brand more infamous than the hangman's, his beauty, the pomp of his dress,—all were alike hateful. I hated him then, scarce knowing why, as I hated him afterward with reason.

He now pulled from the breast of his doublet a packet, which he proffered the Governor. "From the King, sir," he announced, in the half-fierce, half—mocking tone he had made his own. "You may read it at your leisure. He wishes you to further me in a quest upon which I have come."

The Governor took the packet with reverence. "His Majesty's will is our law," he said. "Anything that lies in our power, sir; though if you come for gold"—

The favorite laughed again. "I've come for a thing a deal more precious, Sir Governor,—a thing worth more to me than all the treasure of the Indies with Manoa and El Dorado thrown in,—to wit, the thing upon which I've set my mind. That which I determine to do, I do, sir, and the thing I determine to have, why, sooner or later, by hook or by crook, fair means or foul, I have it! I am not one to be crossed or defied with impunity."

"I do not take your meaning, my lord," said the Governor, puzzled, but courteous. "There are none here who would care to thwart, in any honorable enterprise, a nobleman so high in the King's favor. I trust that my Lord Carnal will make my poor house his own during his stay in Virginia—What's the matter, my lord?"

My lord's face was dark red, his black eyes afire, his mustaches working up and down. His white teeth had closed with a click on the loud oath which had interrupted the Governor's speech. Honest Sir George and his circle stared at this unaccountable guest in amazement not unmixed with dismay. As for myself, I knew before he spoke what had caused the oath and the fierce triumph in that handsome face. Master Jeremy Sparrow had moved a little to one side, thus exposing to view that which his great body had before screened from observation,—namely, Mistress Jocelyn Percy.

In a moment the favorite was before her, hat in hand, bowing to the ground.

"My quest hath ended where I feared it but begun!" he cried, flushed and exultant. "I have found my Manoa sooner than I thought for. Have you no welcome for me, lady?"

She withdrew her arm from mine and curtsied to him profoundly; then stood erect, indignant and defiant, her eyes angry stars, her cheeks carnation, scorn on her smiling lips.

"I cannot welcome you as you should be welcomed, my lord," she said in a clear voice. "I have but my bare hands. Manoa, my lord, lies far to the southward. This land is quite out of your course, and you will find here but your travail for your pains. My lord, permit me to present to you my husband, Captain Ralph Percy. I think that you know his cousin, my Lord of Northumberland."

The red left the favorite's cheeks, and he moved as though a blow had been dealt him by some invisible hand. Recovering himself he bowed to me, and I to him, which done we looked each other in the eyes long enough for each to see the thrown gauntlet.

"I raise it," I said.

"And I raise it," he answered.

"A l'outrance, I think, sir?" I continued.

"A l'outrance," he assented.

"And between us two alone," I suggested.

His answering smile was not good to see, nor was the tone in which he spoke to the Governor good to hear.

"It is now some weeks, sir," he said, "since there disappeared from court a jewel, a diamond of most inestimable worth. It in some sort belonged to the King, and his Majesty, in the goodness of his heart, had promised it to a certain one,—nay, had sworn by his kingdom that it should be his. Well, sir, that man put forth his hand to claim his own—when lo! the jewel vanished! Where it went no man could tell. There was, as you may believe, a mighty running up and down and looking into dark corners, all for naught,—it was clean gone. But the man to whom that bright gem had been promised was not one easily hoodwinked or baffled. He swore to trace it, follow it, find it, and wear it."

His bold eyes left the Governor, to rest upon the woman beside me; had he pointed to her with his hand, he could not have more surely drawn upon her the regard of that motley throng. By degrees the crowd had fallen back, leaving us three—the King's minion, the masquerading lady, and myself— the centre of a ring of staring faces; but now she became the sole target at which all eyes were directed.

In Virginia, at this time, the women of our own race were held in high esteem. During the first years of our planting they were a greater rarity than the mocking-birds and flying squirrels, or than that weed the eating of which made fools of men. The man whose wife was loving and daring enough, or jealous enough of Indian maids, to follow him into the wilderness counted his friends by the score and never lacked for company. The first marriage in Virginia was between a laborer and a waiting maid, and yet there was as great a deal of candy stuff as if it had been the nuptials of a lieutenant of the shire. The brother of my Lord de la Warre stood up with the groom, the brother of my Lord of Northumberland gave away the bride and was the first to kiss her, and the President himself held the caudle to their lips that night. Since that wedding there had been others. Gentlewomen made the Virginia voyage with husband or father; women signed as servants and came over, to marry in three weeks' time, the husband paying good tobacco for the wife's freedom; in the cargoes of children sent for apprentices there were many girls. And last, but not least, had come Sir Edwyn's doves. Things had changed since that day—at the memory of which men still held their sides—when Madam West, then the only woman in the town with youth and beauty, had marched down the street to the pillory, mounted it, called to her the drummer, and ordered him to summon to the square by tuck of drum every man in the place. Which done, and the amazed population at hand, gaping at the spectacle of the wife of their commander (then absent from home) pilloried before them, she gave command, through the crier, that they should take their fill of gazing, whispering, and nudging then and there, forever and a day, and then should go about their business and give her leave to mind her own.

That day was gone, but men still dropped their work to see a woman pass, still cheered when a farthingale appeared over a ship's side, and at church still devoted their eyes to other service than staring at the minister. In our short but crowded history few things had made a greater stir than the coming in of Sir Edwyn's maids. They were married now, but they were still the observed of all observers; to be pointed out to strangers, run after by children, gaped at by the vulgar, bowed to with broad smiles by Burgess, Councilor, and commander, and openly contemned by those dames who had attained to a husband in somewhat more regular fashion. Of the ninety who had arrived two weeks before, the greater number had found husbands in the town itself or in the neighboring hundreds, so that in the crowd that had gathered to withstand the Spaniard, and had stayed to welcome the King's favorite, there were farthingales not a few.

But there were none like the woman whose hand I had kissed in the courting meadow. In the throng, that day, in her Puritan dress and amid the crowd of meaner beauties, she had passed without overmuch comment, and since that day none had seen her save Rolfe and the minister, my servants and myself; and when "The Spaniard!" was cried, men thought of other things than the beauty of women; so that until this moment she had escaped any special notice. Now all that was changed. The Governor, following the pointing of those insolent eyes, fixed his own upon her in a stare of sheer amazement; the gold-laced quality about him craned necks, lifted eyebrows, and whispered; and the rabble behind followed their betters' example with an emphasis quite their own.

"Where do you suppose that jewel went, Sir Governor," said the favorite,— "that jewel which was overnice to shine at court, which set up its will against the King's, which would have none of that one to whom it had been given?"

"I am a plain man, my lord," replied the Governor bluntly. "An it please you, give me plain words."

My lord laughed, his eyes traveling round the ring of greedily intent faces. "So be it, sir," he assented. "May I ask who is this lady?"

"She came in the Bonaventure," answered the Governor. "She was one of the treasurer's poor maids."

"With whom I trod a measure at court not long ago," said the favorite. "I had to wait for the honor until the prince had been gratified."

The Governor's round eyes grew rounder. Young Hamor, a-tiptoe behind him, drew a long, low whistle.

"In so small a community," went on my lord, "sure you must all know one another. There can be no masks worn, no false colors displayed. Everything must be as open as daylight. But we all have a past as well as a present. Now, for instance"—

I interrupted him. "In Virginia, my lord, we live in the present. At present, my lord, I like not the color of your lordship's cloak."

He stared at me, with his black brows drawn together. "It is not of your choosing nor for your wearing, sir," he rejoined haughtily.

"And your sword knot is villainously tied," I continued. "And I like not such a fire-new, bejeweled scabbard. Mine, you see, is out at heel."

"I see," he said dryly.

"The pinking of your doublet suits me not, either," I declared. "I could make it more to my liking," and I touched his Genoa three-pile with the point of my rapier.

A loud murmur arose from the crowd, and the Governor started forward, crying out, "Captain Percy! Are you mad?"

"I was never saner in my life, sir," I answered. "French fashions like me not,—that is all,—nor Englishmen that wear them. To my thinking such are scarcely true-born."

That thrust went home. All the world knew the story of my late Lord Carnal and the waiting woman in the service of the French ambassador's wife. A gasp of admiration went up from the crowd. My lord's rapier was out, the hand that held it shaking with passion. I had my blade in my hand, but the point was upon the ground. "I'll lesson you, you madman!" he said thickly. Suddenly, without any warning, he thrust at me; had he been less blind with rage, the long score which each was to run up against the other might have ended where it began. I swerved, and the next instant with my own point sent his rapier whirling. It fell at the Governor's feet.

"Your lordship may pick it up," I remarked. "Your grasp is as firm as your honor, my lord."

He glared at me, foam upon his lips. Men were between us now,—the Governor, Francis West, Master Pory, Hamor, Wynne,—and a babel of excited voices arose. The diversion I had aimed to make had been made with a vengeance. West had me by the arm. "What a murrain is all this coil about, Ralph Percy? If you hurt hair of his head, you are lost!"

The favorite broke from the Governor's detaining hand and conciliatory speech.

"You'll fight, sir?" he cried hoarsely.

"You know that I need not now, my lord," I answered.

He stamped upon the ground with rage and shame; not true shame for that foul thrust, but shame for the sword upon the grass, for that which could be read in men's eyes, strive to hide it as they might, for the open scorn upon one face. Then, during the minute or more in which we faced each other in silence, he exerted to some effect that will of which he had boasted. The scarlet faded from his face, his frame steadied, and he forced a smile. Also he called to his aid a certain soldierly, honest-seeming frankness of speech and manner which he could assume at will.

"Your Virginian sunshine dazzleth the eyes, sir," he said. "Of a verity it made me think you on guard. Forgive me my mistake."

I bowed. "Your lordship will find me at your service. I lodge at the minister's house, where your lordship's messenger will find me. I am going there now with my wife, who hath ridden a score of miles this morning and is weary. We give you good-day, my lord."

I bowed to him again and to the Governor, then gave my hand to Mistress Percy. The crowd opening before us, we passed through it, and crossed the parade by the west bulwark. At the further end was a bit of rising ground. This we mounted; then, before descending the other side into the lane leading to the minister's house, we turned as by one impulse and looked back. Life is like one of those endless Italian corridors, painted, picture after picture, by a master hand; and man is the traveler through it, taking his eyes from one scene but to rest them upon another. Some remain a blur in his mind; some he remembers not; for some he has but to close his eyes and he sees them again, line for line, tint for tint, the whole spirit of the piece. I close my eyes, and I see the sunshine hot and bright, the blue of the skies, the sheen of the river. The sails are white again upon boats long lost; the Santa Teresa, sunk in a fight with an Algerine rover two years afterward, rides at anchor there forever in the James, her crew in the waist and the rigging, her master and his mates on the poop, above them the flag. I see the plain at our feet and the crowd beyond, all staring with upturned faces; and standing out from the group of perplexed and wondering dignitaries a man in black and scarlet, one hand busy at his mouth, the other clenched upon the newly restored and unsheathed sword. And I see, standing on the green hillock, hand in hand, us two, myself and the woman so near to me, and yet so far away that a common enemy seemed our only tie.

We turned and descended to the green lane and the deserted houses. When we were quite hidden from those we had left on the bank below the fort, she dropped my hand and moved to the other side of the lane; and thus, with never a word to spare, we walked sedately on until we reached the minister's house.

CHAPTER IX IN
WHICH TWO DRINK OF ONE CUP

WAITING for us in the doorway we found Master Jeremy Sparrow, relieved of his battered armor, his face wreathed with hospitable smiles, and a posy in his hand.

"When the Spaniard turned out to be only the King's minion, I slipped away to see that all was in order," he said genially. "Here are roses, madam, that you are not to treat as you did those others."

She took them from him with a smile, and we went into the house to find three fair large rooms, something bare of furnishing, but clean and sweet, with here and there a bow pot of newly gathered flowers, a dish of wardens on the table, and a cool air laden with the fragrance of the pine blowing through the open window.

"This is your demesne," quoth the minister. "I have worthy Master Bucke's own chamber upstairs. Ah, good man, I wish he may quickly recover his strength and come back to his own, and so relieve me of the burden of all this luxury. I, whom nature meant for an eremite, have no business in kings' chambers such as these."

His devout faith in his own distaste for soft living and his longings after a hermit's cell was an edifying spectacle. So was the evident pride which he took in his domain, the complacence with which he pointed out the shady, well-stocked garden, and the delight with which he produced and set upon the table a huge pasty and a flagon of wine.

"It is a fast day with me," he said. "I may neither eat nor drink until the sun goes down. The flesh is a strong giant, very full of pride and lust of living, and the spirit must needs keep watch and ward, seizing every opportunity to mortify and deject its adversary. Goodwife Allen is still gaping with the crowd at the fort, and your man and maid have not yet come, but I shall be overhead if you need aught. Mistress Percy must want rest after her ride."

He was gone, leaving us two alone together. She stood opposite me, beside the window, from which she had not moved since entering the room. The color was still in her cheeks, the light in her eyes, and she still held the roses with which Sparrow had heaped her arms. I was moving to the table.

"Wait!" she said, and I turned toward her again.

"Have you no questions to ask?" she demanded.

I shook my head. "None, madam."

"I was the King's ward!" she cried.

I bowed, but spoke no word, though she waited for me.

"If you will listen," she said at last, proudly, and yet with a pleading sweetness,—"if you will listen, I will tell you how it was that I—that I came to wrong you so."

"I am listening, madam," I replied.

She stood against the light, the roses pressed to her bosom, her dark eyes upon me, her head held high. "My mother died when I was born; my father, years ago. I was the King's ward. While the Queen lived she kept me with her,—she loved me, I think; and the King too was kind,—would have me sing to him, and would talk to me about witchcraft and the Scriptures, and how rebellion to a king is rebellion to God. When I was sixteen, and he tendered me marriage with a Scotch lord, I, who loved the gentleman not, never having seen him, prayed the King to take the value of my marriage and leave me my freedom. He was so good to me then that the Scotch lord was wed elsewhere, and I danced at the wedding with a mind at ease. Time passed, and the King was still my very good lord. Then, one black day, my Lord Carnal came to court, and the King looked at him oftener than at his Grace of Buckingham. A few months, and my lord's wish was the King's will. To do this new favorite pleasure he forgot his ancient kindness of heart; yea, and he made the law of no account. I was his kinswoman, and under my full age; he would give my hand to whom he chose. He chose to give it to my Lord Carnal."

She broke off, and turned her face from me toward the slant sunshine without the window. Thus far she had spoken quietly, with a certain proud patience of voice and bearing; but as she stood there in a silence which I did not break, the memory of her wrongs brought the crimson to her cheeks and the anger to her eyes. Suddenly she burst forth passionately: "The King is the King! What is a subject's will to clash with his? What weighs a woman's heart against his whim? Little cared he that my hand held back, grew cold at the touch of that other hand in which he would have put it. What matter if my will was against that marriage? It was but the will of a girl, and must be broken. All my world was with the King; I, who stood alone, was but a woman, young and untaught. Oh, they pressed me sore, they angered me to the very heart! There was not one to fight my battle, to help me in that strait, to show me a better path than that I took. With all my heart, with all my soul, with all my might, I hate that man which that ship brought here to-day! You know what I did to escape them all, to escape that man. I fled from England in the dress of my waiting maid and under her name. I came to Virginia in that guise. I let myself be put up, appraised, cried for sale, in that meadow yonder, as if I had been indeed the piece of merchandise I professed myself. The one man who approached me with respect I gulled and cheated. I let him, a stranger, give me his name. I shelter myself now behind his name. I have foisted on him my quarrel. I have—Oh, despise me, if you will! You cannot despise me more than I despise myself!"

I stood with my hand upon the table and my eyes studying the shadow of the vines upon the floor. All that she said was perfectly true, and yet—I had a vision of a scarlet and black figure and a dark and beautiful face. I too hated my Lord Carnal.

"I do not despise you, madam," I said at last. "What was done two weeks ago in the meadow yonder is past recall. Let it rest. What is mine is yours: it's little beside my sword and my name. The one is naturally at my wife's service; for the other, I have had some pride in keeping it untarnished. It is now in your keeping as well as my own. I do not fear to leave it there, madam."

I had spoken with my eyes upon the garden outside the window, but now I looked at her, to see that she was trembling in every limb,—trembling so that I thought she would fall. I hastened to her. "The roses," she said,—"the roses are too heavy. Oh, I am tired—and the room goes round."

I caught her as she fell, and laid her gently upon the floor. There was water on the table, and I dashed some in her face and moistened her lips; then turned to the door to get woman's help, and ran against Diccon.

"I got that bag of bones here at last, sir," he began. "If ever I"—His eyes traveled past me, and he broke off.

"Don't stand there staring," I ordered. "Go bring the first woman you meet."

"Is she dead?" he asked under his breath. "Have you killed her?"

"Killed her, fool!" I cried. "Have you never seen a woman swoon?"

"She looks like death," he muttered. "I thought"—

"You thought!" I exclaimed. "You have too many thoughts. Begone, and call for help!"

"Here is Angela," he said sullenly and without offering to move, as, light of foot, soft of voice, ox-eyed and docile, the black woman entered the room. When I saw her upon her knees beside the motionless figure, the head pillowed on her arm, her hand busy with the fastenings about throat and bosom, her dark face as womanly tender as any English mother's bending over her nursling; and when I saw my wife, with a little moan, creep further into the encircling arms, I was satisfied.

"Come away!" I said, and, followed by Diccon, went out and shut the door.

My Lord Carnal was never one to let the grass grow beneath his feet. An hour later came his cartel, borne by no less a personage than the Secretary of the colony.

I took it from the point of that worthy's rapier. It ran thus: "SIR,—At what hour to-morrow and at what place do you prefer to die? And with what weapon shall I kill you?"

"Captain Percy will give me credit for the profound reluctance with which I act in this affair against a gentleman and an officer so high in the esteem of the colony," said Master Pory, with his hand upon his heart. "When I tell him that I once fought at Paris in a duel of six on the same side with my late Lord Carnal, and that when I was last at court my Lord Warwick did me the honor to present me to the present lord, he will see that I could not well refuse when the latter requested my aid."

"Master Pory's disinterestedness is perfectly well known," I said, without a smile. "If he ever chooses the stronger side, sure he has strong reasons for so doing. He will oblige me by telling his principal that I ever thought sunrise a pleasant hour for dying, and that there could be no fitter place than the field behind the church, convenient as it is to the graveyard. As for weapons, I have heard that he is a good swordsman, but I have some little reputation that way myself. If he prefers pistols or daggers, so be it."

"I think we may assume the sword," said Master Pory.

I bowed.

"You'll bring a friend?" he asked.

"I do not despair of finding one," I answered, "though my second, Master Secretary, will put himself in some jeopardy."

"It is combat... outrance, I believe?"

"I understand it so."

"Then we'd better have Bohun. The survivor may need his services."

"As you please," I replied, "though my man Diccon dresses my scratches well enough."

He bit his lip, but could not hide the twinkle in his eye.

"You are cocksure," he said. "Curiously enough, so is my lord. There are no further formalities to adjust, I believe? To-morrow at sunrise, behind the church, and with rapiers?"

"Precisely."

He slapped his blade back into its sheath. "Then that's over and done with, for the nonce at least! Sufficient unto the day, etcetera. 'S life! I'm hot and dry! You've sacked cities, Ralph Percy; now sack me the minister's closet and bring out his sherris I'll be at charges for the next communion."

We sat us down upon the doorstep with a tankard of sack between us, and Master Pory drank, and drank, and drank again.

"How's the crop?" he asked. "Martin reports it poorer in quality than ever, but Sir George will have it that it is very Varinas."

"It's every whit as good as the Spanish," I answered. "You may tell my Lord Warwick so, when next you write."

He laughed. If he was a timeserver and leagued with my Lord Warwick's faction in the Company, he was a jovial sinner. Traveler and student, much of a philosopher, more of a wit, and boon companion to any beggar with a pottle of ale,—while the drink lasted,—we might look askance at his dealings, but we liked his company passing well. If he took half a poor rustic's crop for his fee, he was ready enough to toss him sixpence for drink money; and if he made the tenants of the lands allotted to his office leave their tobacco uncared for whilst they rowed him on his innumerable roving expeditions up creeks and rivers, he at least lightened their labors with most side-splitting tales, and with bottle songs learned in a thousand taverns.

"After to-morrow there'll be more interesting news to write," he announced. "You're a bold man, Captain Percy."

He looked at me out of the corners of his little twinkling eyes. I sat and smoked in silence.

"The King begins to dote upon him," he said; "leans on his arm, plays with his hand, touches his cheek. Buckingham stands by, biting his lip, his brow like a thundercloud. You'll find in to-morrow's antagonist, Ralph Percy, as potent a conjurer as your cousin Hotspur found in Glendower. He'll conjure you up the Tower, and a hanging, drawing, and quartering. Who touches the King's favorite had safer touch the King. It's lese-majeste, you contemplate."

He lit his pipe and blew out a great cloud of smoke, then burst into a roar of laughter. "My Lord High Admiral may see you through. Zooks! there'll be a raree-show worth the penny, behind the church to-morrow, a Percy striving with all his might and main to serve a Villiers! Eureka! There is something new under the sun, despite the Preacher!" He blew out another cloud of smoke. By this the tankard was empty, and his cheeks were red, his eyes moist, and his laughter very ready.

"Where's the Lady Jocelyn Leigh?" he asked. "May I not have the honor to kiss her hand before I go?"

I stared at him. "I do not understand you," I said coldly. "There 's none within but Mistress Percy. She is weary, and rests after her journey. We came from Weyanoke this morning."

He shook with laughter. "Ay, ay, brave it out!" he cried. "It's what every man Jack of us said you would do! But all's known, man! The Governor read the King's letters in full Council an hour ago. She's the Lady Jocelyn Leigh; she 's a ward of the King's; she and her lands are to wed my Lord Carnal!"

"She was all that," I replied. "Now she 's my wife."

"You'll find that the Court of High Commission will not agree with you."

My rapier lay across my knees, and I ran my hand down its worn scabbard. "Here 's one that agrees with me," I said. "And up there is Another," and I lifted my hat.

He stared. "God and my good sword!" he cried. "A very knightly dependence, but not to be mentioned nowadays in the same breath with gold and the King's favor. Better bend to the storm, man; sing low while it roars past. You can swear that you did n't know her to be of finer weave than dowlas. Oh, they'll call it in some sort a marriage, for the lady's own sake; but they'll find flaws enough to crack a thousand such mad matches. The divorce is the thing! There's precedent, you know. A fair lady was parted from a brave man not a thousand years ago, because a favorite wanted her. True, Frances Howard wanted the favorite, whilst this beauty of yours"—

"You will please not couple the name of my wife with the name of that adulteress!" I interrupted fiercely.

He started; then cried out somewhat hurriedly: "No offense, no offense! I meant no comparisons; comparisons are odorous, saith Dogberry. All at court know the Lady Jocelyn Leigh for a very Britomart, a maid as cold as Dian!"

I rose, and began to pace up and down the bit of green before the door. "Master Pory," I said at last, coming to a stop before him, "if, without breach of faith, you can tell me what was said or done at the Council to-day anent this matter, you will lay me under an obligation that I shall not forget."

He studied the lace on his sleeve in silence for a while; then glanced up at me out of those small, sly, merry eyes. "Why," he answered, "the King demands that the lady be sent home forthwith, on the ship that gave us such a turn to-day, in fact, with a couple of women to attend her, and under the protection of the only other passenger of quality, to wit, my Lord Carnal. His Majesty cannot conceive it possible that she hath so far forgotten her birth, rank, and duty as to have maintained in Virginia this mad masquerade, throwing herself into the arms of any petty planter or broken adventurer who hath chanced to have an hundred and twenty pounds of filthy tobacco with which to buy him a wife. If she hath been so mad, she is to be sent home none the less, where she will be tenderly dealt with as one surely in this sole matter under the spell of witchcraft. The ship is to bring home also—and in irons—the man who married her. If he swears to have been ignorant of her quality, and places no straws in the way of the King's Commissioners, then shall he be sent honorably back to Virginia with enough in his hand to get him another wife. Per contra, if he erred with open eyes, and if he remain contumacious, he will have to deal with the King and with the Court of High Commission, to say nothing of the King's favorite. That's the sum and substance, Ralph Percy."

"Why was my Lord Carnal sent?" I asked.

"Probably because my Lord Carnal would come. He hath a will, hath my Lord, and the King is more indulgent than Eli to those upon whom he dotes. Doubtless, my Lord High Admiral sped him on his way, gave him the King's best ship, wished him a favorable wind—to hell."

"I was not ignorant that she was other than she seemed, and I remain contumacious."

"Then," he said shamelessly, "you'll forgive me if in public, at least, I forswear your company? You're plague-spotted, Captain Percy, and your friends may wish you well, but they must stay at home and burn juniper before their own doors."

"I'll forgive you," I said, "when you 've told me what the Governor will do."

"Why, there's the rub," he answered. "Yeardley is the most obstinate man of my acquaintance. He who at his first coming, beside a great deal of worth in his person, brought only his sword hath grown to be as very a Sir Oracle among us as ever I saw. It's 'Sir George says this,' and 'Sir George says that,' and so there's an end on't. It's all because of that leave to cut your own throats in your own way that he brought you last year. Sir George and Sir Edwyn! Zooks! you had better dub them St. George and St. Edwyn at once, and be done with it. Well, on this occasion Sir George stands up and says roundly, with a good round oath to boot: 'The King's commands have always come to us through the Company. The Company obeys the King; we obey the Company. His Majesty's demand (with reverence I speak it) is out of all order. Let the Company, through the treasurer, command us to send Captain Percy home in irons to answer for this passing strange offense, or to return, willy nilly, the lady who is now surely his wife, and we will have no choice but to obey. Until the Company commands us we will do nothing; nay we can do nothing.' And every one of my fellow Councilors (for myself, I was busy with my pens) saith, 'My opinion, Sir George.' The upshot of it all is that the Due

Return is to sail in two days with our humble representation to his Majesty that though we bow to his lightest word as the leaf bows to the zephyr, yet we are, in this sole matter, handfast, compelled by his Majesty's own gracious charter to refer our slightest official doing to that noble Company which owes its very being to its rigid adherence to the terms of said charter. Wherefore, if his Majesty will be graciously pleased to command us as usual through the said Company—and so on. Of course, not a soul in the Council, or in Jamestown, or in Virginia dreams of a duel behind the church at sunrise to-morrow." He knocked the ashes from his pipe, and by degrees got his fat body up from the doorstep. "So there's a reprieve for you, Ralph Percy, unless you kill or are killed to-morrow morning. In the latter case, the problem's solved; in the former, the best service you can do yourself, and maybe the Company, is to walk out of the world of your own accord, and that as quickly as possible. Better a cross-roads and a stake through a dead heart than a hangman's hands upon a live one."

"One moment," I said. "Doth my Lord Carnal know of this decision of the Governor's?"

"Ay, and a fine passion it put him into. Stormed and swore and threatened, and put the Governor's back up finely. It seems that he thought to 'bout ship to-morrow, lady and all. He refuseth to go without the lady, and so remaineth in Virginia until he can have his will. Lord! but Buckingham would be a happy man if he were kept here forever and a day! My lord knows what he risks, and he's in as black a humor as ever you saw. But I have striven to drop oil on the troubled waters. 'My lord,' I told him, 'you have but to posses your soul with patience for a few short weeks, just until the ship the Governor sends can return. Then all must needs be as your lordship wishes. In the meantime, you may find existence in these wilds and away from that good company which is the soul of life endurable, and perhaps pleasant. You may have daily sight of the lady who is to become your wife, and that should count for much with so ardent and determined a lover as your lordship hath shown yourself to be. You may have the pleasure of contemplating your rival's grave, if you kill him. If he kills you, you will care the less about the date of the Santa Teresa's sailing. The land, too, hath inducements to offer to a philosophical and contemplative mind such as one whom his Majesty delighteth to honor must needs possess. Beside these crystal rivers and among these odoriferous woods, my lord, one escapes much expense, envy, contempt, vanity, and vexation of mind.'"

The hoary sinner laughed and laughed. When he had gone away, still in huge enjoyment of his own mirth, I, who had seen small cause for mirth, went slowly indoors. Not a yard from the door, in the shadow of the vines that draped the window, stood the woman who was bringing this fate upon me.

"I thought that you were in your own room," I said harshly, after a moment of dead silence.

"I came to the window," she replied. "I listened. I heard all." She spoke haltingly, through dry lips. Her face was as white as her ruff, but a strange light burned in her eyes, and there was no trembling. "This morning you said that all that you had—your name and your sword—were at my service. You may take them both again, sir. I refuse the aid you offer. Swear what you will, tell them what you please, make your peace whilst you may. I will not have your blood upon my soul."

There was yet wine upon the table. I filled a cup and brought it to her. "Drink!" I commanded.

"I have much of forbearance, much of courtesy, to thank you for," she said. "I will remember it when—Do not think that I shall blame you"—

I held the cup to her lips. "Drink!" I repeated. She touched the red wine with her lips. I took it from her and put it to my own. "We drink of the same cup," I said, with my eyes upon hers, and drained it to the bottom. "I am weary of swords and courts and kings. Let us go into the garden and watch the minister's bees."

CHAPTER X
IN WHICH MASTER PORY GAINS TIME TO SOME PURPOSE

ROLFE coming down by boat from Varina, had reached the town in the dusk of that day which had seen the arrival of the Santa Teresa, and I had gone to him before I slept that night. Early morning found us together again in the field behind the church. We had not long to wait in the chill air and dew-drenched grass. When the red rim of the sun showed like a fire between the trunks of the pines came my Lord Carnal, and with him Master Pory and Dr. Lawrence Bohun.

My lord and I bowed to each other profoundly. Rolfe with my sword and Master Pory with my lord's stepped aside to measure the blades. Dr. Bohun, muttering something about the feverishness of the early air, wrapped his cloak about him, and huddled in among the roots of a gigantic cedar. I stood with my back to the church, and my face to the red water between us and the illimitable forest; my lord opposite me, six feet away. He was dressed again splendidly in black and scarlet, colors he much affected, and, with the dark beauty of his face and the arrogant grace with which he stood there waiting for his sword, made a picture worth looking upon.

Rolfe and the Secretary came back to us. "If you kill him, Ralph," said the former in a low voice, as he took my doublet from me, "you are to put yourself in my hands and do as you are bid."

"Which means that you will try to smuggle me north to the Dutch. Thanks, friend, but I'll see the play out here."

"You were ever obstinate, self-willed, reckless—and the man most to my heart," he continued. "Have your way, in God's name, but I wish not to see what will come of it! All's ready, Master Secretary."

Very slowly that worthy stooped down and examined the ground, narrowly and quite at his leisure. "I like it not, Master Rolfe," he declared at length. "Here is a molehill, and there a fairy ring."

"I see neither," said Rolfe. "It looks as smooth as a table. But we can easily shift under the cedars where there is no grass."

"Here's a projecting root," announced the Secretary, when the new ground had been reached.

Rolfe shrugged his shoulders, but we moved again.

"The light comes jaggedly through the branches," objected my lord's second. "Better try the open again."

Rolfe uttered an exclamation of impatience, and my lord stamped his foot on the ground. "What is this foolery, sir?" the latter cried fiercely. "The ground's well enough, and there 's sufficient light to die by."

"Let the light pass, then," said his second resignedly. "Gentlemen, are you read—Ods blood! my lord, I had not noticed the roses upon your lordship's shoes! They are so large and have such a fall that they sweep the ground on either side your foot; you might stumble in all that dangling ribbon and lace. Allow me to remove them."

He unsheathed his knife, and, sinking upon his knees, began leisurely to sever the threads that held the roses to the leather. As he worked, he looked neither at the roses nor at my lord's angry face, but beneath his own bent arm toward the church and the town beyond.

How long he would have sawed away at the threads there is no telling; for my lord, amongst whose virtues patience was not one, broke from him, and with an oath stooped and tore away the offending roses with his own hand, then straightened himself and gripped his sword more closely. "I've learned one thing in this d———d land," he snarled, "and that is where not to choose a second. You, sir," to Rolfe, "give the word."

Master Pory rose from his knees, unruffled and unabashed, and still with a curiously absent expression upon his fat face and with his ears cocked in the direction of the church. "One moment, gentlemen," he said. "I have just bethought me"—

"On guard!" cried Rolfe, and cut him short.

The King's favorite was no mean antagonist. Once or twice the thought crossed my mind that here, where I least desired it, I had met my match. The apprehension passed. He fought as he lived, with a fierce intensity, a headlong passion, a brute force, bearing down and overwhelming most obstacles. But that I could tire him out I soon knew.

The incessant flash and clash of steel, the quick changes in position, the need to bring all powers of body and mind to aid of eye and wrist, the will to win, the shame of loss, the rage and lust of blood,—there was no sight or sound outside that trampled circle that could force itself upon our brain or make us glance aside. If there was a sudden commotion amongst the three witnesses, if an expression of immense relief and childlike satisfaction reigned in Master Pory's face, we knew it not. We were both bleeding,—I from a pin prick on the shoulder, he from a touch beneath the arm. He made a desperate thrust, which I parried, and the blades clashed. A third came down upon them with such force that the sparks flew.

"In the King's name!" commanded the Governor.

We fell apart, panting, white with rage, staring at the unexpected disturbers of our peace. They were the Governor, the commander, the Cape Merchant, and the watch.

"Lord, now lettest thou thy servant depart in peace!" exclaimed Master Pory, and retired to the cedar and Dr. Bohun.

"This ends here, gentlemen," said the Governor firmly. "You are both bleeding. It is enough."

"Out of my way, sir!" cried my lord, foaming at the mouth. He made a mad thrust over the Governor's extended arm at me, who was ready enough to meet him. "Have at thee, thou bridegroom!" he said between his teeth.

The Governor caught him by the wrist. "Put up your sword, my lord, or, as I stand here, you shall give it into the commander's hands!"

"Hell and furies!" ejaculated my lord. "Do you know who I am, sir?"

"Ay," replied the Governor sturdily, "I do know. It is because of that knowledge, my Lord Carnal, that I interfere in this affair. Were you other than you are, you and this gentleman might fight until doomsday, and meet with no hindrance from me. Being what you are, I will prevent any renewal of this duel, by fair means if I may, by foul if I must."

He left my lord, and came over to me. "Since when have you been upon my Lord Warwick's side, Ralph Percy?" he demanded, lowering his voice.

"I am not so," I said.

"Then appearances are mightily deceitful," he retorted.

"I know what you mean, Sir George," I answered. "I know that if the King's darling should meet death or maiming in this fashion, upon Virginian soil, the Company, already so out of favor, might find some difficulty in explaining things to his Majesty's satisfaction. But I think my Lord Southampton and Sir Edwyn Sandys and Sir George Yeardley equal to the task, especially if they are able to deliver to his Majesty the man whom his Majesty will doubtless consider the true and only rebel and murderer. Let us fight it out, sir. You can all retire to a distance and remain in profound ignorance of any such affair. If I fall, you have nothing to fear. If he falls,— why, I shall not run away, and the Due Return sails to-morrow."

He eyed me closely from under frowning brows.

"And when your wife's a widow, what then?" he asked abruptly.

I have not known many better men than this simple, straightforward, soldierly Governor. The manliness of his character begot trust, invited confidence. Men told him of their hidden troubles almost against their will, and afterward felt neither shame nor fear, knowing the simplicity of his thoughts and the reticence of his speech. I looked him in the eyes, and let him read what I would have shown to no other, and felt no shame. "The Lord may raise her up a helper," I said. "At least she won't have to marry him."

He turned on his heel and moved back to his former station between us two. "My Lord Carnal," he said, "and you, Captain Percy, heed what I say; for what I say I will do. You may take your choice: either you will sheathe your swords here in my presence, giving me your word of honor that you will not draw them upon each other before his Majesty shall have made known his will in this matter to the Company, and the Company shall have transmitted it to me, in token of which truce between you you shall touch each other's hands; or you will pass the time between this and the return of the ship with the King's and the Company's will in strict confinement,—you, Captain Percy, in gaol, and you, my Lord Carnal, in my own poor house, where I will use my best endeavors to make the days pass as pleasantly as possible for your lordship. I have spoken, gentlemen."

There was no protest. For my own part, I knew Yeardley too well to attempt any; moreover, had I been in his place, his course should have been mine. For my Lord Carnal,—what black thoughts visited that fierce and sullen brain I know not, but there was acquiescence in his face, haughty, dark, and vengeful though it was. Slowly and as with one motion we sheathed our swords, and more slowly still repeated the few words after the Governor. His Honor's countenance shone with relief. "Take each other by the hand, gentlemen, and then let 's all to breakfast at my own house, where there shall be no feud save with good capon pasty and jolly good ale." In dead silence my lord and I touched each other's finger tips.

The world was now a flood of sunshine, the mist on the river vanishing, the birds singing, the trees waving in the pleasant morning air. From the town came the roll of the drum summoning all to the week-day service. The bells too began to ring, sounding sweetly through the clear air. The Governor took off his hat. "Let's all to church, gentlemen," he said gravely. "Our cheeks are flushed as with a fever and our pulses run high this morning. There be some among us, perhaps, that have in their hearts discontent, anger, and hatred. I know no better place to take such passions, provided we bring them not forth again."

We went in and sat down. Jeremy Sparrow was in the pulpit. Singly or in groups the town folk entered. Down the aisle strode bearded men, old soldiers, adventurers, sailors, scarred body and soul; young men followed, younger sons and younger brothers, prodigals whose portion had been spent, whose souls now ate of the husks; to the servants' benches came dull laborers, dimly comprehending, groping in the twilight; women entered softly and slowly, some with children clinging to their skirts. One came alone and knelt alone, her face shadowed by her mantle. Amongst the servants stood a slave or two, blindly staring, and behind them all one of that felon crew sent us by the King.

Through the open windows streamed the summer sunshine, soft and fragrant, impartial and unquestioning, caressing alike the uplifted face of the minister, the head of the convict, and all between. The minister's voice was grave and tender when he read and prayed, but in the hymn it rose above the people's like the voice of some mighty archangel. That triumphant singing shook the air, and still rang in the heart while we said the Creed.

When the service was over, the congregation waited for the Governor to pass out first. At the door he pressed me to go with him and his party to his own house, and I gave him thanks, but made excuse to stay away. When he and the nobleman who was his guest had left the churchyard, and the townspeople too were gone, I and my wife and the minister walked home together through the dewy meadow, with the splendor of the morning about us, and the birds caroling from every tree and thicket.

CHAPTER XI
IN WHICH I MEET AN ITALIAN DOCTOR

THE summer slipped away, and autumn came, with the purple of the grape and the yellowing corn, the nuts within the forest, and the return of the countless wild fowl to the marshes and reedy river banks, and still I stayed in Jamestown, and my wife with me, and still the Santa Teresa rode at anchor in the river below the fort. If the man whom she brought knew that by tarrying in Virginia he risked his ruin with the King, yet, with a courage worthy of a better cause, he tarried.

Now and then ships came in, but they were small, belated craft. The most had left England before the sailing of the Santa Teresa; the rest, private ventures, trading for clapboard or sassafras, knew nothing of court affairs. Only the Sea Flower, sailing from London a fortnight after the Santa Teresa, and much delayed by adverse winds, brought a letter from the deputy treasurer to Yeardley and the Council. From Rolfe I learned its contents. It spoke of the stir that was made by the departure from the realm of the King's favorite. "None know where he hath gone. The King looks dour; 't is hinted that the privy council are as much at sea as the rest of the world; my Lord of Buckingham saith nothing, but his following—which of late hath somewhat decayed—is so increased that his antechambers cannot hold the throngs that come to wait upon him. Some will have it that my Lord Carnal hath fled the kingdom to escape the Tower; others, that the King hath sent him on a mission to the King of Spain about this detested Spanish match; others, that the gadfly hath stung him and he is gone to America,—to search for Raleigh's gold mine, maybe. This last most improbable; but if 't is so, and he should touch at Virginia, receive him with all honor. If indeed he is not out of favor, the Company may find in him a powerful friend; of powerful enemies, God knows, there is no lack!"

Thus the worthy Master Ferrar. And at the bottom of the letter, among other news of city and court, mention was made of the disappearance of a ward of the King's, the Lady Jocelyn Leigh. Strict search had been made, but the unfortunate lady had not been found. "'T is whispered that she hath killed herself; also, that his Majesty had meant to give her in marriage to my Lord Carnal. But that all true love and virtue and constancy have gone from the age, one might conceive that the said lord had but fled the court for a while, to indulge his grief in some solitude of hill and stream and shady vale,—the lost lady being right worthy of such dole."

In sooth she was, but my lord was not given to such fashion of mourning.

The summer passed, and I did nothing. What was there I could do? I had written by the Due Return to Sir Edwyn, and to my cousin, the Earl of

Northumberland. The King hated Sir Edwyn as he hated tobacco and witchcraft. "Choose the devil, but not Sir Edwyn Sandys!" had been his passionate words to the Company the year before. A certain fifth of November had despoiled my Lord of Northumberland of wealth, fame, and influence. Small hope there was in those two. That the Governor and Council, remembering old dangers shared, wished me well I did not doubt, but that was all. Yeardley had done all he could do, more than most men would have dared to do, in procuring this delay. There was no further help in him; nor would I have asked it. Already out of favor with the Warwick faction, he had risked enough for me and mine. I could not flee with my wife to the Indians, exposing her, perhaps, to a death by fierce tortures; moreover, Opechancanough had of late strangely taken to returning to the settlements those runaway servants and fugitives from justice which before we had demanded from him in vain. If even it had been possible to run the gauntlet of the Indian villages, war parties, and hunting bands, what would have been before us but endless forest and a winter which for us would have had no spring? I could not see her die of hunger and cold, or by the teeth of the wolves. I could not do what I should have liked to do,—take, single-handed, that King's ship with its sturdy crew and sail with her south and ever southwards, before us nothing more formidable than Spanish ships, and beyond them blue waters, spice winds, new lands, strange islands of the blest.

There seemed naught that I could do, naught that she could do. Our Fate had us by the hands, and held us fast. We stood still, and the days came and went like dreams.

While the Assembly was in session I had my part to act as Burgess from my hundred. Each day I sat with my fellows in the church, facing the Governor in his great velvet chair, the Council on either hand, and listened to the droning of old Twine, the clerk, like the droning of the bees without the window; to the chant of the sergeant-at-arms; to long and windy discourses from men who planted better than they spoke; to remarks by the Secretary, witty, crammed with Latin and traveled talk; to the Governor's slow, weighty words. At Weyanoke we had had trouble with the Indians. I was one who loved them not and had fought them well, for which reason the hundred chose me its representative. In the Assembly it was my part to urge a greater severity toward those our natural enemies, a greater watchfulness on our part, the need for palisades and sentinels, the danger that lay in their acquisition of firearms, which, in defiance of the law, men gave them in exchange for worthless Indian commodities. This Indian business was the chief matter before the Assembly. I spoke when I thought speech was needed, and spoke strongly; for my heart foreboded that which was to come upon us too soon and too surely. The Governor listened gravely, nodding his head; Master Pory, too, the Cape Merchant, and West were of my mind; but the remainder were besotted by their own conceit, esteeming the very name of Englishman sentinel and palisade enough, or trusting in the smooth words and vows of brotherhood poured forth so plentifully by that red Apollyon, Opechancanough.

When the day's work was done, and we streamed out of the church,—the Governor and Council first, the rest of us in order,—it was to find as often as not a red and black figure waiting for us among the graves. Sometimes it joined itself to the Governor, sometimes to Master Pory; sometimes the whole party, save one, went off with it to the guest house, there to eat, drink, and make merry.

If Virginia and all that it contained, save only that jewel of which it had robbed the court, were out of favor with the King's minion, he showed it not. Perhaps he had accepted the inevitable with a good grace; perhaps it was but his mode of biding his time; but he had shifted into that soldierly frankness of speech and manner, that genial, hail-fellow-well-met air, behind which most safely hides a villain's mind. Two days after that morning behind the church, he had removed himself, his French valets, and his Italian physician from the Governor's house to the newly finished guest house. Here he lived, cock of the walk, taking his ease in his inn, elbowing out all guests save those of his own inviting. If, what with his open face and his open hand, his dinners and bear-baitings and hunting parties, his tales of the court and the wars, his half hints as to the good he might do Virginia with the King, extending even to the lightening of the tax upon our tobacco and the prohibition of the Spanish import, his known riches and power, and the unknown height to which they might attain if his star at court were indeed in the ascendant,—if with these things he slowly, but surely, won to his following all save a very few of those I had thought my fast friends, it was not a thing marvelous or without precedent. Upon his side was good that might be seen and handled; on mine was only a dubious right and a not at all dubious danger. I do not think it plagued me much. The going of those who had it in their heart to wish to go left me content, and for those who fawned upon him from the first, or for the rabble multitude who flung up their caps and ran at his heels, I cared not a doit. There were still Rolfe and West and the Governor, Jeremy Sparrow and Diccon.

My lord and I met, perforce, in the street, at the Governor's house, in church, on the river, in the saddle. If we met in the presence of others, we spoke the necessary formal words of greeting or leave-taking, and he kept his countenance; if none were by, off went the mask. The man himself and I looked each other in the eyes and passed on. Once we encountered on a late evening among the graves, and I was not alone. Mistress Percy had been restless, and had gone, despite the minister's protests, to sit upon the river bank. When I returned from the assembly and found her gone, I went to fetch her. A storm was rolling slowly up. Returning the long way through the churchyard, we came upon him sitting beside a sunken grave, his knees drawn up to meet his chin, his eyes gloomily regardful of the dark broad river, the unseen ocean, and the ship that could not return for weeks to come. We passed him in silence,—I with a slight bow, she with a slighter curtsy. An hour later, going down the street in the dusk of the storm, I ran against Dr. Lawrence Bohun. "Don't stop me!" he panted. "The Italian doctor is away in the woods gathering simples, and they found my Lord Carnal in a fit among the graves, half an hour agone." My lord was bled, and the next morning went hunting.

The lady whom I had married abode with me in the minister's house, held her head high, and looked the world in the face. She seldom went from home, but when she did take the air it was with pomp and circumstance. When that slender figure and exquisite face, set off by as rich apparel as could be bought from a store of finery brought in by the Southampton, and attended by a turbaned negress and a serving man who had been to the wars, and had escaped the wheel by the skin of his teeth, appeared in the street, small wonder if a greater commotion arose than had been since the days of the Princess Pocahontas and her train of dusky beauties. To this fairer, more imperial dame gold lace doffed its hat and made its courtliest bow, and young planters bent to their saddlebows, while the common folk nudged and stared and had their say. The beauty, the grace, the pride, that deigned small response to well-meant words,—all that would have been intolerable in plain Mistress Percy, once a waiting maid, then a piece of merchandise to be sold for one hundred and twenty pounds of tobacco, then the wife of a poor gentleman, was pardoned readily enough to the Lady Jocelyn Leigh, the ward of the King, the bride to be (so soon as the King's Court of High Commission should have snapped in twain an inconvenient and ill-welded fetter) of the King's minion.

So she passed like a splendid vision through the street perhaps once a week. On Sundays she went with me to church, and the people looked at her instead of at the minister, who rebuked them not, because his eyes were upon the same errand.

The early autumn passed and the leaves began to turn, and still all things were as they had been, save that the Assembly sat no longer. My fellow Burgesses went back to their hundreds, but my house at Weyanoke knew me no more. In a tone that was apologetic, but firm, the Governor had told me that he wished my company at Jamestown. I was pleased enough to stay, I assured him,—as indeed I was. At Weyanoke, the thunderbolt would fall without warning; at Jamestown, at least I could see, coming up the river, the sails of the Due Return or what other ship the Company might send.

The color of the leaves deepened, and there came a season of a beauty singular and sad, like a smile left upon the face of the dead summer. Over all things, near and far, the forest where it met the sky, the nearer woods, the great river, and the streams that empty into it, there hung a blue haze, soft and dream-like. The forest became a painted forest, with an ever thinning canopy and an ever thickening carpet of crimson and gold; everywhere there was a low rustling underfoot and a slow rain of color. It was neither cold nor hot, but very quiet, and the birds went by like shadows,—a listless and forgetful weather, in which we began to look, every hour of every day, for the sail which we knew we should not see for weeks to come.

Good Master Bucke tarried with Master Thorpe at Henricus, recruiting his strength, and Jeremy Sparrow preached in his pulpit, slept in his chamber, and worked in his garden. This garden ran down to the green bank of the river; and here, sitting idly by the stream, her chin in her hand and her dark eyes watching the strong, free sea birds as they came and went, I found my wife one evening, as I came from the fort, where had been some martial exercise. Thirty feet away Master Jeremy Sparrow worked among the dying flowers, and hummed:—

"There is a garden in her face,

Where roses and white lilies grow."

He and I had agreed that when I must needs be absent he should be within call of her; for I believed my Lord Carnal very capable of intruding himself into her presence. That house and garden, her movements and mine, were spied upon by his foreign hirelings, I knew perfectly well.

As I sat down upon the bank at her feet, she turned to me with a sudden passion. "I am weary of it all!" she cried. "I am tired of being pent up in this house and garden, and of the watch you keep upon me. And if I go abroad, it is worse! I hate all those shameless faces that stare at me as if I were in the pillory. I am pilloried before you all, and I find the experience sufficiently bitter. And when I think that that man whom I hate, hate, hate, breathes the air that I breathe, it stifles me! If I could fly away like those birds, if I could only be gone from this place for even a day!"

"I would beg leave to take you home, to Weyanoke," I said after a pause, "but I cannot go and leave the field to him."

"And I cannot go," she answered. "I must watch for that ship and that King's command that my Lord Carnal thinks potent enough to make me his wife. King's commands are strong, but a woman's will is stronger. At the last I shall know what to do. But now why may I not take Angela and cross that strip of sand and go into the woods on the other side? They are so fair and strange,— all red and yellow,—and they look very still and peaceful. I could walk in them, or lie down under the trees and forget awhile, and they are not at all far away." She looked at me eagerly.

"You could not go alone," I told her. "There would be danger in that. But to-morrow, if you choose, I and Master Sparrow and Diccon will take you there. A day in the woods is pleasant enough, and will do none of us harm. Then you may wander as you please, fill your arms with colored leaves, and forget the world. We will watch that no harm comes nigh you, but otherwise you shall not be disturbed."

She broke into delighted laughter. Of all women the most steadfast of soul, her outward moods were as variable as a child's. "Agreed!" she cried. "You and the minister and Diccon Demon shall lay your muskets across your knees, and Angela shall witch you into stone with her old, mad, heathen charms. And then—and then—I will gather more gold than had King Midas; I will dance with the hamadryads; I will find out Oberon and make Titania jealous!"

"I do not doubt that you could do so," I said, as she sprang to her feet, childishly eager and radiantly beautiful.

I rose to go in with her, for it was supper time, but in a moment changed my mind, and resumed my seat on the bank of turf. "Do you go in," I said. "There's a snake near by, in those bushes below the bank. I'll kill the creature, and then I'll come to supper."

When she was gone, I walked to where, ten feet away, the bank dipped to a clump of reeds and willows planted in the mud on the brink of the river. Dropping on my knees I leaned over, and, grasping a man by the collar, lifted him from the slime where he belonged to the bank beside me.

It was my Lord Carnal's Italian doctor that I had so fished up. I had seen him before, and had found in his very small, mean figure clad all in black, and his narrow face with malignant eyes, and thin white lips drawn tightly over gleaming teeth, something infinitely repulsive, sickening to the sight as are certain reptiles to the touch.

"There are no simples or herbs of grace to be found amongst reeds and half-drowned willows," I said. "What did so learned a doctor look for in so unlikely a place?"

He shrugged his shoulders and made play with his clawlike hands, as if he understood me not. It was a lie, for I knew that he and the English tongue were sufficiently acquainted. I told him as much, and he shot at me a most venomous glance, but continued to shrug, gesticulate, and jabber in Italian. At last I saw nothing better to do than to take him, still by the collar, to the edge of the garden next the churchyard, and with the toe of my boot to send him tumbling among the graves. I watched him pick himself up, set his attire to rights, and go away in the gathering dusk, winding in and out among the graves; and then I went in to supper, and told Mistress Percy that the snake was dead.

CHAPTER XII
IN WHICH I RECEIVE A WARNING AND REPOSE A TRUST

SHORTLY before daybreak I was wakened by a voice beneath my window. "Captain Percy," it cried, "the Governor wishes you at his house!" and was gone.

I dressed and left the house, disturbing no one. Hurrying through the chill dawn, I reached the square not much behind the rapid footsteps of the watch who had wakened me. About the Governor's door were horses, saddled and bridled, with grooms at their heads, men and beasts gray and indistinct, wrapped in the fog. I went up the steps and into the hall, and knocked at the door of the Governor's great room. It opened, and I entered to find Sir George, with Master Pory, Rolfe, West, and others of the Council gathered about the great centre table and talking eagerly. The Governor was but half dressed; West and Rolfe were in jack boots and coats of mail. A man, breathless with hard riding, spattered with swamp mud and torn by briers, stood, cap in hand, staring from one to the other.

"In good time, Captain Percy!" cried the Governor. "Yesterday you called the profound peace with the Indians, of which some of us boasted, the lull before the storm. Faith, it looks to-day as though you were in the right, after all!"

"What 's the matter, sir?" I asked, advancing to the table.

"Matter enough!" he answered. "This man has come, post haste, from the plantations above Paspahegh. Three days ago, Morgan, the trader, was decoyed into the woods by that Paspahegh fool and bully, Nemattanow, whom they call Jack of the Feather, and there murdered. Yesterday, out of sheer bravado, the Indian turned up at Morgan's house, and Morgan's men shot him down. They buried the dog, and thought no more of it. Three hours ago, Chanco the Christian went to the commander and warned him that the Paspaheghs were in a ferment, and that the warriors were painting themselves black. The commander sent off at once to me, and I see naught better to do than to dispatch you with a dozen men to bring them to their senses. But there 's to be no harrying nor battle. A show of force is all that 's needed,— I'll stake my head upon it. Let them see that we are not to be taken unawares, but give them fair words. That they may be the sooner placated I send with you Master Rolfe,—they'll listen to him. See that the black paint is covered with red, give them some beads and a knife or two, then come home. If you like not the look of things, find out where Opechancanough is, and I'll send him an embassy. He loves us well, and will put down any disaffection."

"There's no doubt that he loves us," I said dryly. "He loves us as a cat loves the mouse that it plays with. If we are to start at once, sir, I'll go get my horse."

"Then meet us at the neck of land," said Rolfe.

I nodded, and left the room. As I descended the steps into the growing light outside, I found Master Pory at my side.

"I kept late hours last night," he remarked, with a portentous yawn. "Now that this business is settled, I'll go back to bed."

I walked on in silence.

"I am in your black books," he continued, with his sly, merry, sidelong glance. "You think that I was overcareful of the ground, that morning behind the church, and so unfortunately delayed matters until the Governor happened by and brought things to another guess conclusion."

"I think that you warned the Governor," I said bluntly.

He shook with laughter. "Warned him? Of course I warned him. Youth would never have seen that molehill and fairy ring and projecting root, but wisdom cometh with gray hairs, my son. D' ye not think I'll have the King's thanks?"

"Doubtless," I answered. "An the price contents you, I do not know why I should quarrel with it."

By this we were halfway down the street, and we now came upon the guest house. A window above us was unshuttered, and in the room within a light still burned. Suddenly it was extinguished. A man's face looked down upon us for a moment, then drew back; a skeleton hand was put out softly and slowly, and the shutter drawn to. Hand and face belonged to the man I had sent tumbling among the graves the evening before.

"The Italian doctor," said Master Pory.

There was something peculiar in his tone. I glanced at him, but his broad red face and twinkling eyes told me nothing. "The Italian doctor," he repeated. "If I had a friend in Captain Percy's predicament, I should bid him beware of the Italian doctor."

"Your friend would be obliged for the warning," I replied.

We walked a little further. "And I think," he said, "that I should inform this purely hypothetical friend of mine that the Italian and his patron had their heads mighty close together, last night."

"Last night?"

"Ay, last night. I went to drink with my lord, and so broke up their tete-a-tete. My lord was boisterous in his cups and not oversecret. He dropped some hints"—He broke off to indulge in one of his endless silent laughs. "I don't know why I tell you this, Captain Percy. I am on the other side, you know,—quite on the other side. But now I bethink me, I am only telling you what I should tell you were I upon your side. There's no harm in that, I hope, no disloyalty to my Lord Carnal's interests which happen to be my interests?"

I made no answer. I gave him credit both for his ignorance of the very hornbook of honor and for his large share of the milk of human kindness.

"My lord grows restive," he said, when we had gone a little further. "The Francis and John, coming in yesterday, brought court news. Out of sight, out of mind. Buckingham is making hay while the sun shines. Useth angel water for his complexion, sleepeth in a medicated mask such as the Valois used, and is grown handsomer than ever; changeth the fashion of his clothes thrice a week, which mightily pleaseth his Majesty. Whoops on the Spanish match, too, and, wonderful past all whooping, from the prince's detestation hath become his bosom friend. Small wonder if my Lord Carnal thinks it's time he was back at Whitehall."

"Let him go, then," I said. "There's his ship that brought him here."

"Ay, there 's his ship," rejoined Master Pory. "A few weeks more, and the Due Return will be here with the Company's commands. D' ye think, Captain Percy, that there's the slightest doubt as to their tenor?"

"No."

"Then my lord has but to possess his soul with patience and wait for the Due Return. No doubt he'll do so."

"No doubt he'll do so," I echoed.

By this we had reached the Secretary's own door. "Fortune favor you with the Paspaheghs!" he said, with another mighty yawn. "As for me, I'll to bed. Do you ever dream, Captain Percy? I don't; mine is too good a conscience. But if I did, I should dream of an Italian doctor."

The door shut upon his red face and bright eyes. I walked rapidly on down the street to the minister's house. The light was very pale as yet, and house and garden lay beneath a veil of mist. No one was stirring. I went on through the gray wet paths to the stable, and roused Diccon.

"Saddle Black Lamoral quickly," I ordered. "There's trouble with the Paspaheghs, and I am off with Master Rolfe to settle it."

"Am I to go with you?" he asked.

I shook my head. "We have a dozen men. There's no need of more."

I left him busy with the horse, and went to the house. In the hall I found the negress strewing the floor with fresh rushes, and asked her if her mistress yet slept. In her soft half English, half Spanish, she answered in the affirmative. I went to my own room and armed myself; then ran upstairs to the comfortable chamber where abode Master Jeremy Sparrow, surrounded by luxuries which his soul contemned. He was not there. At the foot of the stair I was met by Goodwife Allen. "The minister was called an hour ago, sir," she announced. "There's a man dying of the fever at Archer's Hope, and they sent a boat for him. He won't be back until afternoon."

I hurried past her back to the stable. Black Lamoral was saddled, and Diccon held the stirrup for me to mount.

"Good luck with the vermin, sir!" he said. "I wish I were going, too."

His tone was sullen, yet wistful. I knew that he loved danger as I loved it, and a sudden remembrance of the dangers we had faced together brought us nearer to each other than we had been for many a day.

"I don't take you," I explained, "because I have need of you here. Master Sparrow has gone to watch beside a dying man, and will not be back for hours. As for myself, there's no telling how long I may be kept. Until I come you are to guard house and garden well. You know what I mean. Your mistress is to be molested by no one."

"Very well, sir."

"One thing more. There was some talk yesterday of my taking her across the neck to the forest. When she awakes, tell her from me that I am sorry for her to lose her pleasure, but that now she could not go even were I here to take her."

"There 's no danger from the Paspaheghs there," he muttered.

"The Paspaheghs happen not to be my only foes," I said curtly. "Do as I bid you without remark. Tell her that I have good reasons for desiring her to remain within doors until my return. On no account whatever is she to venture without the garden."

I gathered up the reins, and he stood back from the horse's head. When I had gone a few paces I drew rein, and, turning in my saddle, spoke to him across the dew-drenched grass. "This is a trust, Diccon," I said.

The red came into his tanned face. He raised his hand and made our old military salute. "I understand it so, my captain," he answered, and I rode away satisfied.

CHAPTER XIII
IN WHICH THE SANTA TERESA DROPS
DOWNSTREAM

AN hour's ride brought us to the block house standing within the forest, midway between the white plantations at Paspahegh and the village of the tribe. We found it well garrisoned, spies out, and the men inclined to make light of the black paint and the seething village.

Amongst them was Chanco the Christian. I called him to me, and we listened to his report with growing perturbation. "Thirty warriors!" I said, when he had finished. "And they are painted yellow as well as black, and have dashed their cheeks with puccoon: it's *l'outrance*, then! And the war dance is toward! If we are to pacify this hornets' nest, it's high time we set about it. Gentlemen of the block house, we are but twelve, and they may beat us back, in which case those that are left of us will fight it out with you here. Watch for us, therefore, and have a sally party ready. Forward, men!"

"One moment, Captain Percy," said Rolfe. "Chanco, where's the Emperor?"

"Five suns ago he was with the priests at Uttamussac," answered the Indian. "Yesterday, at the full sun power, he was in the lodge of the werowance of the Chickahominies. He feasts there still. The Chickahominies and the Powhatans have buried the hatchet."

"I regret to hear it," I remarked. "Whilst they took each other's scalps, mine own felt the safer."

"I advise going direct to Opechancanough," said Rolfe.

"Since he's only a league away, so do I," I answered.

We left the block house and the clearing around it, and plunged into the depths of the forest. In these virgin woods the trees are set well apart, though linked one to the other by the omnipresent grape, and there is little undergrowth, so that we were able to make good speed. Rolfe and I rode well in front of our men. By now the sun was shining through the lower branches of the trees, and the mist was fast vanishing. The forest—around us, above us, and under the hoofs of the horses where the fallen leaves lay thick—was as yellow as gold and as red as blood.

"Rolfe," I asked, breaking a long silence, "do you credit what the Indians say of Opechancanough?"

"That he was brother to Powhatan only by adoption?"

"That, fleeing for his life, he came to Virginia, years and years ago, from some mysterious land far to the south and west?"

"I do not know," he replied thoughtfully. "He is like, and yet not like, the people whom he rules. In his eye there is the authority of mind; his features are of a nobler cast "—

"And his heart is of a darker," I said. "It is a strange and subtle savage."

"Strange enough and subtle enough, I admit," he answered, "though I believe not with you that his friendliness toward us is but a mask."

"Believe it or not, it is so," I said. "That dark, cold, still face is a mask, and that simple-seeming amazement at horses and armor, guns and blue beads, is a mask. It is in my mind that some fair day the mask will be dropped. Here's the village."

Until our interview with Chanco the Christian, the village of the Paspaheghs, and not the village of the Chickahominies, had been our destination, and since leaving the block house we had made good speed; but now, within the usual girdle of mulberries, we were met by the werowance and his chief men with the customary savage ceremonies. We had long since come to the conclusion that the birds of the air and the fish of the streams were Mercuries to the Indians.

The werowance received us in due form, with presents of fish and venison, cakes of chinquapin meal and gourds of pohickory, an uncouth dance by twelve of his young men and a deal of hellish noise; then, at our command, led us into the village, and to the lodge which marked its centre. Around it were gathered Opechancanough's own warriors, men from Orapax and Uttamussac and Werowocomoco, chosen for their strength and cunning; while upon the grass beneath a blood-red gum tree sat his wives, painted and tattooed, with great strings of pearl and copper about their necks. Beyond them were the women and children of the Chickahominies, and around us all the red forest.

The mat that hung before the door of the lodge was lifted, and an Indian, emerging, came forward, with a gesture of welcome. It was Nantauquas, the Lady Rebekah's brother, and the one Indian—saving always his dead sister— that was ever to my liking; a savage, indeed, but a savage as brave and chivalrous, as courteous and truthful, as a Christian knight.

Rolfe sprang from his horse, and advancing to meet the young chief embraced him. Nantauquas had been much with his sister during those her happy days at Varina, before she went with Rolfe that ill-fated voyage to England, and Rolfe loved him for her sake and for his own. "I thought you at Orapax, Nantauquas!" he exclaimed.

"I was there, my brother," said the Indian, and his voice was sweet, deep, and grave, like that of his sister. "But Opechancanough would go to Uttamussac, to the temple and the dead kings. I lead his war parties now, and I came with him. Opechancanough is within the lodge. He asks that my brother and Captain Percy come to him there."

He lifted the mat for us, and followed us into the lodge. There was the usual winding entrance, with half a dozen mats to be lifted one after the other, but at last we came to the central chamber and to the man we sought.

He sat beside a small fire burning redly in the twilight of the room. The light shone now upon the feathers in his scalp lock, now upon the triple row of pearls around his neck, now upon knife and tomahawk in his silk grass belt, now on the otterskin mantle hanging from his shoulder and drawn across his knees. How old he was no man knew. Men said that he was older than Powhatan, and Powhatan was very old when he died. But he looked a man in the prime of life; his frame was vigorous, his skin unwrinkled, his eyes bright and full. When he rose to welcome us, and Nantauquas stood beside him, there seemed not a score of years between them.

The matter upon which we had come was not one that brooked delay. We waited with what patience we might until his long speech of welcome was finished, when, in as few words as possible, Rolfe laid before him our complaint against the Paspaheghs. The Indian listened; then said, in that voice that always made me think of some cold, still, bottomless pool lying black beneath overhanging rocks: "My brothers may go in peace. The Paspaheghs have washed off the black paint. If my brothers go to the village, they will find the peace pipe ready for their smoking."

Rolfe and I stared at each other. "I have sent messengers," continued the Emperor. "I have told the Paspaheghs of my love for the white man, and of the goodwill the white man bears the Indian. I have told them that Nemattanow was a murderer, and that his death was just. They are satisfied. Their village is as still as this beast at my feet." He pointed downward to a tame panther crouched against his moccasins. I thought it an ominous comparison.

Involuntarily we looked at Nantauquas. "It is true," he said. "I am but come from the village of the Paspaheghs. I took them the word of Opechancanough."

"Then, since the matter is settled, we may go home," I remarked, rising as I spoke. "We could, of course, have put down the Paspaheghs with one hand, giving them besides a lesson which they would not soon forget, but in the kindness of our hearts toward them and to save ourselves trouble we came to Opechancanough. For his aid in this trifling business the Governor gives him thanks."

A smile just lit the features of the Indian. It was gone in a moment. "Does not Opechancanough love the white men?" he said. "Some day he will do more than this for them."

We left the lodge and the dark Emperor within it, got to horse, and quitted the village, with its painted people, yellowing mulberries, and blood-red gum trees. Nantauquas went with us, keeping pace with Rolfe's horse, and giving us now and then, in his deep musical voice, this or that bit of woodland news. At the block house we found confirmation of the Emperor's statement. An embassy from the Paspaheghs had come with presents, and the peace pipe had been smoked. The spies, too, brought news that all war-like preparations had ceased in the village. It had sunk once more into a quietude befitting the sleepy, dreamy, hazy weather.

Rolfe and I held a short consultation. All appeared safe, but there was the possibility of a ruse. At the last it seemed best that he, who by virtue of his peculiar relations with the Indians was ever our negotiator, should remain with half our troop at the block house, while I reported to the Governor. So I left him, and Nantauquas with him, and rode back to Jamestown, reaching the town some hours sooner than I was expected.

It was after nooning when I passed through the gates of the palisade, and an hour later when I finished my report to the Governor. When he at last dismissed me, I rode quickly down the street toward the minister's house. As I passed the guest house, I glanced up at the window from which, at daybreak, the Italian had looked down upon me. No one looked out now; the window was closely shuttered, and at the door beneath my lord's French rascals were conspicuously absent. A few yards further on I met my lord face to face, as he emerged from a lane that led down to the river. At sight of me he started violently, and his hand went to his mouth. I slightly bent my head, and rode on past him. At the gate of the churchyard, a stone's throw from home, I met Master Jeremy Sparrow.

"Well met!" he exclaimed. "Are the Indians quiet?"

"For the nonce. How is your sick man?"

"Very well," he answered gravely. "I closed his eyes two hours ago."

"He's dead, then," I said. "Well, he 's out of his troubles, and hath that advantage over the living. Have you another call, that you travel from home so fast?"

"Why, to tell the truth," he replied, "I could not but feel uneasy when I learned just now of this commotion amongst the heathen. You must know best, but I should not have thought it a day for madam to walk in the woods; so I e'en thought I would cross the neck and bring her home."

"For madam to walk in the woods?" I said slowly. "So she walks there? With whom?"

"With Diccon and Angela," he answered. "They went before the sun was an hour high, so Goodwife Allen says. I thought that you—" "No," I told him. "On the contrary, I left command that she should not venture outside the garden. There are more than Indians abroad."

I was white with anger; but besides anger there was fear in my heart.

"I will go at once and bring her home," I said. As I spoke, I happened to glance toward the fort and the shipping in the river beyond. Something seemed wrong with the prospect. I looked again, and saw what hated and familiar object was missing.

"Where is the Santa Teresa?" I demanded, the fear at my heart tugging harder.

"She dropped downstream this morning. I passed her as I came up from Archer's Hope, awhile ago. She's anchored in midstream off the big spring. Why did she go?"

We looked each other in the eyes, and each read the thought that neither cared to put into words.

"You can take the brown mare," I said, speaking lightly because my heart was as heavy as lead, "and we'll ride to the forest. It is all right, I dare say. Doubtless we'll find her garlanding herself with the grape, or playing with the squirrels, or asleep on the red leaves, with her head in Angela's lap."

"Doubtless," he said. "Don't lose time. I'll saddle the mare and overtake you in two minutes."

CHAPTER XIV
IN WHICH WE SEEK A LOST LADY

BESIDE the minister and myself, nothing human moved in the crimson woods. Blue haze was there, and the steady drift of colored leaves, and the sunshine freely falling through bared limbs, but no man or woman. The fallen leaves rustled as the deer passed, the squirrels chattered and the foxes barked, but we heard no sweet laughter or ringing song.

We found a bank of moss, and lying upon it a chaplet of red-brown oak leaves; further on, the mint beside a crystal streamlet had been trodden underfoot; then, flung down upon the brown earth beneath some pines, we came upon a long trailer of scarlet vine. Beyond was a fairy hollow, a cuplike depression, curtained from the world by the red vines that hung from the trees upon its brim, and carpeted with the gold of a great maple; and here Fear became a giant with whom it was vain to wrestle.

There had been a struggle in the hollow. The curtain of vines was torn, the boughs of a sumach bent and broken, the fallen leaves groun underfoot. In one place there was blood upon the leaves.

The forest seemed suddenly very quiet,—quite soundless save for the beating of our hearts. On every side opened red and yellow ways, sunny glades, labyrinthine paths, long aisles, all dim with the blue haze like the cloudy incense in stone cathedrals, but nothing moved in them save the creatures of the forest. Without the hollow there was no sign. The leaves looked undisturbed, or others, drifting down, had hidden any marks there might have been; no footprints, no broken branches, no token of those who had left the hollow. Down which of the painted ways had they gone, and where were they now?

Sparrow and I sat our horses, and stared now down this alley, now down that, into the blue that closed each vista.

"The Santa Teresa is just off the big spring," he said at last. "She must have dropped down there in order to take in water quietly."

"The man that came upon her is still in town,—or was an hour agone," I replied.

"Then she has n't sailed yet," he said.

In the distance something grew out of the blue mist. I had not lived thirteen years in the woodland to be dim of sight or dull of hearing.

"Some one is coming," I announced. "Back your horse into this clump of sumach."

The sumach grew thick, and was draped, moreover, with some broad-leafed vine. Within its covert we could see with small danger of being seen, unless the approaching figure should prove to be that of an Indian. It was not an Indian; it was my Lord Carnal. He came on slowly, glancing from side to side, and pausing now and then as if to listen. He was so little of a woodsman that he never looked underfoot.

Sparrow touched my arm and pointed down a glade at right angles with the path my lord was pursuing. Up this glade there was coming toward us another figure,—a small black figure that moved swiftly, looking neither to the right nor to the left.

Black Lamoral stood like a stone; the brown mare, too, had learned what meant a certain touch upon her shoulder. Sparrow and I, with small shame for our eavesdropping, bent to our saddlebows and looked sideways through tiny gaps in the crimson foliage.

My lord descended one side of the hollow, his heavy foot bringing down the dead leaves and loose earth; the Italian glided down the opposite side, disturbing the economy of the forest as little as a snake would have done.

"I thought I should never meet you," growled my lord. "I thought I had lost you and her and myself. This d-d red forest and this blue haze are enough to"—He broke off with an oath.

"I came as fast as I could," said the other. His voice was strange, thin and dreamy, matching his filmy eyes and his eternal, very faint smile. "Your poor physician congratulates your lordship upon the success that still attends you. Yours is a fortunate star, my lord."

"Then you have her safe?" cried my lord.

"Three miles from here, on the river bank, is a ring of pines, in which the trees grow so thick that it is always twilight. Ten years ago a man was murdered there, and Sir Thomas Dale chained the murderer to the tree beneath which his victim was buried, and left him to perish of hunger and thirst. That is the tale they tell at Jamestown. The wood is said to be haunted by murdered and murderer, and no one enters it or comes nearer to it than he can avoid: which makes it an excellent resort for those whom the dead cannot scare. The lady is there, my lord, with your four knaves to guard her. They do not know that the gloom and quiet of the place are due to more than nature."

My lord began to laugh. Either he had been drinking, or the success of his villainy had served for wine. "You are a man in a thousand, Nicolo!" he said. "How far above or below the ship is this fortunate wood?"

"Just opposite, my lord."

"Can a boat land easily?"

"A creek runs through the wood to the river. There needs but the appointed signal from the bank, and a boat from the Santa Teresa can be rowed up the stream to the very tree beneath which the lady sits."

My lord's laughter rang out again. "You're a man in ten thousand, Nicolo! Nicolo, the bridegroom's in town."

"Back so soon?" said the Italian. "Then we must change your lordship's plan. With him on the ground, you can no longer wait until nightfall to row downstream to the lady and the Santa Teresa. He'll come to look for her."

"Ay he'll come to look for her, curse him!" echoed my lord.

"Do you think the dead will scare him?" continued the Italian.

"No, I don't!" answered my lord, with an oath. "I would he were among them! An I could have killed him before I went"—

"I had devised a way to do it long ago, had not your lordship's conscience been so tender. And yet, before now, our enemies—yours and mine, my lord—have met with sudden and mysterious death. Men stared, but they ended by calling it a dispensation of Providence." He broke off to laugh with silent, hateful laughter, as mirthful as the grin of a death's-head.

"I know, I know!" said my lord impatiently. "We are not overnice, Nicolo. But between me and those who then stood in my way there had passed no challenge. This is my mortal foe, through whose heart I would drive my sword. I would give my ruby to know whether he's in the town or in the forest."

"He's in the forest," I said.

Black Lamoral and the brown mare were beside them before either moved hand or foot, or did aught but stare and stare, as though men and horses had risen from the dead. All the color was gone from my lord's face,—it looked white, drawn, and pinched; as for his companion, his countenance did not change,—never changed, I believe,—but the trembling of the feather in his hat was not caused by the wind.

Jeremy Sparrow bent down from his saddle, seized the Italian under the armpits, and swung him clean from the ground up to the brown mare's neck. "Divinity and medicine," he said genially, "soul healer and body poisoner, we'll ride double for a time," and proceeded to bind the doctor's hands with his own scarf. The creature of venom before him writhed and struggled, but the minister's strength was as the strength of ten, and the minister's hand held him down. By this I was off Black Lamoral and facing my lord. The color had come back to his lip and cheek, and the flash to his eye. His hand went to his sword hilt.

"I shall not draw mine, my lord," I told him. "I keep troth."

He stared at me with a frown that suddenly changed into a laugh, forced and unnatural enough. "Then go thy ways, and let me go mine!" he cried. "Be complaisant, worthy captain of trainbands and Burgess from a dozen huts! The King and I will make it worth your while."

"I will not draw my sword upon you," I replied, "but I will try a fall with you," and I seized him by the wrist.

He was a good wrestler as he was a good swordsman, but, with bitter anger in my heart and a vision of the haunted wood before my eyes, I think I could have wrestled with Hercules and won. Presently I threw him, and, pinning him down with my knee upon his breast, cried to Sparrow to cut the bridle reins from Black Lamoral and throw them to me. Though he had the Italian upon his hands, he managed to obey. With my free hand and my teeth I drew a thong about my lord's arms and bound them to his sides; then took my knee from his chest and my hand from his throat, and rose to my feet. He rose too with one spring. He was very white, and there was foam on his lips.

"What next, captain?" he demanded thickly. "Your score is mounting up rather rapidly. What next?"

"This," I replied, and with the other thong fastened him, despite his struggles, to the young maple beneath which we had wrestled. When the task was done, I first drew his sword from its jeweled scabbard and laid it on the ground at his feet, and then cut the leather which restrained his arms, leaving him only tied to the tree. "I am not Sir Thomas Dale," I said, "and therefore I shall not gag you and leave you bound for an indefinite length of time, to contemplate a grave that you thought to dig. One haunted wood is enough for one county. Your lordship will observe that I have knotted your bonds in easy reach of your hands, the use of which I have just restored to you. The knot is a peculiar one; an Indian taught it to me. If you set to work at once, you will get it untied before nightfall. That you may not think it the Gordian knot and treat it as such, I have put your sword where you can get it only when you have worked for it. Your familiar, my lord, may prove of use to us; therefore we will take him with us to the haunted wood. I have the honor to wish your lordship a very good day."

I bowed low, swung myself into my saddle, and turned my back upon his glaring eyes and bared teeth. Sparrow, his prize flung across his saddlebow, turned with me. A minute more saw us out of the hollow, and entered upon the glade up which had come the Italian. When we had gone a short distance, I turned in my saddle and looked back. The tiny hollow had vanished; all the forest looked level, dreamy and still, barren of humanity, given over to its own shy children, nothing moving save the slow-falling leaves. But from beyond a great clump of sumach, set like a torch in the vaporous blue, came a steady stream of words, happily rendered indistinguishable by distance, and I knew that the King's minion was cursing the Italian, the Governor, the Santa Teresa, the Due Return, the minister, the forest, the haunted wood, his sword, the knot that I had tied, and myself.

I admit that the sound was music in mine ears.

CHAPTER XV
IN WHICH WE FIND THE HAUNTED WOOD

ON the outskirts of the haunted wood we dismounted, fastening the horses to two pines. The Italian we gagged and bound across the brown mare's saddle. Then, as noiselessly as Indians, we entered the wood.

Once within it, it was as though the sun had suddenly sunk from the heavens. The pines, of magnificent height and girth, were so closely set that far overhead, where the branches began, was a heavy roof of foliage, impervious to the sunshine, brooding, dark and sullen as a thundercloud, over the cavernous world beneath. There was no undergrowth, no clinging vines, no bloom, no color; only the dark, innumerable tree trunks and the purplish-brown, scented, and slippery earth. The air was heavy, cold, and still, like cave air; the silence as blank and awful as the silence beneath the earth.

The minister and I stole through the dusk, and for a long time heard nothing but our own breathing and the beating of our hearts. But coming to a sluggish stream, as quiet as the wood through which it crept, and following its slow windings, we at last heard a voice, and in the distance made out dark forms sitting on the earth beside that sombre water. We went on with caution, gliding from tree to tree and making no noise. In the cheerless silence of that place any sound would have shattered the stillness like a pistol shot.

Presently we came to a halt, and, ourselves hidden by a giant trunk, looked out on stealers and stolen. They were gathered on the bank of the stream, waiting for the boat from the Santa Teresa. The lady whom we sought lay like a fallen flower on the dark ground beneath a pine. She did not move, and her eyes were shut. At her head crouched the negress, her white garments showing ghostlike through the gloom. Beneath the next tree sat Diccon, his hands tied behind him, and around him my Lord Carnal's four knaves. It was Diccon's voice that we had heard. He was still speaking, and now we could distinguish the words.

"So Sir Thomas chains him there," he said,—"right there to that tree under which you are sitting, Jacky Bonhomme." Jacques incontinently shifted his position. "He chains him there, with one chain around his neck, one around his waist, and one around his ankles. Then he sticks me a bodkin through his tongue." A groan of admiration from his audience. "Then they dig, before his very eyes, a grave,—shallow enough they make it, too,—and they put into it, uncoffined, with only a long white shroud upon him, the man he murdered. Then they cover the grave. You're sitting on it now, you other Jacky."

"Godam!" cried the rascal addressed, and removed with expedition to a less storied piece of ground.

"Then they go away," continued Diccon in graveyard tones. "They all go away together,—Sir Thomas and Captain Argall, Captain West, Lieutenant George Percy and his cousin, my master, and Sir Thomas's men; they go out of the wood as though it were accursed, though indeed it was not half so gloomy then as it is now. The sun shone into it then, sometimes, and the birds sang. You would n't think it from the looks of things now, would you? As the dead man rotted in his grave, and the living man died by inches above him, they say the wood grew darker, and darker, and darker. How dark it's getting now, and cold,—cold as the dead!"

His auditors drew closer together, and shivered. Sparrow and I were so near that we could see the hands of the ingenious story-teller, bound behind his back, working as he talked. Now they strained this way, and now that, at the piece of rope that bound them.

"That was ten years ago," he said, his voice becoming more and more impressive. "Since that day nothing comes into this wood,—nothing human, that is. Neither white man nor Indian comes, that's certain. Then why are n't there chains around that tree, and why are there no bones beneath it, on the ground there? Because, Jackies all, the man that did that murder walks! It is not always deadly still here; sometimes there 's a clanking of chains! And a bodkin through the tongue can't keep the dead from wailing! And the murdered man walks, too; in his shroud he follows the other—Is n't that something white in the distance yonder?"

My lord's four knaves looked down the arcade of trees, and saw the something white as plainly as if it had been verily there. Each moment the wood grew darker,—a thing in nature, since the sun outside was swiftly sinking to the horizon. But to those to whom that tale had been told it was a darkening unearthly and portentous, bringing with it a colder air and a deepened silence.

"Oh, Sir Thomas Dale, Sir Thomas Dale!"

The voice seemed to come from the distance, and bore in its dismal cadence the melancholy of the damned. For a moment my heart stood still, and the hair of my head commenced to rise; the next, I knew that Diccon had found an ally, not in the dead, but in the living. The minister, standing beside me, opened his mouth again, and again that dismal voice rang through the wood, and again it seemed, by I know not what art, to come from any spot rather than from that particular tree behind whose trunk stood Master Jeremy Sparrow.

"Oh, the bodkin through my tongue! Oh, the bodkin through my tongue!"

Two of the guard sat with hanging lip and lacklustre eyes, turned to stone; one, at full length upon the ground, bruised his face against the pine needles and called on the Virgin; the fourth, panic-stricken, leaped to his feet and dashed off into the darkness, to trouble us no more that day.

"Oh, the heavy chains!" cried the unseen spectre. "Oh, the dead man in his grave!"

The man on his face dug his nails into the earth and howled; his fellows were too frightened for sound or motion. Diccon, a hardy rogue, with little fear of God or man, gave no sign of perturbation beyond a desperate tugging at the rope about his wrists. He was ever quick to take suggestion, and he had probably begun to question the nature of the ghost who was doing him such yeoman service.

"D' ye think they've had enough?" said Sparrow in my ear. "My invention flaggeth."

I nodded, too choked with laughter for speech, and drew my sword. The next moment we were upon the men like wolves upon the fold.

They made no resistance. Amazed and shaken as they were, we might have dispatched them with all ease, to join the dead whose lamentations yet rang in their ears; but we contented ourselves with disarming them and bidding them begone for their lives in the direction of the Pamunkey. They went like frightened deer, their one goal in life escape from the wood.

"Did you meet the Italian?"

I turned to find my wife at my side. The King's ward had a kingly spirit; she was not one that the dead or the living could daunt. To her, as to me, danger was a trumpet call to nerve heart and strengthen soul. She had been in peril of that which she most feared, but the light in her eye was not quenched, and the hand with which she touched mine, though cold, was steady.

"Is he dead?" she asked. "At court they called him the Black Death. They said"—

"I did not kill him," I answered, "but I will if you desire it."

"And his master?" she demanded. "What have you done with his master?"

I told her. At the vision my words conjured up her strained nerves gave way, and she broke into laughter as cruel as it was sweet. Peal after peal rang through the haunted wood, and increased the eeriness of the place.

"The knot that I tied he will untie directly," I said. "If we would reach Jamestown first, we had best be going."

"Night is upon us, too," said the minister, "and this place hath the look of the very valley of the shadow of death. If the spirits walk, it is hard upon their time—and I prefer to walk elsewhere."

"Cease your laughter, madam," I said. "Should a boat be coming up this stream, you would betray us."

I went over to Diccon, and in a silence as grim as his own cut the rope which bound his hands, which done we all moved through the deepening gloom to where we had left the horses, Jeremy Sparrow going on ahead to have them in readiness. Presently he came hurrying back. "The Italian is gone!" he cried.

"Gone!" I exclaimed. "I told you to tie him fast to the saddle!"

"Why, so I did," he replied. "I drew the thongs so tight that they cut into his flesh. He could not have endured to pull against them."

"Then how did he get away?"

"Why," he answered, with a rueful countenance, "I did bind him, as I have said; but when I had done so, I bethought me of how the leather must cut, and of how pain is dreadful even to a snake, and of the injunction to do as you would be done by, and so e'en loosened his bonds. But, as I am a christened man, I thought that they would yet hold him fast!"

I began to swear, but ended in vexed laughter. "The milk's spilt. There 's no use in crying over it. After all, we must have loosed him before we entered the town."

"Will you not bring the matter before the Governor?" he asked.

I shook my head. "If Yeardley did me right, he would put in jeopardy his office and his person. This is my private quarrel, and I will draw no man into it against his will. Here are the horses, and we had best be gone, for by this time my lord and his physician may have their heads together again."

I mounted Black Lamoral, and lifted Mistress Percy to a seat behind me. The brown mare bore the minister and the negress, and Diccon, doggedly silent, trudged beside us.

We passed through the haunted wood and the painted forest beyond without adventure. We rode in silence: the lady behind me too weary for speech, the minister revolving in his mind the escape of the Italian, and I with my own thoughts to occupy me. It was dusk when we crossed the neck of land, and as we rode down the street torches were being lit in the houses. The upper room in the guest house was brightly illumined, and the window was open. Black Lamoral and the brown mare made a trampling with their hoofs, and I began to whistle a gay old tune I had learnt in the wars. A figure in scarlet and black came to the window, and stood there looking down upon us. The lady riding with me straightened herself and raised her weary head. "The next time we go to the forest, Ralph," she said in a clear, high voice, "thou 'lt show me a certain tree," and she broke into silvery laughter. She laughed until we had left behind the guest house and the figure in the upper window, and then the laughter changed to something like a sob. If there were pain and anger in her heart, pain and anger were in mine also. She had never called me by my name before. She had only used it now as a dagger with which to stab at that fierce heart above us.

At last we reached the minister's house, and dismounted before the door. Diccon led the horses away, and I handed my wife into the great room. The minister tarried but for a few words anent some precautions that I meant to take, and then betook himself to his own chamber. As he went out of the door Diccon entered the room.

"Oh, I am weary!" sighed Mistress Jocelyn Percy. "What was the mighty business, Captain Percy, that made you break tryst with a lady? You should go to court, sir, to be taught gallantry."

"Where should a wife go to be taught obedience?" I demanded. "You know where I went and why I could not keep tryst. Why did you not obey my orders?"

She opened wide her eyes. "Your orders? I never received any,—not that I should have obeyed them if I had. Know where you went? I know neither why nor where you went!"

I leaned my hand upon the table, and looked from her to Diccon.

"I was sent by the Governor to quell a disturbance amongst the nearest Indians. The woods today have been full of danger. Moreover, the plan that we made yesterday was overheard by the Italian. When I had to go this morning without seeing you, I left you word where I had gone and why, and also my commands that you should not stir outside the garden. Were you not told this, madam?"

"No!" she cried.

I looked at Diccon. "I told madam that you were called away on business," he said sullenly. "I told her that you were sorry you could not go with her to the woods."

"You told her nothing more?"

"No."

"May I ask why?"

He threw back his head. "I did not believe the Paspaheghs would trouble her," he answered, with hardihood, "and you had n't seen fit, sir, to tell me of the other danger. Madam wanted to go, and I thought it a pity that she should lose her pleasure for nothing."

I had been hunting the day before, and my whip yet lay upon the table. "I have known you for a hardy rogue," I said, with my hand upon it; "now I know you for a faithless one as well. If I gave you credit for all the vices of the soldier, I gave you credit also for his virtues. I was the more deceived. The disobedient servant I might pardon, but the soldier who is faithless to his trust"—

I raised the whip and brought it down again and again across his shoulders. He stood without a word, his face dark red and his hands clenched at his sides. For a minute or more there was no sound in the room save the sound of the blows; then my wife suddenly cried out: "It is enough! You have beaten him enough! Let him go, sir!"

I threw down the whip. "Begone, sirrah!" I ordered. "And keep out of my sight to-morrow!"

With his face still dark red and with a pulse beating fiercely in his cheek, he moved slowly toward the door, turned when he had reached it and saluted, then went out and closed it after him.

"Now he too will be your enemy," said Mistress Percy, "and all through me. I have brought you many enemies, have I not? Perhaps you count me amongst them? I should not wonder if you did. Do you not wish me gone from Virginia?"

"So I were with you, madam," I said bluntly, and went to call the minister down to supper.

CHAPTER XVI
IN WHICH I AM RID OF AN UNPROFITABLE SERVANT

THE next day, Governor and Councilors sat to receive presents from the Paspaheghs and to listen to long and affectionate messages from Opechancanough, who, like the player queen, did protest too much. The Council met at Yeardley's house, and I was called before it to make my report of the expedition of the day before. It was late afternoon when the Governor dismissed us, and I found myself leaving the house in company with Master Pory.

"I am bound for my lord's," said that worthy as we neared the guest house. "My lord hath Xeres wine that is the very original nectar of the gods, and he drinks it from goblets worth a king's ransom. We have heard a deal to-day about burying hatchets: bury thine for the nonce, Ralph Percy, and come drink with us."

"Not I," I said. "I would sooner drink with—some one else."

He laughed. "Here's my lord himself shall persuade you."

My lord, dressed with his usual magnificence and darkly handsome as ever, was indeed standing within the guest-house door. Pory drew up beside him. I was passing on with a slight bow, when the Secretary caught me by the sleeve. At the Governor's house wine had been set forth to revive the jaded Council, and he was already half seas over. "Tarry with us, captain!" he cried. "Good wine's good wine, no matter who pours it! 'S bud! in my young days men called a truce and forgot they were foes when the bottle went round!"

"If Captain Percy will stay," quoth my lord, "I will give him welcome and good wine. As Master Pory says, men cannot be always fighting. A breathing spell to-day gives to-morrow's struggle new zest."

He spoke frankly, with open face and candid eyes. I was not fooled. If yesterday he would have slain me only in fair fight, it was not so to-day. Under the lace that fell over his wrist was a red cirque, the mark of the thong with which I had bound him. As if he had told me, I knew that he had thrown his scruples to the winds, and that he cared not what foul play he used to sweep me from his path. My spirit and my wit rose to meet the danger. Of a sudden I resolved to accept his invitation.

"So be it," I said, with a laugh and a shrug of my shoulders. "A cup of wine is no great matter. I'll take it at your hands, my lord, and drink to our better acquaintance."

We all three went up into my lord's room. The King had fitted out his minion bravely for the Virginia voyage, and the riches that had decked the state cabin aboard the Santa Teresa now served to transform the bare room in the guest house at Jamestown into a corner of Whitehall. The walls were hung with arras, there was a noble carpet beneath as well as upon the table, and against the wall stood richly carved trunks. On the table, beside a bowl of late flowers were a great silver flagon and a number of goblets, some of chased silver and some of colored glass, strangely shaped and fragile as an eggshell. The late sun now shining in at the open window made the glass to glow like precious stones.

My lord rang a little silver bell, and a door behind us was opened. "Wine, Giles!" cried my lord in a raised voice. "Wine for Master Pory, Captain Percy, and myself! And Giles, my two choice goblets."

Giles, whom I had never seen before, advanced to the table, took the flagon, and went toward the door, which he had shut behind him. I negligently turned in my seat, and so came in for a glimpse, as he slipped through the door, of a figure in black in the next room.

The wine was brought, and with it two goblets. My lord broke off in the midst of an account of the morning's bear-baiting which the tediousness of the Indians had caused us to miss. "Who knows if we three shall ever drink together again?" he said. "To honor this bout I use my most precious cups." Voice and manner were free and unconstrained. "This gold cup "—he held it up—"belonged to the Medici. Master Pory, who is a man of taste, will note the beauty of the graven maenads upon this side, and of the Bacchus and Ariadne upon this. It is the work of none other than Benvenuto Cellini. I pour for you, sir." He filled the gold cup with the ruby wine and set it before the Secretary, who eyed it with all the passion of a lover, and waited not for us, but raised it to his lips at once. My lord took up the other cup. "This glass," he continued, "as green as an emerald, freckled inside and out with gold, and shaped like a lily, was once amongst a convent's treasures. My father brought it from Italy, years ago. I use it as he used it, only on gala days. I fill to you, sir." He poured the wine into the green and gold and twisted bauble and set it before me, then filled a silver goblet for himself. "Drink, gentlemen," he said.

"Faith, I have drunken already," quoth the Secretary, and proceeded to fill for himself a second time. "Here's to you, gentlemen!" and he emptied half the measure.

"Captain Percy does not drink," remarked my lord.

I leaned my elbow upon the table, and, holding up the glass against the light, began to admire its beauty. "The tint is wonderful," I said, "as lucent a green as the top of the comber that is to break and overwhelm you. And these knobs of gold, within and without, and the strange shape the tortured glass has been made to take. I find it of a quite sinister beauty, my lord."

"It hath been much admired," said the nobleman addressed.

"I am strangely suited, my lord," I went on, still dreamily enjoying the beauty of the green gem within my clasp. "I am a soldier with an imagination. Sometimes, to give the rein to my fancy pleases me more than wine. Now, this strange chalice,—might it not breed dreams as strange?"

"When I had drunken, I think," replied my lord. "The wine would be a potent spur to my fancy."

"What saith honest Jack Falstaff?" broke in the maudlin Secretary. "Doth he not bear testimony that good sherris maketh the brain apprehensive and quick; filleth it with nimble, fiery, and delectable shapes, which being delivered by the tongue become excellent wit? Wherefore let us drink, gentlemen, and beget fancies." He filled for himself again, and buried his nose in the cup.

"'T is such a cup, methinks," I said, "as Medea may have filled for Theseus. The white hand of Circe may have closed around this stem when she stood to greet Ulysses, and knew not that he had the saving herb in his palm. Goneril may have sent this green and gilded shape to Regan. Fair Rosamond may have drunk from it while the Queen watched her. At some voluptuous feast, Caesar Borgia and his sister, sitting crowned with roses, side by side, may have pressed it upon a reluctant guest, who had, perhaps, a treasure of his own. I dare swear Rene, the Florentine, hath fingered many such a goblet before it went to whom Catherine de' Medici delighted to honor."

"She had the whitest hands," maundered the Secretary. "I kissed them once before she died, in Blois, when I was young. Rene was one of your slow poisoners. Smell a rose, draw on a pair of perfumed gloves, drink from a certain cup, and you rang your own knell, though your bier might not receive you for many and many a day,—not till the rose was dust, the gloves lost, the cup forgotten."

"There's a fashion I have seen followed abroad, that I like," I said. "Host and guest fill to each other, then change tankards. You are my host to-day, my lord, and I am your guest. I will drink to you, my lord, from your silver goblet."

With as frank a manner as his own of a while before, I pushed the green and gold glass over to him, and held out my hand for the silver goblet. That a man may smile and smile and be a villain is no new doctrine. My lord's laugh and gesture of courtesy were as free and ready as if the poisoned splendor he drew toward him had been as innocent as a pearl within the shell. I took the silver cup from before him. "I drink to the King," I said, and drained it to the bottom. "Your lordship does not drink. 'T is a toast no man refuses."

He raised the glass to his lips, but set it down before its rim had touched them. "I have a headache," he declared. "I will not drink to-day."

Master Pory pulled the flagon toward him, tilted it, and found it empty. His rueful face made me laugh. My lord laughed too,—somewhat loudly,—but ordered no more wine. "I would I were at the Mermaid again," lamented the now drunken Secretary. "There we did n't split a flagon in three parts.... The Tsar of Muscovy drinks me down a quartern of aqua vitae at a gulp,—I've seen him do it....I would I were the Bacchus on this cup, with the purple grapes adangle above me.... Wine and women—wine and women... good wine needs no bush... good sherris sack"... His voice died into unintelligible mutterings, and his gray unreverend head sank upon the table.

I rose, leaving him to his drunken slumbers, and, bowing to my lord, took my leave. My lord followed me down to the public room below. A party of upriver planters had been drinking, and a bit of chalk lay upon a settle behind the door upon which the landlord had marked their score. I passed it; then turned back and picked it up. "How long a line shall I draw, my lord?" I asked with a smile.

"How does the length of the door strike you?" he answered.

I drew the chalk from top to bottom of the wood. "A heavy Core makes a heavy reckoning, my lord," I said, and, leaving the mark upon the door, I bowed again and went out into the street.

The sun was sinking when I reached the minister's house, and going into the great room drew a stool to the table and sat down to think. Mistress Percy was in her own chamber; in the room overhead the minister paced up and down, humming a psalm. A fire was burning briskly upon the hearth, and the red light rose and fell,—now brightening all the room, now leaving it to the gathering dusk. Through the door, which I had left open, came the odor of the pines, the fallen leaves, and the damp earth. In the churchyard an owl hooted, and the murmur of the river was louder than usual.

I had sat staring at the table before me for perhaps half an hour, when I chanced to raise my eyes to the opposite wall. Now, on this wall, reflecting the firelight and the open door behind me, hung a small Venetian mirror, which I had bought from a number of such toys brought in by the Southampton, and had given to Mistress Percy. My eyes rested upon it, idly at first, then closely enough as I saw within it a man enter the room. I had heard no footfall; there was no noise now behind me. The fire was somewhat sunken, and the room was almost in darkness; I saw him in the glass dimly, as shadow rather than substance. But the light was not so faint that the mirror could not show me the raised hand and the dagger within its grasp. I sat without motion, watching the figure in the glass grow larger. When it was nearly upon me, and the hand with the dagger drawn back for the blow, I sprang up, wheeled, and caught it by the wrist.

A moment's fierce struggle, and I had the dagger in my own hand and the man at my mercy. The fire upon the hearth seized on a pine knot and blazed up brightly, filling the room with light. "Diccon!" I cried, and dropped my arm.

I had never thought of this. The room was very quiet as, master and man, we stood and looked each other in the face. He fell back to the wall and leaned against it, breathing heavily; into the space between us the past came thronging.

I opened my hand and let the dagger drop to the floor. "I suppose that this was because of last night," I said. "I shall never strike you again."

I went to the table, and sitting down leaned my forehead upon my hand. It was Diccon who would have done this thing! The fire crackled on the hearth as had crackled the old camp fires in Flanders; the wind outside was the wind that had whistled through the rigging of the Treasurer, one terrible night when we lashed ourselves to the same mast and never thought to see the morning. Diccon!

Upon the table was the minister's inkhorn and pen. I drew my tablets from the breast of my doublet and began to write. "Diccon!" I called, without turning, when I had finished.

He came slowly forward to the table, and stood beside it with hanging head. I tore the leaf from the book and pushed it over to him. "Take it," I ordered.

"To the commander?" he asked. "I am to take it to the commander?"

I shook my head. "Read it."

He stared at it vacantly, turning it now this way, now that.

"Did you forget how to read when you forgot all else?" I said sternly.

He read, and the color rushed into his face.

"It is your freedom," I said. "You are no longer man of mine. Begone, sirrah!"

He crumpled the paper in his hand. "I was mad," he muttered.

"I could almost believe it," I replied. "Begone!"

After a moment he went. Sitting still in my place, I heard him heavily and slowly leave the room, descend the step at the door, and go out into the night.

A door opened, and Mistress Jocelyn Percy came into the great room, like a sunbeam strayed back to earth. Her skirt was of flowered satin, her bodice of rich taffeta; between the gossamer walls of her French ruff rose the whitest neck to meet the fairest face. Upon her dark hair sat, as lightly as a kiss, a little pearl-bordered cap. A color was in her cheeks and a laugh on her lips. The rosy light of the burning pine caressed her,—now dwelling on the rich dress, now on the gold chain around the slender waist, now on rounded arms, now on the white forehead below the pearls. Well, she was a fair lady for a man to lay down his life for.

"I held court this afternoon!" she cried. "Where were you, sir? Madam West was here, and my Lady Temperance Yeardley, and Master Wynne, and Master Thorpe from Henricus, and Master Rolfe with his Indian brother,—who, I protest, needs but silk doublet and hose and a month at Whitehall to make him a very fine gentleman."

"If courage, steadfastness, truth, and courtesy make a gentleman," I said, "he is one already. Such an one needs not silk doublet nor court training."

She looked at me with her bright eyes. "No," she repeated, "such an one needs not silk doublet nor court training." Going to the fire, she stood with one hand upon the mantelshelf, looking down into the ruddy hollows. Presently she stooped and gathered up something from the hearth. "You waste paper strangely, Captain Percy," she said. "Here is a whole handful of torn pieces."

She came over to the table, and with a laugh showered the white fragments down upon it, then fell to idly piecing them together. "What were you writing?" she asked. "'To all whom it may concern: I, Ralph Percy, Gentleman, of the Hundred of Weyanoke, do hereby set free from all service to me and mine'"—

I took from her the bits of paper, and fed the fire with them. "Paper is but paper," I said. "It is easily rent. Happily a man's will is more durable."

CHAPTER XVII
IN WHICH MY LORD AND I PLAY AT BOWLS

THE Governor had brought with him from London the year before, a set of boxwood bowls, and had made, between his house and the fort, a noble green. The generality must still use for the game that portion of the street that was not tobacco-planted; but the quality flocked to the Governor's green, and here, one holiday afternoon, a fortnight or more from the day in which I had drunk to the King from my lord's silver goblet, was gathered a very great company. The Governor's match was toward,—ten men to a side, a hogshead of sweet-scented to the victorious ten, and a keg of canary to the man whose bowl should hit the jack.

The season had been one of unusual mildness, and the sunshine was still warm and bright, gilding the velvet of the green, and making the red and yellow leaves swept into the trench to glow like a ribbon of flame. The sky was blue, the water bluer still, the leaves bright-colored, the wind blowing; only the enshrouding forest, wrapped in haze, seemed as dim, unreal, and far away as a last year's dream.

The Governor's gilt armchair had been brought from the church, and put for him upon the bank of turf at the upper end of the green. By his side sat my Lady Temperance, while the gayly dressed dames and the men who were to play and to watch were accommodated with stools and settles or with seats on the green grass. All were dressed in holiday clothes, all tongues spoke, all eyes laughed; you might have thought there was not a heavy heart amongst them. Rolfe was there, gravely courteous, quiet and ready; and by his side, in otterskin mantle, beaded moccasins, and feathered headdress, the Indian chief, his brother-in-law,—the bravest, comeliest, and manliest savage with whom I have ever dealt. There, too, was Master Pory, red and jovial, with an eye to the sack the servants were bringing from the Governor's house; and the commander, with his wife; and Master Jeremy Sparrow, fresh from a most moving sermon on the vanities of this world. Captains, Councilors, and Burgesses aired their gold lace, and their wit or their lack of it; while a swarm of younger adventurers, youths of good blood and bad living, come from home for the weal of England and the woe of Virginia, went here and there through the crowd like gilded summer flies.

Rolfe and I were to play; he sat on the grass at the feet of Mistress Jocelyn Percy, making her now and then some courtly speech, and I stood beside her, my hand on the back of her chair.

The King's ward held court as though she were a king's daughter. In the brightness of her beauty she sat there, as gracious for the nonce as the sunshine, and as much of another world. All knew her story, and to the daring that is in men's hearts her own daring appealed,—and she was young and very beautiful. Some there had not been my friends, and now rejoiced in what seemed my inevitable ruin; some whom I had thought my friends were gone over to the stronger side; many who in secret wished me well still shook their heads and shrugged their shoulders over what they were pleased to call my madness; but for her, I was glad to know, there were only good words. The Governor had left his gilt armchair to welcome her to the green, and had caused a chair to be set for her near his own, and here men came and bowed before her as if she had been a princess indeed.

A stir amongst the crowd, a murmur, and a craning of necks heralded the approach of that other at whom the town gaped with admiration. He came with his retinue of attendants, his pomp of dress, his arrogance of port, his splendid beauty. Men looked from the beauty of the King's ward to the beauty of the King's minion, from her costly silk to his velvet and miniver, from the air of the court that became her well to the towering pride and insolence which to the thoughtless seemed his fortune's proper mantle, and deemed them a pair well suited, and the King's will indeed the will of Heaven.

I was never one to value a man by his outward seeming, but suddenly I saw myself as in a mirror,—a soldier, scarred and bronzed, acquainted with the camp, but not with the court, roughened by a rude life, poor in this world's goods, the first flush of youth gone forever. For a moment my heart was bitter within me. The pang passed, and my hand tightened its grasp upon the chair in which sat the woman I had wed. She was my wife, and I would keep my own.

My lord had paused to speak to the Governor, who had risen to greet him. Now he came toward us, and the crowd pressed and whispered. He bowed low to Mistress Percy, made as if to pass on, then came to a stop before her, his hat in his hand, his handsome head bent, a smile upon his bearded lips.

"When was it that we last sat to see men bowl, lady?" he said. "I remember a gay match when I bowled against my Lord of Buckingham, and fair ladies sat and smiled upon us. The fairest laughed, and tied her colors around my arm."

The lady whom he addressed sat quietly, with hands folded in her silken lap and an untroubled face. "I did not know you then, my lord," she answered him, quite softly and sweetly. "Had I done so, be sure I would have cut my hand off ere it gave color of mine to"—"To whom?" he demanded, as she paused.

"To a coward, my lord," she said clearly.

As if she had been a man, his hand went to his sword hilt. As for her, she leaned back in her chair and looked at him with a smile.

He spoke at last, slowly and with deliberate emphasis. "I won then," he said. "I shall win again, my lady,—my Lady Jocelyn Leigh."

I dropped my hand from her chair and stepped forward. "It is my wife to whom you speak, my Lord Carnal," I said sternly. "I wait to hear you name her rightly."

Rolfe rose from the grass and stood beside me, and Jeremy Sparrow, shouldering aside with scant ceremony Burgess and Councilor, came also. The Governor leaned forward out of his chair, and the crowd became suddenly very still.

"I am waiting, my lord," I repeated.

In an instant, from what he had been he became the frank and guileless nobleman. "A slip of the tongue, Captain Percy!" he cried, his white teeth showing and his hand raised in a gesture of deprecation. "A natural thing, seeing how often, how very often, I have so addressed this lady in the days when we had not the pleasure of your acquaintance." He turned to her and bowed, until the feather in his hat swept the ground. "I won then," he said. "I shall win again—Mistress Percy," and passed on to the seat that had been reserved for him.

The game began. I was to lead one side, and young Clement the other. At the last moment he came over to me. "I am out of it, Captain Percy," he announced with a rueful face. "My lord there asks me to give him my place. When we were hunting yesterday, and the stag turned upon me, he came between and thrust his knife into the brute, which else might have put an end to my hunting forever and a day: so you see I can't refuse him. Plague take it all! and Dorothy Gookin sitting there watching!"

My lord and I stood forward, each with a bowl in his hand. We looked toward the Governor. "My lord first, as becometh his rank," he said. My lord stooped and threw, and his bowl went swiftly over the grass, turned, and rested not a hands'-breadth from the jack. I threw. "One is as near as the other!" cried Master Macocke for the judges. A murmur arose from the crowd, and my lord swore beneath his breath. He and I retreated to our several sides, and Rolfe and West took our places. While they and those that followed bowled, the crowd, attentive though it was, still talked and laughed, and laid wagers upon its favorites; but when my lord and I again stood forth, the noise was hushed, and men and women stared with all their eyes. He delivered, and his bowl touched the jack. He straightened himself, with a smile, and I heard Jeremy Sparrow behind me groan; but my bowl too kissed the jack. The crowd began to laugh with sheer delight, but my lord turned red and his brows drew together. We had but one turn more. While we waited, I marked his black eyes studying every inch of the ground between him and that small white ball, to strike which, at that moment, I verily believe he would have given the King's favor. All men pray, though they pray not to the same god. As he stood there, when his time had come, weighing the bowl in his hand, I knew that he prayed to his daemon, fate, star, whatever thing he raised an altar to and bent before. He threw, and I followed, while the throng held its breath. Master Macocke rose to his feet. "It's a tie, my masters!" he exclaimed.

The excited crowd surged forward, and a babel of voices arose. "Silence, all!" cried the Governor. "Let them play it out!"

My lord threw, and his bowl stopped perilously near the shining mark. As I stepped to my place a low and supplicating "O Lord!" came to my ears from the lips and the heart of the preacher, who had that morning thundered against the toys of this world. I drew back my arm and threw with all my force. A cry arose from the throng, and my lord ground his heel into the earth. The bowl, spurning the jack before it, rushed on, until both buried themselves in the red and yellow leaves that filled the trench.

I turned and bowed to my antagonist. "You bowl well, my lord," I said. "Had you had the forest training of eye and arm, our fortunes might have been reversed."

He looked me up and down. "You are kind, sir," he said thickly. "'To-day to thee, to-morrow to me.' I give you joy of your petty victory."

He turned squarely from me, and stood with his face downstream. I was speaking to Rolfe and to the few—not even all of that side for which I had won—who pressed around me, when he wheeled.

"Your Honor," he cried to the Governor, who had paused beside Mistress Percy, "is not the Due Return high-pooped? Doth she not carry a blue pennant, and hath she not a gilt siren for figurehead?"

"Ay," answered the Governor, lifting his head from the hand he had kissed with ponderous gallantry. "What then, my lord?"

"Then to-morrow has dawned, sir captain," said my lord to me. "Sure, Dame Venus and her blind son have begged for me favorable winds; for the Due Return has come again."

The game that had been played was forgotten for that day. The hogshead of sweet scented, lying to one side, wreathed with bright vines, was unclaimed of either party; the servants who brought forward the keg of canary dropped their burden, and stared with the rest. All looked down the river, and all saw the Due Return coming up the broad, ruffled stream, the wind from the sea filling her sails, the tide with her, the gilt mermaid on her prow just rising from the rushing foam. She came as swiftly as a bird to its nest. None had thought to see her for at least ten days.

Upon all there fell a sudden realization that it was the word of the King, feathered by the command of the Company, that was hurrying, arrow-like, toward us. All knew what the Company's orders would be,—must needs be,—and the Tudor sovereigns were not so long in the grave that men had forgot to fear the wrath of kings. The crowd drew back from me as from a man plague-spotted. Only Rolfe, Sparrow, and the Indian stood their ground.

The Governor turned from staring downstream. "The game is played, gentlemen," he announced abruptly. "The wind grows colder, too, and clouds are gathering. This fair company will pardon me if I dismiss them somewhat sooner than is our wont. The next sunny day we will play again. Give you God den, gentles."

The crowd stood not upon the order of its going, but streamed away to the river bank, whence it could best watch the oncoming ship. My lord, after a most triumphant bow, swept off with his train in the direction of the guest house. With him went Master Pory. The Governor drew nearer to me. "Captain Percy," he said, lowering his voice, "I am going now to mine own house. The letters which yonder ship brings will be in my hands in less than an hour. When I have read them, I shall perforce obey their instructions. Before I have them I will see you, if you so wish."

"I will be with your Honor in five minutes."

He nodded, and strode off across the green to his garden. I turned to Rolfe. "Will you take her home?" I said briefly. She was so white and sat so still in her chair that I feared to see her swoon. But when I spoke to her she answered clearly and steadily enough, even with a smile, and she would not lean upon Rolfe's arm. "I will walk alone," she said. "None that see me shall think that I am stricken down." I watched her move away, Rolfe beside her, and the Indian following with his noiseless step; then I went to the Governor's house. Master Jeremy Sparrow had disappeared some minutes before, I knew not whither.

I found Yeardley in his great room, standing before a fire and staring down into its hollows. "Captain Percy," he said, as I went up to him, "I am most heartily sorry for you and for the lady whom you so ignorantly married."

"I shall not plead ignorance," I told him.

"You married, not the Lady Jocelyn Leigh, but a waiting woman named Patience Worth. The Lady Jocelyn Leigh, a noble lady, and a ward of the King, could not marry without the King's consent. And you, Captain Percy, are but a mere private gentleman, a poor Virginia adventurer; and my Lord

Carnal is—my Lord Carnal. The Court of High Commission will make short work of this fantastic marriage."

"Then they may do it without my aid," I said. "Come, Sir George, had you wed my Lady Temperance in such fashion, and found this hornets' nest about your ears, what would you have done?"

He gave his short, honest laugh. "It's beside the question, Ralph Percy, but I dare say you can guess what I would have done."

"I'll fight for my own to the last ditch," I continued. "I married her knowing her name, if not her quality. Had I known the latter, had I known she was the King's ward, all the same I should have married her, an she would have had me. She is my wife in the sight of God and honest men. Esteeming her honor, which is mine, at stake, Death may silence me, but men shall not bend me."

"Your best hope is in my Lord of Buckingham," he said. "They say it is out of sight, out of mind, with the King, and, thanks to this infatuation of my Lord Carnal's, Buckingham hath the field. That he strains every nerve to oust completely this his first rival since he himself distanced Somerset goes without saying. That to thwart my lord in this passion would be honey to him is equally of course. I do not need to tell you that, if the Company so orders, I shall have no choice but to send you and the lady home to England. When you are in London, make your suit to my Lord of Buckingham, and I earnestly hope that you may find in him an ally powerful enough to bring you and the lady, to whose grace, beauty, and courage we all do homage, out of this coil."

"We give you thanks, sir," I said.

"As you know," he went on, "I have written to the Company, humbly petitioning that I be graciously relieved from a most thankless task, to wit, the governorship of Virginia. My health faileth, and I am, moreover, under my Lord Warwick's displeasure. He waxeth ever stronger in the Company, and if I put not myself out, he will do it for me. If I be relieved at once, and one of the Council appointed in my place, I shall go home to look after certain of my interests there. Then shall I be but a private gentleman, and if I can serve you, Ralph Percy, I shall be blithe to do so; but now, you understand"—

"I understand, and thank you, Sir George," I said. "May I ask one question?"

"What is it?"

"Will you obey to the letter the instructions the Company sends?"

"To the letter," he answered. "I am its sworn officer."

"One thing more," I went on: "the parole I gave you, sir, that morning behind the church, is mine own again when you shall have read those letters and know the King's will. I am free from that bond, at least."

He looked at me with a frown. "Make not bad worse, Captain Percy," he said sternly.

I laughed. "It is my aim to make bad better, Sir George. I see through the window that the Due Return hath come to anchor; I will no longer trespass on your Honor's time." I bowed myself out, leaving him still with the frown upon his face, staring at the fire.

Without, the world was bathed in the glow of a magnificent sunset. Clouds, dark purple and dark crimson, reared themselves in the west to dizzy heights, and hung threateningly over the darkening land beneath. In the east loomed more pallid masses, and from the bastions of the east to the bastions of the west went hurrying, wind-driven cloudless, dark in the east, red in the west. There was a high wind, and the river, where it was not reddened by the sunset, was lividly green. "A storm, too!" I muttered.

As I passed the guest house, there came to me from within a burst of loud and vaunting laughter and a boisterous drinking catch sung by many voices; and I knew that my lord drank, and gave others to drink, to the orders which the Due Return should bring. The minister's house was in darkness. In the great room I struck a light and fired the fresh torches, and found I was not its sole occupant. On the hearth, the ashes of the dead fire touching her skirts, sat Mistress Jocelyn Percy, her arms resting upon a low stool, and her head pillowed upon them. Her face was not hidden: it was cold and pure and still, like carven marble. I stood and gazed at her a moment; then, as she did not offer to move, I brought wood to the fire and made the forlorn room bright again.

"Where is Rolfe?" I asked at last.

"He would have stayed," she answered, "but I made him go. I wished to be alone." She rose, and going to the window leaned her forehead against the bars, and looked out upon the wild sky and the hurrying river. "I would I were alone," she said in a low voice and with a catch of her breath. As she stood there in the twilight by the window, I knew that she was weeping, though her pride strove to keep that knowledge from me. My heart ached for her, and I knew not how to comfort her. At last she turned. A pasty and stoup of wine were upon the table.

"You are tired and shaken," I said, "and you may need all your strength. Come, eat and drink."

"For to-morrow we die," she added, and broke into tremulous laughter. Her lashes were still wet, but her pride and daring had returned. She drank the wine I poured for her, and we spoke of indifferent things,—of the game that afternoon, of the Indian Nantauquas, of the wild night that clouds and wind portended. Supper over, I called Angela to bear her company, and I myself went out into the night, and down the street toward the guest house.

CHAPTER XVIII
IN WHICH WE GO OUT INTO THE NIGHT

THE guest house was aflame with lights. As I neared it, there was borne to my ears a burst of drunken shouts accompanied by a volley of musketry. My lord was pursuing with a vengeance our senseless fashion of wasting in drinking bouts powder that would have been better spent against the Indians. The noise increased. The door was flung open, and there issued a tide of drawers and servants headed by mine host himself, and followed by a hail of such minor breakables as the house contained and by Olympian laughter.

I made my way past the indignant host and his staff, and standing upon the threshold looked at the riot within. The long room was thick with the smoke of tobacco and the smoke of powder, through which the many torches burned yellow. Upon the great table wine had been spilt, and dripped to swell a red pool upon the floor. Underneath the table, still grasping his empty tankard, lay the first of my lord's guests to fall, an up-river Burgess with white hair. The rest of the company were fast reeling to a like fate. Young Hamor had a fiddle, and, one foot upon a settle, the other upon the table, drew across it a fast and furious bow. Master Pory, arrived at the maudlin stage, alternately sang a slow and melancholy ditty and wiped the tears from his eyes with elaborate care. Master Edward Sharpless, now in a high voice, now in an undistinguishable murmur, argued some imaginary case. Peaceable Sherwood was drunk, and Giles Allen, and Pettiplace Clause. Captain John Martin, sitting with outstretched legs, called now for a fresh tankard, which he emptied at a gulp; now for his pistols, which, as fast as my lord's servants brought them to him new primed, he discharged at the ceiling. The loud wind rattled doors and windows, and made the flame of the torches stream sideways. The music grew madder and madder, the shots more frequent, the drunken voices thicker and louder.

The master of the feast carried his wine better than did his guests, or had drunk less, but his spirit too was quite without bounds. A color burned in his cheeks, a wicked light in his eyes; he laughed to himself. In the gray smoke cloud he saw me not, or saw me only as one of the many who thronged the doorway and stared at the revel within. He raised his silver cup with a slow and wavering hand. "Drink, you dogs!" he chanted. "Drink to the Santa Teresa! Drink to to-morrow night! Drink to a proud lady within my arms and an enemy in my power!"

The wine that had made him mad had maddened those others, also. In that hour they were dead to honor. With shameless laughter and as little spilling as might be, they raised their tankards as my lord raised his. A stone thrown by some one behind me struck the cup from my lord's hand, sending it clattering to the floor and dashing him with the red wine. Master Pory roared with drunken laughter. "Cup and lip missed that time!" he cried.

The man who had thrown the stone was Jeremy Sparrow. For one instant I saw his great figure, and the wrathful face beneath his shock of grizzled hair; the next he had made his way through the crowd of gaping menials and was gone.

My lord stared foolishly at the stains upon his hands, at the fallen goblet and the stone beside it. "Cogged dice," he said thickly, "or I had not lost that throw! I'll drink that toast by myself to-morrow night, when the ship does n't rock like this d—d floor, and the sea has no stones to throw. More wine, Giles! To my Lord High Admiral, gentlemen! To his Grace of Buckingham! May he shortly howl in hell, and looking back to Whitehall see me upon the King's bosom! The King 's a good king, gentlemen! He gave me this ruby. D' ye know what I had of him last year? I"—

I turned and left the door and the house. I could not thrust a fight upon a drunken man.

Ten yards away, suddenly and without any warning of his approach, I found beside me the Indian Nantauquas. "I have been to the woods to hunt," he said, in the slow musical English Rolfe had taught him. "I knew where a panther lodged, and to-day I laid a snare, and took him in it. I brought him to my brother's house, and caged him there. When I have tamed him, I shall give him to the beautiful lady."

He expected no answer, and I gave him none. There are times when an Indian is the best company in the world.

Just before we reached the market place we had to pass the mouth of a narrow lane leading down to the river. The night was very dark, though the stars still shone through rifts in the ever moving clouds. The Indian and I walked rapidly on,—my footfalls sounding clear and sharp on the frosty ground, he as noiseless as a shadow. We had reached the further side of the lane, when he put forth an arm and plucked from the blackness a small black figure.

In the middle of the square was kept burning a great brazier filled with pitched wood. It was the duty of the watch to keep it flaming from darkness to dawn. We found it freshly heaped with pine, and its red glare lit a goodly circle. The Indian, pinioning the wrists of his captive with his own hand of steel, dragged him with us into this circle of light.

"Looking for simples once more, learned doctor?" I demanded.

He mowed and jabbered, twisting this way and that in the grasp of the Indian.

"Loose him," I said to the latter, "but let him not come too near you. Why, worthy doctor, in so wild and threatening a night, when fire is burning and wine flowing at the guest house, do you choose to crouch here in the cold and darkness?"

He looked at me with his filmy eyes, and that faint smile that had more of menace in it than a panther's snarl. "I laid in wait for you, it is true, noble sir," he said in his thin, dreamy voice, "but it was for your good. I would give you warning, sir."

He stood with his mean figure bent cringingly forward, and with his hat in his hand. "A warning, sir," he went ramblingly on. "Maybe a certain one has made me his enemy. Maybe I cut myself loose from his service. Maybe I would do him an ill turn. I can tell you a secret, sir." He lowered his voice and looked around, as if in fear of eavesdroppers.

"In your ear, sir," he said.

I recoiled. "Stand back," I cried, "or you will cull no more simples this side of hell!"

"Hell!" he answered. "There's no such place. I will not tell my secret aloud."

"Nicolo the Italian! Nicolo the Poisoner! Nicolo the Black Death! I am coming for the soul you sold me. There is a hell!"

The thundering voice came from underneath our feet. With a sound that was not a groan and not a screech, the Italian reeled back against the heated iron of the brazier. Starting from that fiery contact with an unearthly shriek, he threw up his arms and dashed away into the darkness. The sound of his madly hurrying footsteps came back to us until the guest house had swallowed him and his guilty terrors.

"Can the preacher play the devil too?" I asked, as Sparrow came up to us from the other side of the fire. "I could have sworn that that voice came from the bowels of the earth. 'T is the strangest gift!"

"A mere trick," he said, with his great laugh, "but it has served me well on more occasions than one. It is not known in Virginia, sir, but before ever the word of the Lord came to me to save poor silly souls I was a player. Once I played the King's ghost in Will Shakespeare's 'Hamlet,' and then, I warrant you, I spoke from the cellarage indeed. I so frighted players and playgoers that they swore it was witchcraft, and Burbage's knees did knock together in dead earnest. But to the matter in hand. When I had thrown yonder stone, I walked quietly down to the Governor's house and looked through the window. The Governor hath the Company's letters, and he and the Council—all save the reprobate Pory—sit there staring at them and drumming with their fingers on the table."

"Is Rolfe of the Council?" I asked.

"Ay; he was speaking,—for you, I suppose, though I heard not the words. They all listened, but they all shook their heads."

"We shall know in the morning," I said. "The night grows wilder, and honest folks should be abed. Nantauquas, good-night. When will you have tamed your panther?"

"It is now the moon of cohonks," answered the Indian. "When the moon of blossoms is here, the panther shall roll at the beautiful lady's feet."

"The moon of blossoms!" I said. "The moon of blossoms is a long way off. I have panthers myself to tame before it comes. This wild night gives one wild thoughts, Master Sparrow. The loud wind, and the sound of the water, and the hurrying clouds—who knows if we shall ever see the moon of blossoms?" I broke off with a laugh for my own weakness. "It's not often that a soldier thinks of death," I said. "Come to bed, reverend sir. Nantauquas, again, good-night, and may you tame your panther!"

In the great room of the minister's house I paced up and down; now pausing at the window, to look out upon the fast darkening houses of the town, the ever thickening clouds, and the bending trees; now speaking to my wife, who sat in the chair I had drawn for her before the fire, her hands idle in her lap, her head thrown back against the wood, her face white and still, with wide dark eyes. We waited for we knew not what, but the light still burned in the Governor's house, and we could not sleep and leave it there.

It grew later and later. The wind howled down the chimney, and I heaped more wood upon the fire. The town lay in darkness now; only in the distance burned like an angry star the light in the Governor's house. In the lull between the blasts of wind it was so very still that the sound of my footfalls upon the floor, the dropping of the charred wood upon the hearth, the tapping of the withered vines without the window, jarred like thunder.

Suddenly madam leaned forward in her chair. "There is some one at the door," she said.

As she spoke, the latch rose and some one pushed heavily against the door. I had drawn the bars across. "Who is it?" I demanded, going to it.

"It is Diccon, sir," replied a guarded voice outside. "I beg of you, for the lady's sake, to let me speak to you."

I opened the door, and he crossed the threshold. I had not seen him since the night he would have played the assassin. I had heard of him as being in Martin's Hundred, with which plantation and its turbulent commander the debtor and the outlaw often found sanctuary.

"What is it, sirrah?" I inquired sternly.

He stood with his eyes upon the floor, twirling his cap in his hands. He had looked once at madam when he entered, but not at me. When he spoke there was the old bravado in his voice, and he threw up his head with the old reckless gesture. "Though I am no longer your man, sir," he said, "yet I hope that one Christian may warn another. The marshal, with a dozen men at his heels, will be here anon."

"How do you know?"

"Why, I was in the shadow by the Governor's window when the parson played eavesdropper. When he was gone I drew myself up to the ledge, and with my knife made a hole in the shutter that fitted my ear well enough. The Governor and the Council sat there, with the Company's letters spread upon the table. I heard the letters read. Sir George Yeardley's petition to be released from the governorship of Virginia is granted, but he will remain in office until the new Governor, Sir Francis Wyatt, can arrive in Virginia. The Company is out of favor. The King hath sent Sir Edwyn Sandys to the Tower. My Lord Warwick waxeth greater every day. The very life of the Company dependeth upon the pleasure of the King, and it may not defy him. You are to be taken into custody within six hours of the reading of the letter, to be kept straitly until the sailing of the Santa Teresa, and to be sent home aboard of her in irons. The lady is to go also, with all honor, and with women to attend her. Upon reaching London, you are to be sent to the Tower, the lady to Whitehall. The Court of High Commission will take the matter under consideration at once. My Lord of Southampton writes that, because of the urgent entreaty of Sir George Yeardley, he will do for you all that lieth in his power, but that if you prove not yourself conformable, there will be little that any can do."

"When will the marshal be here?" I demanded.

"Directly. The Governor was sending for him when I left the window. Master Rolfe spoke vehemently for you, and would have left the Council to come to you; but the Governor, swearing that the Company should not be betrayed by its officers, constrained him to remain. I'm not the Company's officer, so I may tell its orders if I please. A masterless man may speak without fear or favor. I have told you all I know." Before I could speak he was gone, closing the door heavily behind him.

I turned to the King's ward. She had risen from the chair, and now stood in the centre of the room, one hand at her bosom, the other clenched at her side, her head thrown up. She looked as she had looked at Weyanoke, that first night.

"Madam," I said under my breath.

She turned her face upon me. "Did you think," she asked in a low, even voice,—"did you think that I would ever set my foot upon that ship,—that ship on the river there? One ship brought me here upon a shameful errand; another shall not take me upon one more shameful still."

She took her hand from her bosom; in it gleamed in the firelight the small dagger I had given her that night. She laid it on the table, but kept her hand upon it. "You will choose for me, sir," she declared.

I went to the door and looked out. "It is a wild night," I said. "I can suit it with as wild an enterprise. Make a bundle of your warmest clothing, madam, and wrap your mantle about you. Will you take Angela?"

"No," she answered. "I will not have her peril too upon me."

As she stood there, her hand no longer upon the dagger, the large tears welled into her eyes and fell slowly over her white cheeks. "It is for mine honor, sir," she said. "I know that I ask your death."

I could not bear to see her weep, and so I spoke roughly. "I have told you before," I said, "that your honor is my honor. Do you think I would sleep to-morrow night, in the hold of the Santa Teresa, knowing that my wife supped with my Lord Carnal?"

I crossed the room to take my pistols from the rack. As I passed her she caught my hand in hers, and bending pressed her lips upon it. "You have been very good to me," she murmured. "Do not think me an ingrate."

Five minutes later she came from her own room, hooded and mantled, and with a packet of clothing in her hand. I extinguished the torches, then opened the door. As we crossed the threshold, we paused as by one impulse and looked back into the firelit warmth of the room; then I closed the door softly behind us, and we went out into the night.

CHAPTER XIX
IN WHICH WE HAVE UNEXPECTED COMPANY

THE wind, which had heretofore come in fierce blasts, was now steadying to a gale. What with the flying of the heaped clouds, the slanting, groaning pines, and the rushing of the river, the whole earth seemed a fugitive, fleeing breathless to the sea. From across the neck of land came the long-drawn howl of wolves, and in the wood beyond the church a catamount screamed and screamed. The town before us lay as dark and as still as the grave; from the garden where we were we could not see the Governor's house.

"I will carry madam's bundle," said a voice behind us.

It was the minister who had spoken, and he now stood beside us. There was a moment's silence, then I said, with a laugh: "We are not going upon a summer jaunt, friend Sparrow. There is a warm fire in the great room, to which your reverence had best betake yourself out of this windy night."

As he made no movement to depart, but instead possessed himself of Mistress Percy's bundle, I spoke again, with some impatience: "We are no longer of your fold, reverend sir, but are bound for another parish. We give you hearty thanks for your hospitality, and wish you a very good night."

As I spoke I would have taken the bundle from him, but he tucked it under his arm, and, passing us, opened the garden gate. "Did I forget to tell you," he said, "that worthy Master Bucke is well of the fever, and returns to his own to-morrow? His house and church are no longer mine. I have no charge anywhere. I am free and footloose. May I not go with you, madam? There may be dragons to slay, and two can guard a distressed princess better than one. Will you take me for your squire, Captain Percy?"

He held out his great hand, and after a moment I put my own in it.

We left the garden and struck into a lane. "The river, then, instead of the forest?" he asked in a low voice.

"Ay," I answered. "Of the two evils it seems the lesser."

"How about a boat?"

"My own is fastened to the piles of the old deserted wharf."

"You have with you neither food nor water."

"Both are in the boat. I have kept her victualed for a week or more."

He laughed in the darkness, and I heard my wife beside me utter a stifled exclamation.

The lane that we were now in ran parallel to the street to within fifty yards of the guest house, when it bent sharply down to the river. We moved silently and with caution, for some night bird might accost us or the watch come upon us. In the guest house all was darkness save one room,—the upper room,—from which came a very pale light. When we had turned with the lane there were no houses to pass; only gaunt pines and copses of sumach. I took my wife by the hand and hurried her on. A hundred yards before us ran the river, dark and turbulent, and between us and it rose an old, unsafe, and abandoned landing. Sparrow laid his hand upon my arm. "Footsteps behind us," he whispered.

Without slackening pace I turned my head and looked. The clouds, high around the horizon, were thinning overhead, and the moon, herself invisible, yet lightened the darkness below. The sandy lane stretched behind us like a ribbon of twilight,—nothing to be seen but it and the ebony mass of bush and tree lining it on either side. We hastened on. A minute later and we heard behind us a sound like the winding of a small horn, clear, shrill, and sweet. Sparrow and I wheeled—and saw nothing. The trees ran down to the very edge of the wharf, upon whose rotten, loosened, and noisy boards we now trod. Suddenly the clouds above us broke, and the moon shone forth, whitening the mountainous clouds, the ridged and angry river, and the low, tree-fringed shore. Below us, fastened to the piles and rocking with the waves, was the open boat in which we were to embark. A few broken steps led from the boards above to the water below. Descending these I sprang into the boat and held out my arms for Mistress Percy. Sparrow gave her to me, and I lifted her down beside me; then turned to give what aid I might to the minister, who was halfway down the steps—and faced my Lord Carnal.

What devil had led him forth on such a night; why he, whom with my own eyes, three hours agone, I had seen drunken, should have chosen, after his carouse, cold air and his own company rather than sleep; when and where he first spied us, how long he had followed us, I have never known. Perhaps he could not sleep for triumph, had heard of my impending arrest, had come forth to add to the bitterness of my cup by his presence, and so had happened upon us. He could only have guessed at those he followed, until he reached the edge of the wharf and looked down upon us in the moonlight. For a moment he stood without moving; then he raised his hand to his lips, and the shrill call that had before startled us rang out again. At the far end of the lane lights appeared. Men were coming down the lane at a run; whether they were the watch, or my lord's own rogues, we tarried not to see. There was not time to loosen the rope from the piles, so I drew my knife to cut it. My lord saw the movement, and sprang down the steps, at the same time shouting to the men behind to hasten. Sparrow, grappling with him, locked him in a giant's embrace, lifted him bodily from the steps, and flung him into the boat. His head struck against a thwart, and he lay, huddled beneath it, quiet enough. The minister sprang after him, and I cut the rope. By now the wharf shook with running feet, and the backward-streaming flame of the torches reddened its boards and the black water beneath; but each instant the water widened between us and our pursuers. Wind and current swept us out, and at that wharf there were no boats to follow us.

Those whom my lord's whistle had brought were now upon the very edge of the wharf. The marshal's voice called upon us in the name of the King to return. Finding that we vouchsafed no answer, he pulled out a pistol and fired, the ball going through my hat; then whipped out its fellow and fired again. Mistress Percy, whose behavior had been that of an angel, stirred in her seat. I did not know until the day broke that the ball had grazed her arm, drenching her sleeve with blood.

"It is time we were away," I said, with a laugh. "If your reverence will keep your hand upon the tiller and your eye upon the gentleman whom you have made our traveling companion, I'll put up the sail."

I was on my way to the foremast, when the boom lying prone before me rose. Slowly and majestically the sail ascended, tapering upward, silvered by the moon,—the great white pinion which should bear us we knew not whither. I stopped short in my tracks, Mistress Percy drew a sobbing breath, and the minister gasped with admiration. We all three stared as though the white cloth had veritably been a monster wing endowed with life.

"Sails don't rise of themselves!" I exclaimed, and was at the mast before the words were out of my lips. Crouched behind it was a man. I should have known him even without the aid of the moon. Often enough, God knows, I had seen him crouched like this beside me, ourselves in ambush awaiting some unwary foe, brute or human; or ourselves in hiding, holding our breath lest it should betray us. The minister who had been a player, the rival who would have poisoned me, the servant who would have stabbed me, the wife who was wife in name only,—mine were strange shipmates.

He rose to his feet and stood there against the mast, in the old half-submissive, half-defiant attitude, with his head thrown back in the old way.

"If you order me, sir, I will swim ashore," he said, half sullenly, half—I know not how.

"You would never reach the shore," I replied. "And you know that I will never order you again. Stay here if you please, or come aft if you please."

I went back and took the tiller from Sparrow. We were now in mid-river, and the swollen stream and the strong wind bore us on with them like a leaf before the gale. We left behind the lights and the clamor, the dark town and the silent fort, the weary Due Return and the shipping about the lower wharf. Before us loomed the Santa Teresa; we passed so close beneath her huge black sides that we heard the wind whistling through her rigging. When she, too, was gone, the river lay bare before us; silver when the moon shone, of an inky blackness when it was obscured by one of the many flying clouds.

My wife wrapped her mantle closer about her, and, leaning back in her seat in the stern beside me, raised her face to the wild and solemn heavens. Diccon sat apart in the bow and held his tongue. The minister bent over, and, lifting the man that lay in the bottom of the boat, laid him at full length upon the thwart before us. The moonlight streamed down upon the prostrate figure. I think it could never have shone upon a more handsome or a more wicked man. He lay there in his splendid dress and dark beauty, Endymion-like, beneath the moon. The King's ward turned her eyes upon him, kept them there a moment, then glanced away, and looked at him no more.

"There's a parlous lump upon his forehead where it struck the thwart," said the minister, "but the life's yet in him. He'll shame honest men for many a day to come. Your Platonists, who from a goodly outside argue as fair a soul, could never have been acquainted with this gentleman."

The subject of his discourse moaned and stirred. The minister raised one of the hanging hands and felt for the pulse. "Faint enough," he went on. "A little more and the King might have waited for his minion forever and a day. It would have been the better for us, who have now, indeed, a strange fish upon our hands, but I am glad I killed him not."

I tossed him a flask. "It's good aqua vitae, and the flask is honest. Give him to drink of it."

He forced the liquor between my lord's teeth, then dashed water in his face. Another minute and the King's favorite sat up and looked around him. Dazed as yet, he stared, with no comprehension in his eyes, at the clouds, the sail, the rushing water, the dark figures about him. "Nicolo!" he cried sharply.

"He's not here, my lord," I said.

At the sound of my voice he sprang to his feet.

"I should advise your lordship to sit still," I said. "The wind is very boisterous, and we are not under bare poles. If you exert yourself, you may capsize the boat."

He sat down mechanically, and put his hand to his forehead. I watched him curiously. It was the strangest trick that fortune had played him.

His hand dropped at last, and he straightened himself, with a long breath. "Who threw me into the boat?" he demanded.

"The honor was mine," declared the minister.

The King's minion lacked not the courage of the body, nor, when passionate action had brought him naught, a certain reserve force of philosophy. He now did the best thing he could have done,—burst into a roar of laughter. "Zooks!" he cried. "It's as good a comedy as ever I saw! How's the play to end, captain? Are we to go off laughing, or is the end to be bloody after all? For instance, is there murder to be done?" He looked at me boldly, one hand on his hip, the other twirling his mustaches.

"We are not all murderers, my lord," I told him. "For the present you are in no danger other than that which is common to us all."

He looked at the clouds piling behind us, thicker and thicker, higher and higher, at the bending mast, at the black water swirling now and again over the gunwales. "It's enough," he muttered.

I beckoned to Diccon, and putting the tiller into his hands went forward to reef the sail. When it was done and I was back in my place, my lord spoke again.

"Where are we going, captain?"

"I don't know."

"If you leave that sail up much longer, you will land us at the bottom of the river."

"There are worse places," I replied.

He left his seat, and moved, though with caution, to one nearer Mistress Percy. "Are cold and storm and peril sweeter to you, lady, than warmth and safety, and a love that would guard you from, not run you into, danger?" he said in a whisper. "Do you not wish this boat the Santa Teresa, these rude boards the velvet cushions of her state cabin, this darkness her many lights, this cold her warmth, with the night shut out and love shut in?"

His audacity, if it angered me, yet made me laugh. Not so with the King's ward. She shrank from him until she pressed against the tiller. Our flight, the pursuing feet, the struggle at the wharf, her wounded arm of which she had not told, the terror of the white sail rising as if by magic, the vision of the man she hated lying as one dead before her in the moonlight, the cold, the hurry of the night,—small wonder if her spirit failed her for some time. I felt her hand touch mine where it rested upon the tiller. "Captain Percy," she murmured, with a little sobbing breath.

I leaned across the tiller and addressed the favorite. "My lord," I said, "courtesy to prisoners is one thing, and freedom from restraint and license of tongue is another. Here at the stern the boat is somewhat heavily freighted.

Your lordship will oblige me if you will go forward where there is room enough and to spare."

His black brows drew together. "And what if I refuse, sir?" he demanded haughtily.

"I have rope here," I answered, "and to aid me the gentleman who once before to-night, and in despite of your struggles, lifted you in his arms like an infant. We will tie you hand and foot, and lay you in the bottom of the boat. If you make too much trouble, there is always the river. My lord, you are not now at Whitehall. You are with desperate men, outlaws who have no king, and so fear no king's minions. Will you go free, or will you go bound? Go you shall, one way or the other."

He looked at me with rage and hatred in his face. Then, with a laugh that was not good to hear and a shrug of the shoulders, he went forward to bear Diccon company in the bow.

CHAPTER XX
IN WHICH WE ARE IN DESPERATE CASE

"GOD walketh upon the sea as he walketh upon the land," said the minister. "The sea is his and we are his. He will do what it liketh him with his own." As he spoke he looked with a steadfast soul into the black hollow of the wave that combed above us, threatening destruction.

The wave broke, and the boat still lived. Borne high upon the shoulder of the next rolling hill, we looked north, south, east, and west, and saw only a waste of livid, ever forming, ever breaking waves, a gray sky streaked with darker gray shifting vapor, and a horizon impenetrably veiled. Where we were in the great bay, in what direction we were being driven, how near we might be to the open sea or to some fatal shore, we knew not. What we did know was that both masts were gone, that we must bail the boat without ceasing if we would keep it from swamping, that the wind was doing an apparently impossible thing and rising higher and higher, and that the waves which buffeted us from one to the other were hourly swelling to a more monstrous bulk.

We had come into the wider waters at dawn, and still under canvas. An hour later, off Point Comfort, a bare mast contented us; we had hardly gotten the sail in when mast and all went overboard. That had been hours ago.

A common peril is a mighty leveler of barriers. Scant time was there in that boat to make distinction between friend and foe. As one man we fought the element which would devour us. Each took his turn at the bailing, each watched for the next great wave before which we must cower, clinging with numbed hands to gunwale and thwart. We fared alike, toiled alike, and suffered alike, only that the minister and I cared for Mistress Percy, asking no help from the others.

The King's ward endured all without a murmur. She was cold, she was worn with watching and terror, she was wounded; each moment Death raised his arm to strike, but she sat there dauntless, and looked him in the face with a smile upon her own. If, wearied out, we had given up the fight, her look would have spurred us on to wrestle with our fate to the last gasp. She sat between Sparrow and me, and as best we might we shielded her from the drenching seas and the icy wind. Morning had shown me the blood upon her sleeve, and I had cut away the cloth from the white arm, and had washed the wound with wine and bound it up. If for my fee, I should have liked to press my lips upon the blue-veined marble, still I did it not.

When, a week before, I had stored the boat with food and drink and had brought it to that lonely wharf, I had thought that if at the last my wife willed to flee I would attempt to reach the bay, and passing out between the capes would go to the north. Given an open boat and the tempestuous seas of November, there might be one chance out of a hundred of our reaching Manhattan and the Dutch, who might or might not give us refuge. She had willed to flee, and we were upon our journey, and the one chance had vanished. That wan, monotonous, cold, and clinging mist had shrouded us for our burial, and our grave yawned beneath us.

The day passed and the night came, and still we fought the sea, and still the wind drove us whither it would. The night passed and the second morning came, and found us yet alive. My wife lay now at my feet, her head pillowed upon the bundle she had brought from the minister's house. Too weak for speech, waiting in pain and cold and terror for death to bring her warmth and life, the knightly spirit yet lived in her eyes, and she smiled when I bent over her with wine to moisten her lips. At length she began to wander in her mind, and to speak of summer days and flowers. A hand held my heart in a slowly tightening grip of iron, and the tears ran down the minister's cheeks. The man who had darkened her young life, bringing her to this, looked at her with an ashen face.

As the day wore on, the gray of the sky paled to a dead man's hue and the wind lessened, but the waves were still mountain high. One moment we poised, like the gulls that now screamed about us, upon some giddy summit, the sky alone above and around us; the next we sank into dark green and glassy caverns. Suddenly the wind fell away, veered, and rose again like a giant refreshed.

Diccon started, put his hand to his ear, then sprang to his feet. "Breakers!" he cried hoarsely.

We listened with straining ears. He was right. The low, ominous murmur changed to a distant roar, grew louder yet, and yet louder, and was no longer distant.

"It will be the sand islets off Cape Charles, sir," he said. I nodded. He and I knew there was no need of words.

The sky grew paler and paler, and soon upon the woof of the clouds a splash of dull yellow showed where the sun would be. The fog rose, laying bare the desolate ocean. Before us were two very small islands, mere handfuls of sand, lying side by side, and encompassed half by the open sea, half by stiller waters diked in by marshes and sand bars. A coarse, scanty grass and a few stunted trees with branches bending away from the sea lived upon them, but nothing else. Over them and over the marshes and the sand banks circled myriads of great white gulls. Their harsh, unearthly voices came to us faintly, and increased the desolation of earth and sky and sea.

To the shell-strewn beach of the outer of the two islets raced long lines of surf, and between us and it lurked a sand bar, against which the great rollers dashed with a bull-like roar. The wind drove us straight upon this bar. A moment of deadly peril and it had us fast, holding us for the waves to beat our life out. The boat listed, then rested, quivering through all its length. The waves pounded against its side, each watery battering-ram dissolving in foam and spray but to give place to another, and yet it held together, and yet we lived. How long it would hold we could not tell; we only knew it could not be for long. The inclination of the boat was not so great but that, with caution, we might move about. There were on board rope and an axe. With the latter I cut away the thwarts and the decking in the bow, and Diccon and I made a small raft. When it was finished, I lifted my wife in my arms and laid her upon it and lashed her to it with the rope. She smiled like a child, then closed her eyes. "I have gathered primroses until I am tired," she said. "I will sleep here a little in the sunshine, and when I awake I will make you a cowslip ball."

Time passed, and the groaning, trembling timbers still held together. The wind fell, the sky became blue, and the sun shone. Another while, and the waves were less mountainous and beat less furiously against the boat. Hope brightened before us. To strong swimmers the distance to the islet was trifling; if the boat would but last until the sea subsided, we might gain the beach. What we would do upon that barren spot, where was neither man nor brute, food nor water, was a thing that we had not the time to consider. It was land that we craved.

Another hour, and the sea still fell. Another, and a wave struck the boat with force. "The sea is coming in!" cried the minister.

"Ay," I answered. "She will go to pieces now."

The minister rose to his feet. "I am no mariner," he said, "but once in the water I can swim you like any fish. There have been times when I have reproached the Lord for that he cased a poor silly humble preacher like me with the strength and seeming of some might man of old, and there have been times when I have thanked him for that strength. I thank him now. Captain Percy, if you will trust the lady to me, I will take her safely to that shore."

I raised my head from the figure over which I was bending, and looked first at the still tumultuous sea, and then at the gigantic frame of the minister. When we had made that frail raft no swimmer could have lived in that shock of waves; now there was a chance for all, and for the minister, with his great strength, the greatest I have ever seen in any man, a double chance. I took her from the raft and gave her into his arms. A minute later the boat went to pieces.

Side by side Sparrow and I buffeted the sea. He held the King's ward in one arm, and he bore her safely over the huge swells and through the onslaught of the breaking waves. I could thank God for his strength, and trust her to it. For the other three of us, we were all strong swimmers, and though bruised and beat about, we held our own. Each wave, overcome, left us nearer the islet,—a little while and our feet touched bottom. A short struggle with the tremendous surf and we were out of the maw of the sea, but out upon a desolate islet, a mere hand's-breadth of sand and shell in a lonely ocean, some three leagues from the mainland of Accomac, and upon it neither food nor water. We had the clothes upon our backs, and my lord and I had kept our swords. I had a knife, and Diccon too was probably armed. The flint and steel and tinder box within my pouch made up our store.

The minister laid the woman whom he carried upon the pebbles, fell upon his knees, and lifted his rugged face to heaven. I too knelt, and with my hand upon her heart said my own prayer in my own way. My lord stood with unbent head, his eyes upon that still white face, but Diccon turned abruptly and strode off to a low ridge of sand, from the top of which one might survey the entire island.

In two minutes he was back again. "There's plenty of driftwood further up the beach," he announced, "and a mort of dried seaweed. At least we need n't freeze."

The great bonfire that we made roared and crackled, sending out a most cheerful heat and light. Under that genial breath the color came slowly back to madam's cheek and lip, and her heart beat more strongly. Presently she turned under my hand, and with a sigh pillowed her head upon her arm and went to sleep in that blessed warmth like a little child.

We who had no mind for sleep sat there beside the fire and watched the sun sink behind the low black line of the mainland, now plainly visible in the cleared air. It dyed the waves blood red, and shot out one long ray to crimson a single floating cloud, no larger than a man's hand, high in the blue. Sea birds, a countless multitude, went to and fro with harsh cries from island to marsh, and marsh to island. The marshes were still green; they lay, a half moon of fantastic shapes, each parted from the other by pink water. Beyond them was the inlet dividing us from the mainland, and that inlet was three leagues in width. We turned and looked seaward. Naught but leaping waves white-capped to the horizon.

"We touched here the time we went against the French at Port Royal and St. Croix," I said. "We had heard a rumor that the Bermuda pirates had hidden gold here. Argall and I went over every foot of it."

"And found no water?" questioned the minister.

"And found no water."

The light died from the west and from the sea beneath, and the night fell. When with the darkness the sea fowl ceased their clamor, a dreadful silence suddenly enfolded us. The rush of the surf made no difference; the ear heard it, but to the mind there was no sound. The sky was thick with stars; every moment one shot, and the trail of white fire it left behind melted into the night silently like snowflakes. There was no wind. The moon rose out of the sea, and lent the sandy isle her own pallor. Here and there, back amongst the dunes, the branches of a low and leafless tree writhed upward like dark fingers thrust from out the spectral earth. The ocean, quiet now, dreamed beneath the moon and cared not for the five lives it had cast upon that span of sand.

We piled driftwood and tangles of seaweed upon our fire, and it flamed and roared and broke the silence. Diccon, going to the landward side of the islet, found some oysters, which we roasted and ate; but we had nor wine nor water with which to wash them down.

"At least there are here no foes to fear," quoth my lord. "We may all sleep to-night; and zooks! we shall need it!" He spoke frankly, with an open face.

"I will take one watch, if you will take the other," I said to the minister.

He nodded. "I will watch until midnight."

It was long past that time when he roused me from where I lay at Mistress Percy's feet.

"I should have relieved you long ago," I told him.

He smiled. The moon, now high in the heavens, shone upon and softened his rugged features. I thought I had never seen a face so filled with tenderness and hope and a sort of patient power. "I have been with God," he said simply. "The starry skies and the great ocean and the little shells beneath my hand,—how wonderful are thy works, O Lord! What is man that thou art mindful of him? And yet not a sparrow falleth"—I rose and sat by the fire, and he laid himself down upon the sand beside me.

"Master Sparrow," I asked, "have you ever suffered thirst?"

"No," he answered. We spoke in low tones, lest we should wake her. Diccon and my lord, upon the other side of the fire, were sleeping heavily.

"I have," I said. "Once I lay upon a field of battle throughout a summer day, sore wounded and with my dead horse across my body. I shall forget the horror of that lost field and the torment of that weight before I forget the thirst."

"You think there is no hope?"

"What hope should there be?"

He was silent. Presently he turned and looked at the King's ward where she lay in the rosy light; then his eyes came back to mine.

"If it comes to the worst I shall put her out of her torment," I said.

He bowed his head and we sat in silence, our gaze upon the ground between us, listening to the low thunder of the surf and the crackling of the fire. "I love her," I said at last. "God help me!"

He put his finger to his lips. She had stirred and opened her eyes. I knelt beside her, and asked her how she did and if she wanted aught.

"It is warm," she said wonderingly.

"You are no longer in the boat," I told her. "You are safe upon the land. You have been sleeping here by the fire that we kindled."

An exquisite smile just lit her face, and her eyelids drooped again. "I am so tired," she said drowsily, "that I will sleep a little longer. Will you bring me some water, Captain Percy? I am very thirsty."

After a moment I said gently, "I will go get it, madam." She made no answer; she was already asleep. Nor did Sparrow and I speak again. He laid himself down with his face to the ocean, and I sat with my head in my hands, and thought and thought, to no purpose.

CHAPTER XXI
IN WHICH A GRAVE IS DIGGED

WHEN the stars had gone out and the moon begun to pale, I raised my face from my hands. Only a few glowing embers remained of the fire, and the driftwood that we had collected was exhausted. I thought that I would gather more, and build up the fire against the time when the others should awake. The driftwood lay in greatest quantity some distance up the beach, against a low ridge of sand dunes. Beyond these the islet tapered off to a long gray point of sand and shell. Walking toward this point in the first pale light of dawn, I chanced to raise my eyes, and beheld riding at anchor beyond the spit of sand a ship.

I stopped short and rubbed my eyes. She lay there on the sleeping ocean like a dream ship, her masts and rigging black against the pallid sky, the mist that rested upon the sea enfolding half her hull. She might have been of three hundred tons burthen; she was black and two-decked, and very high at poop and forecastle, and she was heavily armed. My eyes traveled from the ship to the shore, and there dragged up on the point, the oars within it, was a boat.

At the head of the beach, beyond the line of shell and weed, the sand lay piled in heaps. With these friendly hillocks between me and the sea, I crept on as silently as I might, until I reached a point just above the boat. Here I first heard voices. I went a little further, then knelt, and, parting the long coarse grass that filled the hollow between two hillocks, looked out upon two men who were digging a grave.

They dug in a furious hurry, throwing the sand to left and right, and cursing as they dug. They were powerful men, of a most villainous cast of countenance, and dressed very oddly. One with a shirt of coarsest dowlas, and a filthy rag tying up a broken head, yet wore velvet breeches, and wiped the sweat from his face with a wrought handkerchief; the other topped a suit of shreds and patches with a fine bushy ruff, and swung from one ragged shoulder a cloak of grogram lined with taffeta. On the ground, to one side of them, lay something long and wrapped in white.

As they dug and cursed, the light strengthened. The east changed from gray to pale rose, from rose to a splendid crimson shot with gold. The mist lifted and the sea burned red. Two boats were lowered from the ship, and came swiftly toward the point.

"Here they are at last," growled the gravedigger with the broken head and velvet breeches.

"They've taken their time," snarled his companion, "and us two here on this d-d island with a dead man the whole ghost's hour. Boarding a ship's nothing, but to dig a grave on the land before cockcrow, with the man you're to put in it looking at you! Why could n't he be buried at sea, decent and respectable, like other folk?"

"It was his will,—that's all I know," said the first; "just as it was his will, when he found he was a dying man, to come booming away from the gold seas up here to a land where there is n't no gold, and never will be. Belike he thought he'd find waiting for him at the bottom of the sea, all along from the Lucayas to Cartagena, the many he sent there afore he died. And Captain Paradise, he says, says he: 'It's ill crossing a dead man. We'll obey him this once more'"—

"Captain Paradise!" cried he of the ruff. "Who made him captain?—curse him!"

His fellow straightened himself with a jerk. "Who made him captain? The ship will make him captain. Who else should be captain?"

"Red Gil!"

"Red Gil!" exclaimed the other. "I'd rather have the Spaniard!"

"The Spaniard would do well enough, if the rest of us were n't English. If hating every other Spaniard would do it, he'd be English fast enough."

The scoundrel with the broken head burst into a loud laugh. "D' ye remember the bark we took off Porto Bello, with the priests aboard? Oho! Oho!"

The rogue with the ruff grinned. "I reckon the padres remember it, and find hell easy lying. This hole's deep enough, I'm thinking."

They both clambered out, and one squatted at the head of the grave and mopped his face with his delicate handkerchief, while the other swung his fine cloak with an air and dug his bare toes in the sand.

The two boats now grated upon the beach, and several of their occupants, springing out, dragged them up on the sand.

"We'll never get another like him that's gone," said the worthy at the head of the grave, gloomily regarding the something wrapped in white.

"That's gospel truth," assented the other, with a prodigious sigh. "He was a man what was a man. He never stuck at nothing. Don or priest, man or woman, good red gold or dirty silver,—it was all one to him. But he's dead and gone!"

"Now, if we had a captain like Kirby," suggested the first.

"Kirby keeps to the Summer Isles," said the second. "'T is n't often now that he swoops down as far as the Indies."

The man with the broken head laughed. "When he does, there's a noise in that part of the world."

"And that's gospel truth, too," swore the other, with an oath of admiration.

By this the score or more who had come in the two boats were halfway up the beach. In front, side by side, as each conceding no inch of leadership, walked three men: a large man, with a villainous face much scarred, and a huge, bushy, dark red beard; a tall dark man, with a thin fierce face and bloodshot eyes, the Spaniard by his looks; and a slight man, with the face and bearing of an English gentleman. The men behind them differed no whit from the two gravediggers, being as scoundrelly of face, as great of strength, and as curiously attired. They came straight to the open grave, and the dead man beside it. The three who seemed of most importance disposed themselves, still side by side, at the head of the grave, and their following took the foot.

"It's a dirty piece of work," said Red Gil in a voice like a raven's, "and the sooner it's done with, and we are aboard again and booming back to the Indies, the better I'll like it. Over with him, brave boys!"

"Is it yours to give the word?" asked the slight man, who was dressed point-device, and with a finical nicety, in black and silver. His voice was low and clear, and of a somewhat melancholy cadence, going well with the pensiveness of fine, deeply fringed eyes.

"Why should n't I give the word?" growled the personage addressed, adding with an oath, "I've as good a right to give it as any man,—maybe a better right!"

"That would be scanned," said he of the pensive eyes. "Gentlemen, we have here the pick of the ship. For the captain that these choose, those on board will throw up their caps. Let us bury the dead, and then let choice be made of one of us three, each of whom has claims that might be put forward"— He broke off and picking up a delicate shell began to study its pearly spirals with a tender, thoughtful, half-pleased, half-melancholy countenance.

The gravedigger with the wrought handkerchief looked from him to the rascal crew massed at the foot of the grave, and, seeing his own sentiments mirrored in the countenances of not a few, snatched the bloody clout from his head, waved it, and cried out, "Paradise!" Whereupon arose a great confusion. Some bawled for Paradise, some for Red Gil, a few for the Spaniard. The two gravediggers locked horns, and a brawny devil with a woman's mantle swathed about his naked shoulders drew a knife, and made for a partisan of the Spaniard, who in his turn skillfully interposed between himself and the attack the body of a bawling well-wisher to Red Gil.

The man in black and silver tossed aside the shell, rose, and entered the lists. With one hand he seized the gravedigger of the ruff, and hurled him apart from him of the velvet breeches; with the other he presented a dagger with a jeweled haft at the breast of the ruffian with the woman's mantle, while in tones that would have befitted Astrophel plaining of his love to rocks, woods, and streams, he poured forth a flood of wild, singular, and filthy oaths, such as would have disgraced a camp follower. His interference was effectual. The combatants fell apart and the clamor was stilled, whereupon the gentleman of contrarieties at once resumed the gentle and indifferent melancholy of manner and address.

"Let us off with the old love before we are on with the new, gentlemen," he said. "We'll bury the dead first, and choose his successor afterward,— decently and in order, I trust, and with due submission to the majority."

"I'll fight for my rights," growled Red Gil.

"And I for mine," cried the Spaniard.

"And each of us'll back his own man," muttered in an aside the gravedigger with the broken head.

The one they called Paradise sighed. "It is a thousand pities that there is not amongst us some one of so preeminent that faction should hide its head before it. But to the work in hand, gentlemen."

They gathered closer around the yawning grave, and some began to lift the corpse. As for me, I withdrew as noiselessly as an Indian from my lair of grass, and, hidden by the heaped-up sand, made off across the point and down the beach to where a light curl of smoke showed that some one was mending the fire I had neglected. It was Sparrow, who alternately threw on driftwood and seaweed and spoke to madam, who sat at his feet in the blended warmth of fire and sunshine. Diccon was roasting the remainder of the oysters he had gathered the night before, and my lord stood and stared with a frowning face at the nine-mile distant mainland. All turned their eyes upon me as I came up to the fire.

"A little longer, Captain Percy, and we would have had out a search warrant," began the minister cheerfully. "Have you been building a bridge?"

"If I build one," I said, "it will be a perilous one enough. Have you looked seaward?"

"We waked but a minute agone," he answered. As he spoke, he straightened his great form and lifted his face from the fire to the blue sea. Diccon, still on his knees at his task, looked too; and my lord, turning from his contemplation of the distant kingdom of Accomac; and Mistress Percy, one hand shading her eyes, the slender fingers of the other still immeshed in her long dark hair which she had been braiding. They stared at the ship in silence until my lord laughed.

"Conjure us on board at once, captain," he cried. "We are thirsty."

I drew the minister aside. "I am going up the beach, beyond that point, again; you will one and all stay here. If I do not come back, do the best you can, and sell her life as dearly as you can. If I come back,—you are quick of wit and have been a player; look that you take the cue I give you!"

I returned to the fire, and he followed me, amazement in his face. "My Lord Carnal," I said, "I must ask you for your sword."

He started, and his black brows drew together. "Though the fortunes of war have made me in some sort your captive, sir," he said at last, and not without dignity, "I do not see, upon this isle to which we are all prisoners, the need of so strong testimony to the abjectness of my condition, nor deem it generous"—

"We will speak of generosity another day, my lord," I interrupted. "At present I am in a hurry. That you are my prisoner in verity is enough for me, but not for others. I must have you so in seeming as well as in truth. Moreover, Master Sparrow is weaponless, and I must needs disarm an enemy to arm a friend. I beg that you will give what else we must take."

He looked at Diccon, but Diccon stood with his face to the sea. I thought we were to have a struggle, and I was sorry for it, but my lord could and did add discretion to a valor that I never doubted. He shrugged his shoulders, burst into a laugh, and turned to Mistress Percy.

"What can one do, lady, when one is doubly a prisoner, prisoner to numbers and to beauty? E'en laugh at fate, and make the best of a bad job. Here, sir! Some day it shall be the point!"

He drew his rapier from its sheath, and presented the hilt to me. I took it with a bow, and handed it to Sparrow.

The King's ward had risen, and now leant against the bank of sand, her long dark hair, half braided, drawn over either shoulder, her face marble white between the waves of darkness.

"I do not know that I shall ever come back," I said, stopping before her. "May I kiss your hand before I go?"

Her lips moved, but she did not speak. I knelt and kissed her clasped hands. They were cold to my lips. "Where are you going?" she whispered. "Into what danger are you going? I—I—take me with you!"

I rose, with a laugh at my own folly that could have rested brow and lips on those hands, and let the world wag. "Another time," I said. "Rest in the sunshine now, and think that all is well. All will be well, I trust."

A few minutes later saw me almost upon the party gathered about the grave. The grave had received that which it was to hold until the crack of doom, and was now being rapidly filled with sand. The crew of deep-dyed villains worked or stood or sat in silence, but all looked at the grave, and saw me not. As the last handful of sand made it level with the beach, I walked into their midst, and found myself face to face with the three candidates for the now vacant captaincy.

"Give you good-day, gentlemen," I cried. "Is it your captain that you bury or one of your crew, or is it only pezos and pieces of eight?"

CHAPTER XXII
IN WHICH I CHANGE MY NAME AND OCCUPATION

"THE sun shining on so much bare steel hurts my eyes," I said. "Put up, gentlemen, put up! Cannot one rover attend the funeral of another without all this crowding and display of cutlery? If you will take the trouble to look around you, you will see that I have brought to the obsequies only myself."

One by one cutlass and sword were lowered, and those who had drawn them, falling somewhat back, spat and swore and laughed. The man in black and silver only smiled gently and sadly. "Did you drop from the blue?" he asked. "Or did you come up from the sea?"

"I came out of it," I said. "My ship went down in the storm yesterday. Your little cockboat yonder was more fortunate." I waved my hand toward that ship of three hundred tons, then twirled my mustaches and stood at gaze.

"Was your ship so large, then?" demanded Paradise, while a murmur of admiration, larded with oaths, ran around the circle.

"She was a very great galleon," I replied, with a sigh for the good ship that was gone.

A moment's silence, during which they all looked at me. "A galleon," then said Paradise softly.

"They that sailed her yesterday are to-day at the bottom of the sea," I continued. "Alackaday! so are one hundred thousand pezos of gold, three thousand bars of silver, ten frails of pearls, jewels uncounted, cloth of gold and cloth of silver. She was a very rich prize."

The circle sucked in their breath. "All at the bottom of the sea?" queried Red Gil, with gloating eyes fixed upon the smiling water. "Not one pezo left, not one little, little pearl?"

I shook my head and heaved a prodigious sigh. "The treasure is gone," I said, "and the men with whom I took it are gone. I am a captain with neither ship nor crew. I take you, my friends, for a ship and crew without a captain. The inference is obvious."

The ring gaped with wonder, then strange oaths arose. Red Gil broke into a bellow of angry laughter, while the Spaniard glared like a catamount about to spring. "So you would be our captain?" said Paradise, picking up another shell, and poising it upon a hand as fine and small as a woman's.

"Faith, you might go farther and fare worse," I answered, and began to hum a tune. When I had finished it, "I am Kirby," I said, and waited to see if that shot should go wide or through the hull.

For two minutes the dash of the surf and the cries of the wheeling sea fowl made the only sound in that part of the world; then from those half-clad rapscallions arose a shout of "Kirby!"—a shout in which the three leaders did not join. That one who looked a gentleman rose from the sand and made me a low bow. "Well met, noble captain," he cried in those his honey tones. "You will doubtless remember me who was with you that time at Maracaibo when you sunk the galleasses. Five years have passed since then, and yet I see you ten years younger and three inches taller."

"I touched once at the Lucayas, and found the spring de Leon sought," I said. "Sure the waters have a marvelous effect, and if they give not eternal youth at least renew that which we have lost."

"Truly a potent aqua vitae," he remarked, still with thoughtful melancholy. "I see that it hath changed your eyes from black to gray."

"It hath that peculiar virtue," I said, "that it can make black seem white."

The man with the woman's mantle drawn about him now thrust himself from the rear to the front rank. "That's not Kirby!" he bawled. "He's no more Kirby than I am Kirby! Did n't I sail with Kirby from the Summer Isles to Cartagena and back again? He's a cheat, and I am agoing to cut his heart out!" He was making at me with a long knife, when I whipped out my rapier.

"Am I not Kirby, you dog?" I cried, and ran him through the shoulder.

He dropped, and his fellows surged forward with a yell. "Yet a little patience, my masters!" said Paradise in a raised voice and with genuine amusement in his eyes. "It is true that that Kirby with whom I and our friend there on the ground sailed was somewhat short and as swart as a raven, besides having a cut across his face that had taken away a part of his lip and the top of his ear, and that this gentleman who announces himself as Kirby hath none of Kirby's marks. But we are fair and generous and open to conviction"—

"He'll have to convince my cutlass!" roared Red Gil.

I turned upon him. "If I do convince it, what then?" I demanded. "If I convince your sword, you of Spain, and yours, Sir Black and Silver?"

The Spaniard stared. "I was the best sword in Lima," he said stiffly. "I and my Toledo will not change our minds."

"Let him try to convince Paradise; he's got no reputation as a swordsman!" cried out the gravedigger with the broken head.

A roar of laughter followed this suggestion, and I gathered from it and from the oaths and allusions to this or that time and place that Paradise was not without reputation.

I turned to him. "If I fight you three, one by one, and win, am I Kirby?"

He regarded the shell with which he was toying with a thoughtful smile, held it up that the light might strike through its rose and pearl, then crushed it to dust between his fingers.

"Ay," he said with an oath. "If you win against the cutlass of Red Gil, the best blade of Lima, and the sword of Paradise, you may call yourself the devil an you please, and we will all subscribe to it."

I lifted my hand. "I am to have fair play?"

As one man that crew of desperate villains swore that the odds should be only three to one. By this the whole matter had presented itself to them as an entertainment more diverting than bullfight or bearbaiting. They that follow the sea, whether honest men or black-hearted knaves, have in their composition a certain childlikeness that makes them easily turned, easily led, and easily pleased. The wind of their passion shifts quickly from point to point, one moment blowing a hurricane, the next sinking to a happy-go-lucky summer breeze. I have seen a little thing convert a crew on the point of mutiny into a set of rollicking, good-natured souls who—until the wind veered again—would not hurt a fly. So with these. They spread themselves into a circle, squatting or kneeling or standing upon the white sand in the bright sunshine, their sinewy hands that should have been ingrained red clasped over their knees, or, arms akimbo, resting upon their hips, on their scoundrel faces a broad smile, and in their eyes that had looked on nameless horrors a pleasurable expectation as of spectators in a playhouse awaiting the entrance of the players.

"There is really no good reason why we should gratify your whim," said Paradise, still amused. "But it will serve to pass the time. We will fight you, one by one."

"And if I win?"

He laughed. "Then, on the honor of a gentleman, you are Kirby and our captain. If you lose, we will leave you where you stand for the gulls to bury."

"A bargain," I said, and drew my sword.

"I first!" roared Red Gil. "God's wounds! there will need no second!"

As he spoke he swung his cutlass and made an arc of blue flame. The weapon became in his hands a flail, terrible to look upon, making lightnings and whistling in the air, but in reality not so deadly as it seemed. The fury of his

- 133 -

onslaught would have beaten down the guard of any mere swordsman, but that I was not. A man, knowing his weakness and insufficiency in many and many a thing, may yet know his strength in one or two and his modesty take no hurt. I was ever master of my sword, and it did the thing I would have it do. Moreover, as I fought I saw her as I had last seen her, standing against the bank of sand, her dark hair, half braided, drawn over her bosom and hanging to her knees. Her eyes haunted me, and my lips yet felt the touch of her hand. I fought well,—how well the lapsing of oaths and laughter into breathless silence bore witness.

The ruffian against whom I was pitted began to draw his breath in gasps. He was a scoundrel not fit to die, less fit to live, unworthy of a gentleman's steel. I presently ran him through with as little compunction and as great a desire to be quit of a dirty job as if he had been a mad dog. He fell, and a little later, while I was engaged with the Spaniard, his soul went to that hell which had long gaped for it. To those his companions his death was as slight a thing as would theirs have been to him. In the eyes of the two remaining would-be leaders he was a stumbling-block removed, and to the squatting, open-mouthed commonality his taking off weighed not a feather against the solid entertainment I was affording them. I was now a better man than Red Gil,—that was all.

The Spaniard was a more formidable antagonist. The best blade of Lima was by no means to be despised; but Lima is a small place, and its blades can be numbered. The sword that for three years had been counted the best in all the Low Countries was its better. But I fought fasting and for the second time that morning, so maybe the odds were not so great. I wounded him slightly, and presently succeeded in disarming him. "Am I Kirby?" I demanded, with my point at his breast.

"Kirby, of course, senor," he answered with a sour smile, his eyes upon the gleaming blade.

I lowered my point and we bowed to each other, after which he sat down upon the sand and applied himself to stanching the bleeding from his wound. The pirate ring gave him no attention, but stared at me instead. I was now a better man than the Spaniard.

The man in black and silver rose and removed his doublet, folding it very carefully, inside out, that the sand might not injure the velvet, then drew his rapier, looked at it lovingly, made it bend until point and hilt well-nigh met, and faced me with a bow.

"You have fought twice, and must be weary," he said. "Will you not take breath before we engage, or will your long rest afterward suffice you?"

"I will rest aboard my ship," I made reply. "And as I am in a hurry to be gone we won't delay."

Our blades had no sooner crossed than I knew that in this last encounter I should need every whit of my skill, all my wit, audacity, and strength. I had met my equal, and he came to it fresh and I jaded. I clenched my teeth and prayed with all my heart; I set her face before me, and thought if I should fail her to what ghastly fate she might come, and I fought as I had never fought before. The sound of the surf became a roar in my ears, the sunshine an intolerable blaze of light; the blue above and around seemed suddenly beneath my feet as well. We were fighting high in the air, and had fought thus for ages. I knew that he made no thrust I did not parry, no feint I could not interpret. I knew that my eye was more quick to see, my brain to conceive, and my hand to execute than ever before; but it was as though I held that knowledge of some other, and I myself was far away, at Weyanoke, in the minister's garden, in the haunted wood, anywhere save on that barren islet. I heard him swear under his breath, and in the face I had set before me the eyes brightened. As if she had loved me I fought for her with all my powers of body and mind. He swore again, and my heart laughed within me. The sea now roared less loudly, and I felt the good earth beneath my feet. Slowly but surely I wore him out. His breath came short, the sweat stood upon his forehead, and still I deferred my attack. He made the thrust of a boy of fifteen, and I smiled as I put it by.

"Why don't you end it?" he breathed. "Finish and be d-d to you!"

For answer I sent his sword flying over the nearest hillock of sand. "Am I Kirby?" I said. He fell back against the heaped-up sand and leaned there, panting, with his hand to his side. "Kirby or devil," he replied. "Have it your own way."

I turned to the now highly excited rabble. "Shove the boats off, half a dozen of you!" I ordered. "Some of you others take up that carrion there and throw it into the sea. The gold upon it is for your pains. You there with the wounded shoulder you have no great hurt. I'll salve it with ten pieces of eight from the captain's own share, the next prize we take."

A shout of acclamation arose that scared the sea fowl. They who so short a time before had been ready to tear me limb from limb now with the greatest apparent delight hailed me as captain. How soon they might revert to their former mood was a question that I found not worth while to propound to myself.

By this the man in black and silver had recovered his breath and his equanimity. "Have you no commission with which to honor me, noble captain?" he asked in gently reproachful tones. "Have you forgot how often you were wont to employ me in those sweet days when your eyes were black?"

"By no means, Master Paradise," I said courteously. "I desire your company and that of the gentleman from Lima. You will go with me to bring up the rest of my party. The three gentlemen of the broken head, the bushy ruff, which I protest is vastly becoming, and the wounded shoulder will escort us."

"The rest of your party?" said Paradise softly.

"Ay," I answered nonchalantly. "They are down the beach and around the point warming themselves by a fire which this piled-up sand hides from you. Despite the sunshine it is a biting air. Let us be going! This island wearies me, and I am anxious to be on board ship and away."

"So small an escort scarce befits so great a captain," he said. "We will all attend you." One and all started forward.

I called to mind and gave utterance to all the oaths I had heard in the wars. "I entertain you for my subordinate whom I command, and not who commands me!" I cried, when my memory failed me. "As for you, you dogs, who would question your captain and his doings, stay where you are, if you would not be lessoned in earnest!"

Sheer audacity is at times the surest steed a man can bestride. Now at least it did me good service. With oaths and grunts of admiration the pirates stayed where they were, and went about their business of launching the boats and stripping the body of Red Gil, while the man in black and silver, the Spaniard, the two gravediggers, the knave with the wounded shoulder, and myself walked briskly up the beach.

With these five at my heels I strode up to the dying fire and to those who had sprung to their feet at our approach. "Sparrow," I said easily, "luck being with us as usual, I have fallen in with a party of rovers. I have told them who I am,—that Kirby, to wit, whom an injurious world calls the blackest pirate unhanged,—and have recounted to them how the great galleon which I took some months ago went down yesterday with all on board, you and I with these others being the sole survivors. By dint of a little persuasion they have elected me their captain, and we will go on board directly and set sail for the Indies, a hunting ground which we never should have left. You need not look so blank; you shall be my mate and right hand still." I turned to the five who formed my escort. "This, gentlemen, is my mate, Jeremy Sparrow by name, who hath a taste for divinity that in no wise interferes with his taste for a galleon or a guarda costa. This man, Diccon Demon by name, was of my crew. The gentleman without a sword is my prisoner, taken by me from the last ship I sunk. How he, an Englishman, came to be upon a Spanish bark I have not found leisure to inquire. The lady is my prisoner, also."

"Sure by rights she should be gaoler and hold all men's hearts in ward," said Paradise, with a low bow to my unfortunate captive.

While he spoke a most remarkable transformation was going on. The minister's grave, rugged, and deeply lined face smoothed itself and shed ten years at least; in the eyes that I had seen wet with noble tears a laughing devil now lurked, while his strong mouth became a loose-lipped, devil-may-care one. His head with its aureole of bushy, grizzled hair set itself jauntily upon one side, and from it and from his face and his whole great frame breathed a wicked jollity quite indescribable.

"Odsbodikins, captain!" he cried. "Kirby's luck!—'t will pass into a saw! Adzooks! and so you're captain once more, and I'm mate once more, and we've a ship once more, and we're off once more

sail the Spanish Main

give the Spaniard pain,

ho, bully boy, heave ho!

By 'r lakin! I'm too dry to sing. It will take all the wine of Xeres in the next galleon to unparch my tongue!"

CHAPTER XXIII
IN WHICH WE WRITE UPON THE SAND

DAY after day the wind filled our sails and sang in the rigging, and day after day we sailed through blue seas toward the magic of the south. Day after day a listless and voluptuous world seemed too idle for any dream of wrong, and day after day we whom a strange turn of Fortune's wheel had placed upon a pirate ship held our lives in our hands, and walked so close with Death that at length that very intimacy did breed contempt. It was not a time to think; it was a time to act, to laugh and make others laugh, to bluster and brag, to estrange sword and scabbard, to play one's hand with a fine unconcern, but all the time to watch, watch, watch, day in and day out, every minute of every hour. That ship became a stage, and we, the actors, should have been applauded to the echo. How well we played let witness the fact that the ship came to the Indies, with me for captain and the minister for mate, and with the woman that was on board unharmed; nay, reverenced like a queen. The great cabin was hers, and the poop deck; we made for her a fantastic state with doffing of hats and bowings and backward steps. We were her guard,— the gentlemen of the Queen,—I and my Lord Carnal, the minister and Diccon, and we kept between her and the rest of the ship.

We did our best, and our best was very much. When I think of the songs the minister sang; of the roars of laughter that went up from the lounging pirates when, sitting astride one of the main-deck guns, he made his voice call to them, now from the hold, now from the stern gallery, now from the masthead, now from the gilt sea maid upon the prow, I laugh too. Sometimes a space was cleared for him, and he played to them as to the pit at Blackfriars. They laughed and wept and swore with delight,—all save the Spaniard, who was ever like a thundercloud, and Paradise, who only smiled like some languid, side-box lord. There was wine on board, and during the long, idle days, when the wind droned in the rigging like a bagpipe, and there was never a cloud in the sky, and the galleons were still far away, the pirates gambled and drank. Diccon diced with them, and taught them all the oaths of a free company. So much wine, and no more, should they have; when they frowned, I let them see that their frowning and their half-drawn knives mattered no doit to me. It was their whim—a huge jest of which they could never have enough—still to make believe that they sailed under Kirby. Lest it should spoil the jest, and while the jest outranked all other entertainment, they obeyed as though I had been indeed that fierce sea wolf.

Time passed, though it passed like a tortoise, and we came to the Lucayas, to the outposts of the vast hunting ground of Spaniard and pirate and buccaneer, the fringe of that zone of beauty and villainy and fear, and sailed slowly past the islands, looking for our prey.

The sea was blue as blue could be. Only in the morning and the evening it glowed blood red, or spread upon its still bosom all the gold of all the Indies, or became an endless mead of palest green shot with amethyst. When night fell, it mirrored the stars, great and small, or was caught in a net of gold flung across it from horizon to horizon. The ship rent the net with a wake of white fire. The air was balm; the islands were enchanted places, abandoned by Spaniard and Indian, overgrown, serpent-haunted. The reef, the still water, pink or gold, the gleaming beach, the green plume of the palm, the scarlet birds, the cataracts of bloom,—the senses swooned with the color, the steaming incense, the warmth, the wonder of that fantastic world. Sometimes, in the crystal waters near the land, we sailed over the gardens of the sea gods, and, looking down, saw red and purple blooms and shadowy waving forests, with rainbow fish for humming birds. Once we saw below us a sunken ship. With how much gold she had endowed the wealthy sea, how many long drowned would rise from her rotted decks when the waves gave up their dead, no man could tell. Away from the ship darted many-hued fish, gold-disked, or barred and spotted with crimson, or silver and purple. The dolphin and the tunny and the flying fish swam with us. Sometimes flights of small birds came to us from the land. Sometimes the sea was thickly set with full-blown pale red bloom, the jellyfish that was a flower to the sight and a nettle to the touch. If a storm arose, a fury that raged and threatened, it presently swept away, and the blue laughed again. When the sun sank, there arose in the east such a moon as might have been sole light to all the realms of faery. A beauty languorous and seductive was most absolute empress of the wonderful land and the wonderful sea.

We were in the hunting grounds, and men went not there to gather flowers. Day after day we watched for Spanish sails; for the plate fleets went that way, and some galleass or caravel or galleon might stray aside. At last, in the clear green bay of a nameless island at which we stopped for water, we found two carracks come upon the same errand, took them, and with them some slight treasure in rich cloths and gems. A week later, in a strait between two islands like tinted clouds, we fought a very great galleon from sunrise to noon, pierced her hull through and through and silenced her ordnance, then boarded her and found a king's ransom in gold and silver. When the fighting had ceased and the treasure was ours, then we four stood side by side on the deck of the slowly sinking galleon, in front of our prisoners,—of the men who had fought well, of the ashen priests and the trembling women. Those whom we faced were in high good humor: they had gold with which to gamble, and wine to drink, and rich clothing with which to prank their villainous bodies, and prisoners with whom to make merry. When I ordered the Spaniards to lower their boats, and taking with them their priests and women row off to one of those two islands, the weather changed.

We outlived that storm, but how I scarcely know. As Kirby would have done, so did I; rating my crew like hounds, turning my point this way and that, daring them to come taste the red death upon it, braving it out like some devil who knows he is invulnerable. My lord, swinging the cutlass with which he was armed, stood beside me, knee to knee, and Diccon cursed after me, making quarterstaff play with his long pike. But it was the minister that won us through. At length they laughed, and Paradise, standing forward, swore that such a captain and such a mate were worth the lives of a thousand Spaniards. To pleasure Kirby, they would depart this once from their ancient usage and let the prisoners go, though it was passing strange,—it being Kirby's wont to clap prisoners under hatches and fire their ship above them. At the end of which speech the Spaniard began to rave, and sprang at me like a catamount. Paradise put forth a foot and tripped him up, whereat the pirates laughed again, and held him back when he would have come at me a second time.

From the deck of the shattered galleon I watched her boats, with their heavy freight of cowering humanity, pull off toward the island. Back upon my own poop, the grappling irons cast loose, and a swiftly widening ribbon of blue between us and the sinking ship, I looked at the pirates thronging the waist below me, and knew that the play was nearly over. How many days, weeks, hours, before the lights would go out, I could not tell: they might burn until we took or lost another ship; the next hour might see that brief tragedy consummated.

I turned, and going below met Sparrow at the foot of the poop ladder.

"I have sworn at these pirates until my hair stood on end," he said ruefully. "God forgive me! And I have bent into circles three half pikes in demonstration of the thing that would occur to them if they tempted me overmuch. And I have sung them all the bloody and lascivious songs that ever I knew in my unregenerate days. I have played the bravo and buffoon until they gaped for wonder. I have damned myself to all eternity, I fear, but there'll be no mutiny this fair day. It may arrive by to-morrow, though."

"Likely enough," I said. "Come within. I have eaten nothing since yesterday."

"I'll speak to Diccon first," he answered, and went on toward the forecastle, while I entered the state cabin. Here I found Mistress Percy kneeling beside the bench beneath the stern windows, her face buried in her outstretched arms, her dark hair shadowing her like a mantle. When I spoke to her she did not answer. With a sudden fear I stooped and touched her clasped hands. A shudder ran through her frame, and she slowly raised a colorless face.

"Are you come back?" she whispered. "I thought you would never come back. I thought they had killed you. I was only praying before I killed myself."

I took her hands and wrung them apart to rouse her, she was so white and cold, and spoke so strangely. "God forbid that I should die yet awhile, madam!" I said. "When I can no longer serve you, then I shall not care how soon I die."

The eyes with which she gazed upon me were still wide and unseeing. "The guns!" she cried, wresting her hands from mine and putting them to her ears. "Oh, the guns! they shake the air. And the screams and the trampling—the guns again!"

I brought her wine and made her drink it; then sat beside her, and told her gently, over and over again, that there was no longer thunder of the guns or screams or trampling. At last the long, tearless sobs ceased, and she rose from her knees, and let me lead her to the door of her cabin. There she thanked me softly, with downcast eyes and lips that yet trembled; then vanished from my sight, leaving me first to wonder at that terror and emotion in her who seldom showed the thing she felt, and finally to conclude that it was not so wonderful after all.

We sailed on,—southwards to Cuba, then north again to the Lucayas and the Florida straits, looking for Spanish ships and their gold. The lights yet burned,—now brightly, now so sunken that it seemed as though the next hour they must flicker out. We, the players, flagged not in that desperate masque; but we knew that, in spite of all endeavor, the darkness was coming fast upon us.

Had it been possible, we would have escaped from the ship, hazarding new fortunes on the Spanish Main, in an open boat, sans food or water. But the pirates watched us very closely. They called me "captain" and "Kirby," and for the jest's sake gave an exaggerated obedience, with laughter and flourishes; but none the less I was their prisoner,—I and those I had brought with me to that ship.

An islet, shaped like the crescent moon, rose from out the sea before us. We needed water, and so we felt our way between the horns of the crescent into the blue crystal of a fairy harbor. One low hill, rose-colored from base to summit, with scarce a hint of the green world below that canopy of giant bloom, a little silver beach with wonderful shells upon it, the sound of a waterfall and a lazy surf,—we smelt the fruits and the flowers, and a longing for the land came upon us. Six men were left on the ship, and all besides went ashore. Some rolled the water casks toward the sound of the cascade; others plunged into the forest, to return laden with strange and luscious fruits, birds, guanas, conies,—whatever eatable thing they could lay hands upon; others scattered along the beach to find turtle eggs, or, if fortune favored them, the turtle itself. They laughed, they sang, they swore, until the isle rang to their merriment. Like wanton children, they called to each other, to the screaming birds, to the echoing bloom-draped hill.

I spread a square of cloth upon the sand, in the shadow of a mighty tree that stood at the edge of the forest, and the King's ward took her seat upon it, and looked, in the golden light of the sinking sun, the very spirit of the isle. By this we two were alone on the beach. The hunters for eggs, led by Diccon, were out upon the farthest gleaming horn; from the wood came the loud laughter of the fruit gatherers, and a most rollicking song issuing from the mighty chest of Master Jeremy Sparrow. With the woodsmen had gone my lord.

I walked a little way into the forest, and shouted a warning to Sparrow against venturing too far. When I returned to the giant tree and the cloth in the shadow of its outer branches, my wife was writing on the sand with a pointed shell. She had not seen or heard me, and I stood behind her and read what she wrote. It was my name. She wrote it three times, slowly and carefully; then she felt my presence, glanced swiftly up, smiled, rubbed out my name, and wrote Sparrow's, Diccon's, and the King's in succession. "Lest I should forget to make my letters," she explained.

I sat down at her feet, and for some time we said no word. The light, falling between the heavy blooms, cast bright sequins upon her dress and dark hair. The blooms were not more pink than her cheeks, the recesses of the forest behind us not deeper or darker than her eyes. The laughter and the song came faintly to us now. The sun was low in the west, and a wonderful light slept upon the sea.

"Last year we had a masque at court," she said at length, breaking the long silence. "We had Calypso's island, and I was Calypso. The island was built of boards covered with green velvet, and there was a mound upon it of pink silk roses. There was a deep blue painted sea below, and a deep blue painted sky above. My nymphs danced around the mound of roses, while I sat upon a real rock beside the painted sea and talked with Ulysses—to wit, my Lord of Buckingham—in gold armor. That was a strange, bright, unreal, and wearisome day, but not so strange and unreal as this."

She ceased to speak, and began again to write upon the sand. I watched her white hand moving to and fro. She wrote, "How long will it last?"

"I do not know. Not long."

She wrote again: "If there is time at the last, when you see that it is best, will you kill me?"

I took the shell from her hand, and wrote my answer beneath her question.

The forest behind us sank into that pause and breathless hush between the noises of the day and the noises of the night. The sun dropped lower, and the water became as pink as the blooms above us.

"An you could, would you change?" I asked. "Would you return to England and safety?"

She took a handful of the sand and let it slowly drift through her white fingers. "You know that I would not," she said; "not if the end were to come to-night. Only—only"—She turned from me and looked far out to sea. I could not see her face, only the dusk of her hair and her heaving bosom. "My blood may be upon your hands," she said in a whisper, "but yours will be upon my soul."

She turned yet further away, and covered her eyes with her hand. I arose, and bent over her until I could have touched with my lips that bowed head. "Jocelyn," I said.

A branch of yellow fruit fell beside us, and my Lord Carnal, a mass of gaudy bloom in his hand, stepped from the wood. "I returned to lay our first-fruits at madam's feet," he explained, his darkly watchful eyes upon us both. "A gift from one poor prisoner to another, madam." He dropped the flowers in her lap. "Will you wear them, lady? They are as fair almost as I could wish."

She touched the blossoms with listless fingers, said they were fair; then, rising, let them drop upon the sand. "I wear no flowers save of my husband's gathering, my lord," she said.

There was a pathos and weariness in her voice, and a mist of unshed tears in her eyes. She hated him; she loved me not, yet was forced to turn to me for help at every point, and she had stood for weeks upon the brink of death and looked unfalteringly into the gulf beneath her.

"My lord," I said, "you know in what direction Master Sparrow led the men. Will you reenter the wood and call them to return? The sun is fast sinking, and darkness will be upon us."

He looked from her to me, with his brows drawn downwards and his lips pressed together. Stooping, he took up the fallen flowers and deliberately tore them to pieces, until the pink petals were all scattered upon the sand.

"I am weary of requests that are but sugared commands," he said thickly. "Go seek your own men, an you will. Here we are but man to man, and I budge not. I stay, as the King would have me stay, beside the unfortunate lady whom you have made the prisoner and the plaything of a pirate ship."

"You wear no sword, my Lord Carnal," I said at last, "and so may lie with impunity."

"But you can get me one!" he cried, with ill-concealed eagerness.

I laughed. "I am not zealous in mine enemy's cause, my lord. I shall not deprive Master Sparrow of your lordship's sword."

Before I knew what he was about he crossed the yard of sand between us and struck me in the face. "Will that quicken your zeal?" he demanded between his teeth.

I seized him by the arm, and we stood so, both white with passion, both breathing heavily. At length I flung his arm from me and stepped back. "I fight not my prisoner," I said, "nor, while the lady you have named abides upon that ship with the nobleman who, more than myself, is answerable for her being there, do I put my life in unnecessary hazard. I will endure the smart as best I may, my lord, until a more convenient season, when I will salve it well."

I turned to Mistress Percy, and giving her my hand led her down to the boats; for I heard the fruit gatherers breaking through the wood, and the hunters for eggs, black figures against the crimson sky, were hurrying down the beach. Before the night had quite fallen we were out of the fairy harbor, and when the moon rose the islet looked only a silver sail against the jeweled heavens.

CHAPTER XXIV
IN WHICH WE CHOOSE THE LESSER OF TWO EVILS

THE luck that had been ours could not hold; when the tide turned, it ebbed fast.

The weather changed. One hurricane followed upon the stride of another, with only a blue day or two between. Ofttimes we thought the ship was lost. All hands toiled like galley slaves; and as the heavens darkened, there darkened also the mood of the pirates.

In sight of the great island of Cuba we gave chase to a bark. The sun was shining and the sea fairly still when first she fled before us; we gained upon her, and there was not a mile between us when a cloud blotted out the sun. The next minute our own sails gave us occupation enough. The storm, not we, was victor over the bark; she sank with a shriek from her decks that rang above the roaring wind. Two days later we fought a large caravel. With a fortunate shot she brought down our foremast, and sailed away from us with small damage of her own. All that day and night the wind blew, driving us out of our course, and by dawn we were as a shuttlecock between it and the sea. We weathered the gale, but when the wind sank there fell on board that black ship a menacing silence.

In the state cabin I held a council of war. Mistress Percy sat beside me, her arm upon the table, her hand shadowing her eyes; my lord, opposite, never took his gaze from her, though he listened gloomily to Sparrow's rueful assertion that the brazen game we had been playing was well-nigh over. Diccon, standing behind him, bit his nails and stared at the floor.

"For myself I care not overmuch," ended the minister. "I scorn not life, but think it at its worst well worth the living; yet when my God calls me, I will go as to a gala day and triumph. You are a soldier, Captain Percy, you and Diccon here, and know how to die. You too, my Lord Carnal, are a brave man, though a most wicked one. For us four, we can drink the cup, bitter though it be, with little trembling. But there is one among us"—His great voice broke, and he sat staring at the table.

The King's ward uncovered her eyes. "If I be not a man and a soldier, Master Sparrow," she said simply, "yet I am the daughter of many valiant gentlemen. I will die as they died before me. And for me, as for you four, it will be only death,—naught else." She looked at me with a proud smile.

"Naught else," I said.

My lord started from his seat and strode over to the window, where he stood drumming his fingers against the casing. I turned toward him. "My Lord Carnal," I said, "you were overheard last night when you plotted with the Spaniard."

He recoiled with a gasp, and his hand went to his side, where it found no sword. I saw his eyes busy here and there through the cabin, seeking something which he might convert into a weapon.

"I am yet captain of this ship," I continued. "Why I do not, even though it be my last act of authority, have you flung to the sharks, I scarcely know."

He threw back his head, all his bravado returned to him. "It is not I that stand in danger," he began loftily; "and I would have you remember, sir, that you are my enemy, and that I owe you no loyalty."

"I am content to be your enemy," I answered.

"You do not dare to set upon me now," he went on, with his old insolent, boastful smile. "Let me cry out, make a certain signal, and they without will be here in a twinkling, breaking in the door"—"The signal set?" I said. "The mine laid, the match burning? Then 't is time that we were gone. When I bid the world good-night, my lord, my wife goes with me."

His lips moved and his black eyes narrowed, but he did not speak.

"An my cheek did not burn so," I said, "I would be content to let you live; live, captain in verity of this ship of devils, until, tired of you, the devils cut your throat, or until some victorious Spaniard hung you at his yardarm; live even to crawl back to England, by hook or crook, to wait, hat in hand, in the antechamber of his Grace of Buckingham. As it is, I will kill you here and now. I restore you your sword, my lord, and there lies my challenge."

I flung my glove at his feet, and Sparrow unbuckled the keen blade which he had worn since the day I had asked it of its owner, and pushed it to me across the table. The King's ward leaned back in her chair, very white, but with a proud, still face, and hands loosely folded in her lap. My lord stood irresolute, his lip caught between his teeth, his eyes upon the door.

"Cry out, my lord," I said. "You are in danger. Cry to your friends without, who may come in time. Cry out loudly, like a soldier and a gentleman!"

With a furious oath he stooped and caught up the glove at his feet; then snatched out of my hand the sword that I offered him.

"Push back the settle, you; it is in the way!" he cried to Diccon; then to me, in a voice thick with passion: "Come on, sir! Here there are no meddling governors; this time let Death throw down the warder!"

"He throws it," said the minister beneath his breath.

From without came a trampling and a sudden burst of excited voices. The next instant the door was burst open, and a most villainous, fiery-red face thrust itself inside. "A ship!" bawled the apparition, and vanished. The clamor increased; voices cried for captain and mate, and more pirates appeared at the door, swearing out the good news, come in search of Kirby, and giving no choice but to go with them at once.

"Until this interruption is over, sir," I said sternly, bowing to him as I spoke. "No longer."

"Be sure, sir, that to my impatience the time will go heavily," he answered as sternly.

We reached the poop to find the fog that had lain about us thick and white suddenly lifted, and the hot sunshine streaming down upon a rough blue sea. To the larboard, a league away, lay a low, endless coast of sand, as dazzling white as the surf that broke upon it, and running back to a matted growth of vivid green.

"That is Florida," said Paradise at my elbow, "and there are reefs and shoals enough between us. It was Kirby's luck that the fog lifted. Yonder tall ship hath a less fortunate star."

She lay between us and the white beach, evidently in shoal and dangerous waters. She too had encountered a hurricane, and had not come forth victorious. Foremast and forecastle were gone, and her bowsprit was broken. She lay heavily, her ports but a few inches above the water. Though we did not know it then, most of her ordnance had been flung overboard to lighten her. Crippled as she was, with what sail she could set, she was beating back to open sea from that dangerous offing.

"Where she went we can follow!" sang out a voice from the throng in our waist. "A d—d easy prize! And we'll give no quarter this time!" There was a grimness in the applause of his fellows that boded little good to some on either ship.

"Lord help all poor souls this day!" ejaculated the minister in undertones; then aloud and more hopefully, "She hath not the look of a don; maybe she's buccaneer."

"She is an English merchantman," said Paradise. "Look at her colors. A Company ship, probably, bound for Virginia, with a cargo of servants, gentlemen out at elbows, felons, children for apprentices, traders, French vignerons, glasswork Italians, returning Councilors and heads of hundreds, with their wives and daughters, men servants and maid servants. I made the Virginia voyage once myself, captain."

I did not answer. I too saw the two crosses, and I did not doubt that the arms upon the flag beneath were those of the Company. The vessel, which was of about two hundred tons, had mightily the look of the George, a ship with which we at Jamestown were all familiar. Sparrow spoke for me.

"An English ship!" he cried out of the simplicity of his heart. "Then she's safe enough for us! Perhaps we might speak her and show her that we are English, too! Perhaps"—He looked at me eagerly.

"Perhaps you might be let to go off to her in one of the boats," finished Paradise dryly. "I think not, Master Sparrow."

"It's other guess messengers that they'll send," muttered Diccon. "They're uncovering the guns, sir."

Every man of those villains, save one, was of English birth; every man knew that the disabled ship was an English merchantman filled with peaceful folk, but the knowledge changed their plans no whit. There was a great hubbub; cries and oaths and brutal laughter, the noise of the gunners with their guns, the clang of cutlass and pike as they were dealt out, but not a voice raised against the murder that was to be done. I looked from the doomed ship, upon which there was now frantic haste and confusion, to the excited throng below me, and knew that I had as well cry for mercy to winter wolves.

The helmsman behind me had not waited for orders, and we were bearing down upon the disabled bark. Ahead of us, upon our larboard bow, was a patch of lighter green, and beyond it a slight hurry and foam of the waters. Half a dozen voices cried warning to the helmsman. It was he of the woman's mantle, whom I had run through the shoulder on the island off Cape Charles, and he had been Kirby's pilot from Maracaibo to Fort Caroline. Now he answered with a burst of vaunting oaths: "We're in deep water, and there's deep water beyond. I've passed this way before, and I'll carry ye safe past that reef were 't hell's gate!"

The desperadoes who heard him swore applause, and thought no more of the reef that lay in wait. Long since they had gone through the gates of hell for the sake of the prize beyond. Knowing the appeal to be hopeless, I yet made it.

"She is English, men!" I shouted. "We will fight the Spaniards while they have a flag in the Indies, but our own people we will not touch!"

The clamor of shouts and oaths suddenly fell, and the wind in the rigging, the water at the keel, the surf on the shore, made themselves heard. In the silence, the terror of the fated ship became audible. Confused voices came to us, and the scream of a woman.

On the faces of a very few of the pirates there was a look of momentary doubt and wavering; it passed, and the most had never worn it. They began to press forward toward the poop, cursing and threatening, working themselves up into a rage that would not care for my sword, the minister's cutlass, or Diccon's pike. One who called himself a wit cried out something about Kirby and his methods, and two or three laughed.

"I find that the role of Kirby wearies me," I said. "I am an English gentleman, and I will not fire upon an English ship."

As if in answer there came from our forecastle a flame and thunder of guns. The gunners there, intent upon their business, and now within range of the merchantman, had fired the three forecastle culverins. The shot cut her rigging and brought down the flag. The pirates' shout of triumph was echoed by a cry from her decks and the defiant roar of her few remaining guns.

I drew my sword. The minister and Diccon moved nearer to me, and the King's ward, still and white and braver than a man, stood beside me. From the pirates that we faced came one deep breath, like the first sigh of the wind before the blast strikes. Suddenly the Spaniard pushed himself to the front; with his gaunt figure and sable dress he had the seeming of a raven come to croak over the dead. He rested his gloomy eyes upon my lord. The latter, very white, returned the look; then, with his head held high, crossed the deck with a measured step and took his place among us. He was followed a moment later by Paradise. "I never thought to die in my bed, captain," said the latter nonchalantly. "Sooner or later, what does it matter? And you must know that before I was a pirate I was a gentleman." Turning, he doffed his hat with a flourish to those he had quitted. "Hell litter!" he cried. "I have run with you long enough. Now I have a mind to die an honest man."

At this defection a dead hush of amazement fell upon that crew. One and all they stared at the man in black and silver, moistening their lips, but saying no word. We were five armed and desperate men; they were fourscore. We might send many to death before us, but at the last we ourselves must die,—we and those aboard the helpless ship.

In the moment's respite I bowed my head and whispered to the King's ward.

"I had rather it were your sword," she answered in a low voice, in which there was neither dread nor sorrow. "You must not let it grieve you; it will be added to your good deeds. And it is I that should ask your forgiveness, not you mine."

Though there was scant time for such dalliance, I bent my knee and rested my forehead upon her hand. As I rose, the minister's hand touched my shoulder and the voice spoke in my ear. "There is another way," he said. "There is God's death, and not man's. Look and see what I mean."

I followed the pointing of his eyes, and saw how close we were to those white and tumbling waters, the danger signal, the rattle of the hidden snake. The eyes of the pirate at the helm, too, were upon them; his brows were drawn downward, his lips pressed together, the whole man bent upon the ship's safe passage.... The low thunder of the surf, the cry of a wheeling sea bird, the gleaming lonely shore, the cloudless sky, the ocean, and the white sand far, far below, where one might sleep well, sleep well, with other valiant dead, long drowned, long changed. "Of their bones are coral made."

The storm broke with fury and outcries, and a blue radiance of drawn steel. A pistol ball sang past my ear.

"Don't shoot!" roared the gravedigger to the man who had fired the shot. "Don't cut them down! Take them and thrust them under hatches until we've time to give them a slow death! And hands off the woman until we've time to draw lots!"

He and the Spaniard led the rush. I turned my head and nodded to Sparrow, then faced them again. "Then may the Lord have mercy upon your souls!" I said.

As I spoke the minister sprang upon the helmsman, and, striking him to the deck with one blow of his huge fist, himself seized the wheel. Before the pirates could draw breath he had jammed the helm to starboard, and the reef lay right across our bows.

A dreadful cry went up from that black ship to a deaf Heaven,—a cry that was echoed by a wild shout of triumph from the merchantman. The mass fronting us broke in terror and rage and confusion. Some ran frantically up and down with shrieks and curses; others sprang overboard. A few made a dash for the poop and for us who stood to meet them. They were led by the Spaniard and the gravedigger. The former I met and sent tumbling back into the waist; the latter whirled past me, and rushing upon Paradise thrust him through with a pike, then dashed on to the wheel, to be met and hewn down by Diccon.

The ship struck. I put my arm around my wife, and my hand before her eyes; and while I looked only at her, in that storm of terrible cries, of flapping canvas, rushing water, and crashing timbers, the Spaniard clambered like a catamount upon the poop, that was now high above the broken forepart of the ship, and fired his pistol at me point-blank.

CHAPTER XXV
IN WHICH MY LORD HATH HIS DAY

I AND Black Lamoral were leading a forlorn hope. With all my old company behind us, we were thundering upon an enemy as thick as ants, covering the face of the earth. Down came Black Lamoral, and the hoofs of every mad charger went over me. For a time I was dead; then I lived again, and was walking with the forester's daughter in the green chase at home. The oaks stretched broad sheltering arms above the young fern and the little wild flowers, and the deer turned and looked at us. In the open spaces, starring the lush grass, were all the yellow primroses that ever bloomed. I gathered them for her, but when I would have given them to her she was no longer the forester's daughter, but a proud lady, heiress to lands and gold, the ward of the King. She would not take the primroses from a poor gentleman, but shook her head and laughed sweetly, and faded into a waterfall that leaped from a pink hill into a waveless sea. Another darkness, and I was captive to the Chickahominies, tied to the stake. My arm and shoulder were on fire, and Opechancanough came and looked at me, with his dark, still face and his burning eyes. The fierce pain died, and I with it, and I lay in a grave and listened to the loud and deep murmur of the forest above. I lay there for ages on ages before I awoke to the fact that the darkness about me was the darkness of a ship's hold, and the murmur of the forest the wash of the water alongside. I put out an arm and touched, not the side of a grave, but a ship's timbers. I stretched forth the other arm, then dropped it with a groan. Some one bent over me and held water to my lips. I drank, and my senses came fully to me. "Diccon!" I said.

"It's not Diccon," replied the figure, setting down a pitcher. "It is Jeremy Sparrow. Thank God, you are yourself again!"

"Where are we?" I asked, when I had lain and listened to the water a little longer.

"In the hold of the George," he answered. "The ship sank by the bows, and well-nigh all were drowned. But when they upon the George saw that there was a woman amongst us who clung to the poop deck, they sent their longboat to take us off."

The light was too dim for me to read his face, so I touched his arm.

"She was saved," he said. "She is safe now. There are gentlewomen aboard, and she is in their care."

I put my unhurt arm across my eyes.

"You are weak yet," said the minister gently. "The Spaniard's ball, you know, went through your shoulder, and in some way your arm was badly torn from shoulder to wrist. You have been out of your head ever since we were brought here, three days ago. The chirurgeon came and dressed your wound, and it is healing well. Don't try to speak,—I'll tell you all. Diccon has been pressed into service, as the ship is short of hands, having lost some by fever and some overboard. Four of the pirates were picked up, and hung at the yardarm next morning."

He moved as he spoke, and something clanked in the stillness. "You are ironed!" I exclaimed.

"Only my ankles. My lord would have had me bound hand and foot; but you were raving for water, and, taking you for a dying man, they were so humane as to leave my hands free to attend you."

"My lord would have had you bound," I said slowly. "Then it's my lord's day."

"High noon and blazing sunshine," he answered, with a rueful laugh. "It seems that half the folk on board had gaped at him at court. Lord! when he put his foot over the side of the ship, how the women screeched and the men stared! He 's cock of the walk now, my Lord Carnal, the King's favorite!"

"And we are pirates."

"That 's the case in a nutshell," he answered cheerfully.

"Do they know how the ship came to strike upon that reef?" I asked.

"Probably not, unless madam has enlightened them. I did n't take the trouble,—they would n't have believed me,—and I can take my oath my lord has n't. He was only our helpless prisoner, you know; and they would think madam mistaken or bewitched."

"It 's not a likely tale," I said grimly, "seeing that we had already opened fire upon them."

"I trust in heaven the sharks got the men who fired the culverins!" he cried, and then laughed at his own savagery.

I lay still and tried to think. "Who are they on board?" I asked at last.

"I don't know," he replied. "I was only on deck until my lord had had his say in the poop cabin with the master and a gentleman who appeared most in authority. Then the pirates were strung up, and we were bundled down here in quick order. But there seems to be more of quality than usual aboard."

"You do not know where we are?"

"We lay at anchor for a day,—whilst they patched her up, I suppose,—and since then there has been rough weather. We must be still off Florida, and that is all I know. Now go to sleep. You'll get your strength best so, and there's nothing to be gotten by waking."

He began to croon a many-versed psalm. I slept and waked, and slept again, and was waked by the light of a torch against my eyes. The torch was held by a much-betarred seaman, and by its light a gentleman of a very meagre aspect, with a weazen face and small black eyes, was busily examining my wounded shoulder and arm.

"It passeth belief," he said in a sing-song voice, "how often wounds, with naught in the world done for them outside of fair water and a clean rag, do turn to and heal out of sheer perversity. Now, if I had been allowed to treat this one properly with scalding oil and melted lead, and to have bled the patient as he should have been bled, it is ten to one that by this time there would have been a pirate the less in the world." He rose to his feet with a highly injured countenance.

"Then he's doing well?" asked Sparrow.

"So well that he could n't do better," replied the other. "The arm was a trifling matter, though no doubt exquisitely painful. The wound in the shoulder is miraculously healing, without either blood-letting or cauteries. You'll have to hang after all, my friend." He looked at me with his little beady eyes. "It must have been a grand life," he said regretfully. "I never expected to see a pirate chief in the flesh. When I was a boy, I used to dream of the black ships and the gold and the fighting. By the serpent of Esculapius, in my heart of hearts I would rather be such a world's thief, uncaught, than Governor of Virginia!" He gathered up the tools of his trade, and motioned to his torchbearer to go before. "I'll have to report you rapidly recovering," he said warningly, as he turned to follow the light.

"Very well," I made answer. "To whom am I indebted for so much kindness?"

"I am Dr. John Pott, newly appointed physician general to the colony of Virginia. It is little of my skill I could give you, but that little I gladly bestow upon a real pirate. What a life it must have been! And to have to part with it when you are yet young! And the good red gold and the rich gems all at the bottom of the sea!"

He sighed heavily and went his way. The hatches were closed after him, and the minister and I were left in darkness while the slow hours dragged themselves past us. Through the chinks of the hatches a very faint light streamed down, and made the darkness gray instead of black. The minister and I saw each other dimly, as spectres. Some one brought us mouldy biscuit that I wanted not, and water for which I thirsted. Sparrow put the small pitcher to his lips, kept it there a moment, then held it to mine. I drank, and with that generous draught tasted pure bliss. It was not until five minutes later that I raised myself upon my elbow and turned on him.

"The pitcher felt full to my lips!" I exclaimed. "Did you drink when you said you did?"

He put out his great hand and pushed me gently down. "I have no wound," he said, "and there was not enough for two."

The light that trembled through the cracks above died away, and the darkness became gross. The air in the hold was stifling; our souls panted for the wind and the stars outside. At the worst, when the fetid blackness lay upon our chests like a nightmare, the hatch was suddenly lifted, a rush of pure air came to us, and with it the sound of men's voices speaking on the deck above. Said one, "True the doctor pronounces him out of all danger, yet he is a wounded man."

"He is a desperate and dangerous man," broke in another harshly. "I know not how you will answer to your Company for leaving him unironed so long."

"I and the Company understand each other, my lord," rejoined the first speaker, with some haughtiness. "I can keep my prisoner without advice. If I now order irons to be put upon him and his accomplice, it is because I see fit to do so, and not because of your suggestion, my lord. You wish to take this opportunity to have speech with him,—to that I can have no objection."

The speaker moved away. As his footsteps died in the distance my lord laughed, and his merriment was echoed by three or four harsh voices. Some one struck flint against steel, and there was a sudden flare of torches and the steadier light of a lantern. A man with a brutal, weather-beaten face—the master of the ship, we guessed—came down the ladder, lantern in hand, turned when he had reached the foot, and held up the lantern to light my lord down. I lay and watched the King's favorite as he descended. The torches held slantingly above cast a fiery light over his stately figure and the face which had raised him from the low estate of a doubtful birth and a most lean purse to a pinnacle too near the sun for men to gaze at with undazzled eyes. In his rich dress and the splendor of his beauty, with the red glow enveloping him, he lit the darkness like a baleful star.

The two torchbearers and a third man descended, closing the hatch after them. When all were down, my lord, the master at his heels, came and stood over me. I raised myself, though with difficulty, for the fever had left me weak as a babe, and met his gaze. His was a cruel look; if I had expected, as assuredly I did not expect, mercy or generosity from this my dearest foe, his look would have struck such a hope dead. Presently he beckoned to the men behind him. "Put the manacles upon him first," he said, with a jerk of his thumb toward Sparrow.

The man who had come down last, and who carried irons enough to fetter six pirates, started forward to do my lord's bidding. The master glanced at Sparrow's great frame, and pulled out a pistol. The minister laughed. "You'll not need it, friend. I know when the odds are too great." He held out his arms, and the men fettered them wrist to wrist. When they had finished he said calmly: "'I have seen the wicked in great power, and spreading himself like a green bay tree. Yet he passed away, and, lo, he was not: yea, I sought him, but he could not be found.'"

My lord turned from him, and pointed to me. He kept his eyes upon my face while they shackled me hand and foot; then said abruptly, "You have cords there: bind his arms to his sides." The men wound the cords around me many times. "Draw them tight," commanded my lord.

There came a wrathful clank of the minister's chains. "The arm is torn and inflamed from shoulder to wrist, as I make no doubt you have been told!" he cried. "For very shame, man!"

"Draw them tighter," said my lord, between his teeth.

The men knotted the cords, and rose to their feet, to be dismissed by my lord with a curt "You may go." They drew back to the foot of the ladder, while the master of the ship went and perched himself upon one of the rungs. "The air is fresher here beneath the hatch," he remarked.

As for me, though I lay at my enemy's feet, I could yet set my teeth and look him in the eyes. The cup was bitter, but I could drink it with an unmoved face.

"Art paid?" he demanded. "Art paid for the tree in the red forest without the haunted wood? Art paid, thou bridegroom?"

"No," I answered. "Bring her here to laugh at me as she laughed in the twilight beneath the guesthouse window."

I thought he would murder me with the poniard he drew, but presently he put it up.

"She is come to her senses," he said. "Up in the state cabin are bright lights, and wine and laughter. There are gentlewomen aboard, and I have been singing to the lute, to them—and to her. She is saved from the peril into which you plunged her; she knows that the King's Court of High Commission, to say nothing of the hangman, will soon snap the fetters which she now shudders to think of; that the King and one besides will condone her past short madness. Her cheeks are roses, her eyes are stars. But now, when I pressed her hand between the verses of my song, she smiled and sighed and blushed. She is again the dutiful ward of the King, the Lady Jocelyn Leigh—she hath asked to be so called"—

"You lie," I said. "She is my true and noble wife. She may sit in the state cabin, in the air and warmth and light, she may even laugh with her lips, but her heart is here with me in the hold."

As I spoke, I knew, and knew not how I knew, that the thing which I had said was true. With that knowledge came a happiness so deep and strong that it swept aside like straw the torment of those cords, and the deeper hurt that I lay at his feet. I suppose my face altered, and mirrored that blessed glow about my heart, for into his own came a white fury, changing its beauty into something inhuman and terrifying. He looked a devil baffled. For a minute he stood there rigid, with hands clenched. "Embrace her heart, if thou canst," he said, in a voice so low that it came like a whisper from the realm he might have left. "I shall press my face against her bosom."

Another minute of a silence that I disdained to break; then he turned and went up the ladder. The seamen and the master followed. The hatch was clapped to and fastened, and we were left to the darkness and the heavy air, and to a grim endurance of what could not be cured.

During those hours of thirst and torment I came indeed to know the man who sat beside me. His hands were so fastened that he could not loosen the cords, and there was no water for him to give me; but he could and did bestow a higher alms,—the tenderness of a brother, the manly sympathy of a soldier, the balm of the priest of God. I lay in silence, and he spoke not often; but when he did so, there was that in the tone of his voice—Another cycle of pain, and I awoke from a half swoon, in which there was water to drink and no anguish, to hear him praying beside me. He ceased to speak, and in the darkness I heard him draw his breath hard and his great muscles crack. Suddenly there came a sharp sound of breaking iron, and a low "Thank Thee, Lord!" Another moment, and I felt his hands busy at the knotted cords. "I will have them off thee in a twinkling, Ralph," he said, "thanks to Him who taught my hands to war, and my arms to break in two a bow of steel." As he spoke, the cords loosened beneath his fingers.

I raised my head and laid it on his knee, and he put his great arm, with the broken chain dangling from it, around me, and, like a mother with a babe, crooned me to sleep with the twenty-third psalm.

CHAPTER XXVI
IN WHICH I AM BROUGHT TO TRIAL

MY lord came not again into the hold, and the untied cords and the broken chain were not replaced. Morning and evening we were brought a niggard allowance of bread and water; but the man who carried it bore no light, and may not even have observed their absence. We saw no one in authority. Hour by hour my wounds healed and my strength returned. If it was a dark and noisome prison, if there were hunger and thirst and inaction to be endured, if we knew not how near to us might be a death of ignominy, yet the minister and I found the jewel in the head of the toad; for in that time of pain and heaviness we became as David and Jonathan.

At last some one came beside the brute who brought us food. A quiet gentleman, with whitening hair and bright dark eyes, stood before us. He had ordered the two men with him to leave open the hatch, and he held in his hand a sponge soaked with vinegar. "Which of you is—or rather was—Captain Ralph Percy?" he asked, in a grave but pleasant voice.

"I am Captain Percy," I answered.

He looked at me with attention. "I have heard of you before," he said. "I read the letter you wrote to Sir Edwyn Sandys, and thought it an excellently conceived and manly epistle. What magic transformed a gentleman and a soldier into a pirate?"

As he waited for me to speak, I gave him for answer, "Necessity."

"A sad metamorphosis," he said. "I had rather read of nymphs changed into laurel and gushing springs. I am come to take you, sir, before the officers of the Company aboard this ship, when, if you have aught to say for yourself, you may say it. I need not tell you, who saw so clearly some time ago the danger in which you then stood, that your plight is now a thousandfold worse."

"I am perfectly aware of it," I said. "Am I to go in fetters?"

"No," he replied, with a smile. "I have no instructions on the subject, but I will take it upon myself to free you from them,—even for the sake of that excellently writ letter."

"Is not this gentleman to go too?" I asked.

He shook his head. "I have no orders to that effect."

While the men who were with him removed the irons from my wrists and ankles he stood in silence, regarding me with a scrutiny so close that it would have been offensive had I been in a position to take offense. When they had finished I turned and held Jeremy's hand in mine for an instant, then followed the new-comer to the ladder and out of the hold; the two men coming after us, and resolving themselves above into a guard. As we traversed the main deck we came upon Diccon, busy with two or three others about the ports. He saw me, and, dropping the bar that he held, started forward, to be plucked back by an angry arm. The men who guarded me pushed in between us, and there was no word spoken by either. I walked on, the gentleman at my side, and presently came to an open port, and saw, with an intake of my breath, the sunshine, a dark blue heaven flecked with white, and a quiet ocean. My companion glanced at me keenly.

"Doubtless it seems fair enough, after that Cimmerian darkness below," he remarked. "Would you like to rest here a moment?"

"Yes," I said, and, leaning against the side of the port, looked out at the beauty of the light.

"We are off Hatteras," he informed me, "but we have not met with the stormy seas that vex poor mariners hereabouts. Those sails you see on our quarter belong to our consort. We were separated by the hurricane that nigh sunk us, and finally drove us, helpless as we were, toward the Florida coast and across your path. For us that was a fortunate reef upon which you dashed. The gods must have made your helmsman blind, for he ran you into a destruction that gaped not for you. Why did every wretch that we hung next morning curse you before he died?"

"If I told you, you would not believe me," I replied.

I was dizzy with the bliss of the air and the light, and it seemed a small thing that he would not believe me. The wind sounded in my ears like a harp, and the sea beckoned. A white bird flashed down into the crystal hollow between two waves, hung there a second, then rose, a silver radiance against the blue. Suddenly I saw a river, dark and ridged beneath thunderclouds, a boat, and in it, her head pillowed upon her arm, a woman, who pretended that she slept. With a shock my senses steadied, and I became myself again. The sea was but the sea, the wind the wind; in the hold below me lay my friend; somewhere in that ship was my wife; and awaiting me in the state cabin were men who perhaps had the will, as they had the right and the might, to hang me at the yardarm that same hour.

"I have had my fill of rest," I said. "Whom am I to stand before?"

"The newly appointed officers of the Company, bound in this ship for Virginia," he answered. "The ship carries Sir Francis Wyatt, the new Governor; Master Davison, the Secretary; young Clayborne, the surveyor general; the knight marshal, the physician general, and the Treasurer, with other gentlemen, and with fair ladies, their wives and sisters. I am George Sandys, the Treasurer."

The blood rushed to my face, for it hurt me that the brother of Sir Edwyn Sandys should believe that the firing of those guns had been my act. His was the trained observation of the traveler and writer, and he probably read the color aright. "I pity you, if I can no longer esteem you," he said, after a pause. "I know no sorrier sight than a brave man's shield reversed."

I bit my lip and kept back the angry word. The next minute saw us at the door of the state cabin. It opened, and my companion entered, and I after him, with my two guards at my back. Around a large table were gathered a number of gentlemen, some seated, some standing. There were but two among them whom I had seen before,—the physician who had dressed my wound and my Lord Carnal. The latter was seated in a great chair, beside a gentleman with a pleasant active face and light brown curling hair,—the new Governor, as I guessed. The Treasurer, nodding to the two men to fall back to the window, glided to a seat upon my lord's other hand, and I went and stood before the Governor of Virginia.

For some moments there was silence in the cabin, every man being engaged in staring at me with all his eyes; then the Governor spoke: "It should be upon your knees, sir."

"I am neither petitioner nor penitent," I said. "I know no reason why I should kneel, your Honor."

"There 's reason, God wot, why you should be both!" he exclaimed. "Did you not, now some months agone, defy the writ of the King and Company, refusing to stand when called upon to do so in the King's name?"

"Yes."

"Did you not, when he would have stayed your lawless flight, lay violent hands upon a nobleman high in the King's favor, and, overpowering him with numbers, carry him out of the King's realm?"

"Yes."

"Did you not seduce from her duty to the King, and force to fly with you, his Majesty's ward, the Lady Jocelyn Leigh?"

"No," I said. "There was with me only my wife, who chose to follow the fortunes of her husband."

He frowned, and my lord swore beneath his breath. "Did you not, falling in with a pirate ship, cast in your lot with the scoundrels upon it, and yourself turn pirate?"

"In some sort."

"And become their chief?"

"Since there was no other situation open,—yes."

"Taking with you as captives upon the pirate ship that lady and that nobleman?"

"Yes."

"You proceeded to ravage the dominions of the King of Spain, with whom his Majesty is at peace"—

"Like Drake and Raleigh,—yes," I said.

He smiled, then frowned "Tempora mutantur," he said dryly. "And I have never heard that Drake or Raleigh attacked an English ship."

"Nor have I attacked one," I said.

He leaned back in his chair and stared at me. "We saw the flame and heard the thunder of your guns, and our rigging was cut by the shot. Did you expect me to believe that last assertion?"

"No."

"Then you might have spared yourself—and us—that lie," he said coldly.

The Treasurer moved restlessly in his seat, and began to whisper to his neighbor the Secretary. A young man, with the eyes of a hawk and an iron jaw,—Clayborne, the surveyor general,—who sat at the end of the table beside the window, turned and gazed out upon the clouds and the sea, as if, contempt having taken the place of curiosity, he had no further interest in the proceedings. As for me, I set my face like a flint, and looked past the man who might have saved me that last speech of the Governor's as if he had never been.

There was a closed door in the cabin, opposite the one by which I had entered. Suddenly from behind it came the sound of a short struggle, followed by the quick turn of a key in the lock. The door was flung open, and two women entered the cabin. One, a fair young gentlewoman, with tears in her brown eyes, came forward hurriedly with outspread hands.

"I did what I could, Frank!" she cried. "When she would not listen to reason, I e'en locked the door; but she is strong, for all that she has been ill, and she forced the key out of my hand!" She looked at the red mark upon the white hand, and two tears fell from her long lashes upon her wild-rose cheeks.

With a smile the Governor put out an arm and drew her down upon a stool beside him, then rose and bowed low to the King's ward. "You are not yet well enough to leave your cabin, as our worthy physician general will assure you, lady," he said courteously, but firmly. "Permit me to lead you back to it."

Still smiling he made as if to advance, when she stayed him with a gesture of her raised hand, at once so majestic and so pleading that it was as though a strain of music had passed through the stillness of the cabin.

"Sir Francis Wyatt, as you are a gentleman, let me speak," she said. It was the voice of that first night at Weyanoke, all pathos, all sweetness, all entreating.

The Governor stopped short, the smile still upon his lips, his hand still outstretched,—stood thus for a moment, then sat down. Around the half circle of gentlemen went a little rustling sound, like wind in dead leaves. My lord half rose from his seat. "She is bewitched," he said, with dry lips. "She will say what she has been told to say. Lest she speak to her shame, we should refuse to hear her."

She had been standing in the centre of the floor, her hands clasped, her body bowed toward the Governor, but at my lord's words she straightened like a bow unbent. "I may speak, your Honor?" she asked clearly.

The Governor, who had looked askance at the working face of the man beside him, slightly bent his head and leaned back in his great armchair. The King's favorite started to his feet. The King's ward turned her eyes upon him. "Sit down, my lord," she said. "Surely these gentlemen will think that you are afraid of what I, a poor erring woman, rebellious to the King, traitress to mine own honor, late the plaything of a pirate ship, may say or do. Truth, my lord, should be more courageous." Her voice was gentle, even plaintive, but it had in it the quality that lurks in the eyes of the crouching panther.

My lord sat down, one hand hiding his working mouth, the other clenched on the arm of his chair as if it had been an arm of flesh.

CHAPTER XXVII
IN WHICH I FIND AN ADVOCATE

SHE came slowly nearer the ring of now very quiet and attentive faces until she stood beside me, but she neither looked at me nor spoke to me. She was thinner and there were heavy shadows beneath her eyes, but she was beautiful.

"I stand before gentlemen to whom, perhaps, I am not utterly unknown," she said. "Some here, perchance, have been to court, and have seen me there. Master Sandys, once, before the Queen died, you came to Greenwich to kiss her Majesty's hands; and while you waited in her antechamber you saw a young maid of honor—scarce more than a child—curled in a window seat with a book. You sat beside her, and told her wonderful tales of sunny lands and gods and nymphs. I was that maid of honor. Master Clayborne, once, hawking near Windsor, I dropped my glove. There were a many out of their saddles before it touched the ground, but a gentleman, not of our party, who had drawn his horse to one side to let us pass, was quicker than they all. Did you not think yourself well paid, sir, when you kissed the hand to which you restored the glove? All here, I think, may have heard my name. If any hath heard aught that ever I did in all my life to tarnish it, I pray him to speak now and shame me before you all!"

Clayborne started up. "I remember that day at Windsor, lady!" he cried. "The man of whom I afterward asked your name was a most libertine courtier, and he raised his hat when he spoke of you, calling you a lily which the mire of the court could not besmirch. I will believe all good, but no harm of you, lady!"

He sat down, and Master Sandys said gravely: "Men need not be courtiers to have known of a lady of great wealth and high birth, a ward of the King's, and both beautiful and pure. I nor no man else, I think, ever heard aught of the Lady Jocelyn Leigh but what became a daughter of her line."

A murmur of assent went round the circle. The Governor, leaning forward from his seat, his wife's hand in his, gravely bent his head. "All this is known, lady," he said courteously.

She did not answer; her eyes were upon the King's favorite, and the circle waited with her.

"It is known," said my lord.

She smiled proudly. "For so much grace, thanks, my lord," she said, then addressed herself again to the Governor: "Your Honor, that is the past, the long past, the long, long past, though not a year has gone by. Then I was a girl, proud and careless; now, your Honor, I am a woman, and I stand here in the dignity of suffering and peril. I fled from England"—She paused, drew herself up, and turned upon my lord a face and form so still, and yet so expressive of noble indignation, outraged womanhood, scorn, and withal a kind of angry pity, that small wonder if he shrank as from a blow. "I left the only world I knew," she said. "I took a way low and narrow and dark and set with thorns, but the only way that I—alone and helpless and bewildered—could find, because that I, Jocelyn Leigh, willed not to wed with you, my Lord Carnal. Why did you follow me, my lord? You knew that I loved you not. You knew my mind, and that I was weak and friendless, and you used your power. I must tell you, my lord, that you were not chivalrous, nor compassionate, nor brave"—

"I loved you!" he cried, and stretched out his arm toward her across the table. He saw no one but her, spoke to none but her. There was a fierce yearning and a hopelessness in his voice and bent head and outstretched arm that lent for the time a tragic dignity to the pageant, evil and magnificent, of his life.

"You loved me," she said. "I had rather you had hated me, my lord. I came to Virginia, your Honor, and men thought me the thing I professed myself. In the green meadow beyond the church they wooed me as such. This one came and that one, and at last a fellow, when I said him nay and bade him begone, did dare to seize my hands and kiss my lips. While I struggled one came and flung that dastard out of the way, then asked me plainly to become his wife, and there was no laugh or insult in his voice. I was wearied and fordone and desperate.... So I met my husband, and so I married him. That same day I told him a part of my secret, and when my Lord Carnal was come I told him all.... I had not met with much true love or courtesy or compassion in my life. When I saw the danger in which he stood because of me, I told him he might free himself from that coil, might swear to what they pleased, whistle me off, save himself, and I would say no word of blame. There was wine upon the table, and he filled a cup and brought it to me, and we drank of it together. We drank of the same cup then, your Honor, and we will drink of it still. We twain were wedded, and the world strove to part us. Which of you here, in such quarrel, would not withstand the world? Lady Wyatt, would not thy husband hold thee, while he lived, against the world? Then speak for mine!"

"Frank, Frank!" cried Lady Wyatt. "They love each other!"

"If he withstood the King," went on the King's ward, "it was for his honor and for mine. If he fled from Virginia, it was because I willed it so. Had he stayed, my Lord Carnal, and had you willed to follow me again, you must have made a yet longer journey to a most distant bourne. That wild night when we fled, why did you come upon us, my lord? The moon burst forth from a black cloud, and you stood there upon the wharf above us, calling to the footsteps behind to hasten. We would have left you there in safety, and gone ourselves alone down that stream as black and strange as death. Why did you spring down the steps and grapple with the minister? And he that might have thrust you beneath the flood and drowned you there did but fling you into the boat. We wished not your company, my lord; we would willingly have gone without you. I trust, my lord, you have made honest report of this matter, and have told these gentlemen that my husband gave you, a prisoner whom he wanted not, all fair and honorable treatment. That you have done this I dare take my oath, my lord"——

She stood silent, her eyes upon his. The men around stirred, and a little flash like the glint of drawn steel went from one pair of eyes to another.

"My lord, my lord!" said the King's ward. "Long ago you won my hatred; an you would not win my contempt, speak truth this day!"

In his eyes, which he had never taken from her face, there leaped to meet the proud appeal in her own a strange fire. That he loved her with a great and evil passion, I, who needs had watched him closely, had long known. Suddenly he burst into jarring laughter. "Yea, he treated me fairly enough, damn him to everlasting hell! But he 's a pirate, sweet bird; he's a pirate, and must swing as such!"

"A pirate!" she cried. "But he was none! My lord, you know he was none! Your Honor"——

The Governor interrupted her: "He made himself captain of a pirate ship, lady. He took and sunk ships of Spain."

"In what sort did he become their chief?" she cried. "In such sort, gentlemen, as the bravest of you, in like straits, would have been blithe to be, an you had had like measure of wit and daring! Your Honor, the wind before which our boat drave like a leaf, the waves that would engulf us, wrecked us upon a desert isle. There was no food or water or shelter. That night, while we slept, a pirate ship anchored off the beach, and in the morning the pirates came ashore to bury their captain. My husband met them alone, fought their would-be leaders one by one, and forced the election to fall upon himself. Well he knew that if he left not that isle their leader, he would leave it their captive; and not he alone! God's mercy, gentlemen, what other could he do? I pray you to hold him absolved from a willing embrace of that life! Sunk ships of Spain! Yea, forsooth; and how long hath it been since other English gentlemen sunk other ships of Spain? The world hath changed indeed if to fight the Spaniard in the Indies, e'en though at home we be at peace with him, be conceived so black a crime! He fought their galleons fair and knightly, with his life in his hand; he gave quarter, and while they called him chief those pirates tortured no prisoner and wronged no woman. Had he not been there, would the ships have been taken less surely? Had he not been there, God wot, ships and ships' boats alike would have sunk or burned, and no Spanish men and women had rowed away and blessed a generous foe. A pirate! He, with me and with the minister and with my Lord Carnal, was prisoner to the pirates, and out of that danger he plucked safety for us all! Who hath so misnamed a gallant gentleman? Was it you, my lord?"

Eyes and voice were imperious, and in her cheeks burned an indignant crimson. My lord's face was set and white; he looked at her, but spoke no word.

"The Spanish ships might pass, lady," said the Governor; "but this is an English ship, with the flag of England above her."

"Yea," she said. "What then?"

The circle rustled again. The Governor loosed his wife's fingers and leaned forward. "You plead well, lady!" he exclaimed. "You might win, an Captain Percy had not seen fit to fire upon us."

A dead silence followed his words. Outside the square window a cloud passed from the face of the sun, and a great burst of sunshine entered the cabin. She stood in the heart of it, and looked a goddess angered. My lord, with his haggard face and burning eyes, slowly rose from his seat, and they faced each other.

"You told them not who fired those guns, who sunk that pirate ship?" she said. "Because he was your enemy, you held your tongue? Knight and gentleman—my Lord Carnal—my Lord Coward!"

"Honor is an empty word to me," he answered. "For you I would dive into the deepest hell,—if there be a deeper than that which burns me, day in, day out.... Jocelyn, Jocelyn, Jocelyn!"

"You love me so?" she said. "Then do me pleasure. Because I ask it of you, tell these men the truth." She came a step nearer, and held out her clasped hands to him. "Tell them how it was, my lord, and I will strive to hate you no longer. The harm that you have done me I will pray for strength to forgive. Ah, my lord, let me not ask in vain! Will you that I kneel to you?"

"I fix my own price," he said. "I will do what you ask, an you will let me kiss your lips."

I sprang forward with an oath. Some one behind caught both my wrists in an iron grasp and pulled me back. "Be not a fool!" growled Clayborne in my ear. "The cord's loosening fast: if you interfere, it may tighten with a jerk!" I freed my hands from his grasp. The Treasurer, sitting next him, leaned across the table and motioned to the two seamen beside the window. They left their station, and each seized me by an arm. "Be guided, Captain Percy," said Master Sandys in a low voice. "We wish you well. Let her win you through."

"First tell the truth, my lord," said the King's ward; "then come and take the reward you ask."

"Jocelyn!" I cried. "I command you"—

She turned upon me a perfectly colorless face. "All my life after I will be to you an obedient wife," she said. "This once I pray you to hold me excused.... Speak, my lord."

There was the mirth of the lost in the laugh with which he turned to the Governor. "That pretty little tale, sir, that I regaled you with, the day you obligingly picked me up, was pure imagination; the wetting must have disordered my reason. A potion sweeter than the honey of Hybla, which I am about to drink, hath restored me beforehand. Gentlemen all, there was mutiny aboard that ship which so providentially sank before your very eyes. For why? The crew, who were pirates, and the captain, who was yonder gentleman, did not agree. The one wished to attack you, board you, rummage you, and slay, after recondite fashions, every mother's son of you; the other demurred,—so strongly, in fact, that his life ceased to be worth a pin's purchase. Indeed, I believe he resigned his captaincy then and there, and, declining to lift a finger against an English ship, defied them to do their worst. He had no hand in the firing of those culverins; the mutineers touched them off without so much as a 'by your leave.' His attention was otherwise occupied. Good sirs, there was not the slightest reason in nature why the ship should have struck upon that sunken reef, to the damnation of her people and the salvation of yours. Why do you suppose she diverged from the path of safety to split into slivers against that fortunate ledge?"

The men around drew in their breath, and one or two sprang to their feet. My lord laughed again. "Have you seen the pious man who left Jamestown and went aboard the pirate ship as this gentleman's lieutenant? He hath the strength of a bull. Captain Percy here had but to nod his head, and hey, presto! the helmsman was bowled over, and the minister had the helm. The ship struck: the pirates went to hell, and you, gentlemen, were preserved to order all things well in Virginia. May she long be grateful! The man who dared that death rather than attack the ship he guessed to be the Company's is my mortal foe, whom I will yet sweep from my path, but he is not a pirate. Ay, take it down, an it please you, Master Secretary! I retreat from a most choice position, to be sure, but what care I? I see a vantage ground more to my liking. I have lost a throw, perhaps, but I will recoup ten such losses with one such kiss. By your leave, lady."

He went up to her where she stood, with hanging arms, her head a little bent, white and cold and yielding as a lady done in snow; gazed at her a moment, with his passion written in his fierce eyes and haggard, handsome face; then crushed her to him.

If I could have struck him dead, I would have done so. When her word had been kept, she released herself with a quiet and resolute dignity. As for him, he sank back into the great chair beside the Governor's, leaned an elbow on the table, and hid his eyes with one shaking hand.

The Governor rose to his feet, and motioned away the two seamen who held me fast. "We'll have no hanging this morning, gentlemen," he announced. "Captain Percy, I beg to apologize to you for words that were never meant for a brave and gallant gentleman, but for a pirate who I find does not exist. I pray you to forget them, quite."

I returned his bow, but my eyes traveled past him.

"I will allow you no words with my Lord Carnal," he said. "With your wife,— that is different." He moved aside with a smile.

She was standing, pale, with downcast eyes, where my lord had left her. "Jocelyn," I said. She turned toward me, crimsoned deeply, uttered a low cry, half laughter, half a sob, then covered her face with her hands. I took them away and spoke her name again, and this time she hid her face upon my breast.

A moment thus; then—for all eyes were upon her—I lifted her head, kissed her, and gave her to Lady Wyatt, whom I found at my side. "I commend my wife to your ladyship's care," I said. "As you are woman, deal sisterly by her!"

"You may trust me, sir," she made answer, the tears upon her cheeks. "I did not know,—I did not understand....Dear heart, come away,—come away with Margaret Wyatt."

Clayborne opened the door of the cabin, and stood aside with a low bow. The men who had sat to judge me rose; only the King's favorite kept his seat. With Lady Wyatt's arm about her, the King's ward passed between the lines of standing gentlemen to the door, there hesitated, turned, and, facing them with I know not what of pride and shame, wistfulness of entreaty and noble challenge to belief in the face and form that were of all women's most beautiful, curtsied to them until her knee touched the floor. She was gone, and the sunlight with her.

When I turned upon that shameless lord where he sat in his evil beauty, with his honor dead before him, men came hastily in between. I put them aside with a laugh. I had but wanted to look at him. I had no sword,—already he lay beneath my challenge,—and words are weak things.

At length he rose, as arrogant as ever in his port, as evilly superb in his towering pride, and as amazingly indifferent to the thoughts of men who lied not. "This case hath wearied me," he said. "I will retire for a while to rest, and in dreams to live over a past sweetness. Give you good-day, gentles! Sir Francis Wyatt, you will remember that this gentleman did resist arrest, and that he lieth under the King's displeasure!" So saying he clapped his hat upon his head and walked out of the cabin. The Company's officers drew a long breath, as if a fresher air had come in with his departure.

"I have no choice, Captain Percy, but to keep you still under restraint, both here and when we shall reach Jamestown," said the Governor. "All that the Company, through me, can do, consistent with its duty to his Majesty, to lighten your confinement shall be done"—

"Then send him not again into the hold, Sir Francis!" exclaimed the Treasurer, with a wry face.

The Governor laughed. "Lighter and sweeter quarters shall be found. Your wife's a brave lady, Captain Percy"—

"And a passing fair one," said Claybourne under his breath.

"I left a friend below in the hold, your Honor," I said. "He came with me from Jamestown because he was my friend. The King hath never heard of him. And he's no more a pirate than I or you, your Honor. He is a minister,— a sober, meek, and godly man"—

From behind the Secretary rose the singsong of my acquaintance of the hold, Dr. John Pott. "He is Jeremy, your Honor, Jeremy who made the town merry at Blackfriars. Your Honor remembers him? He had a sickness, and forsook the life and went into the country. He was known to the Dean of St. Paul's. All the town laughed when it heard that he had taken orders."

"Jeremy!" cried out the Treasurer. "Nick Bottom! Christopher Sly! Sir Toby Belch! Sir Francis, give me Jeremy to keep in my cabin!"

The Governor laughed. "He shall be bestowed with Captain Percy where he'll not lack for company, I warrant! Jeremy! Ben Jonson loved him; they drank together at the Mermaid."

A little later the Treasurer turned to leave my new quarters, to which he had walked beside me, glanced at the men who waited for him without,—Jeremy had not yet been brought from the hold,—and returned to my side to say, in a low voice, but with emphasis: "Captain Percy has been a long time without news from home,—from England. What would he most desire to hear?"

"Of the welfare of his Grace of Buckingham," I replied.

He smiled. "His Grace is as well as heart could desire, and as powerful. The Queen's dog now tuggeth the sow by the ears this way or that, as it pleaseth him. Since we are not to hang you as a pirate, Captain Percy, I incline to think your affairs in better posture than when you left Virginia."

"I think so too, sir," I said, and gave him thanks for his courtesy, and wished him good-day, being anxious to sit still and thank God, with my face in my hands and summer in my heart.

CHAPTER XXVIII
IN WHICH THE SPRINGTIME IS AT HAND

TIRED of dicing against myself, and of the books that Rolfe had sent me, I betook myself to the gaol window, and, leaning against the bars, looked out in search of entertainment. The nearest if not the merriest thing the prospect had to offer was the pillory. It was built so tall that it was but little lower than the low upper story of the gaol, and it faced my window at so short a distance that I could hear the long, whistling breath of the wretch who happened to occupy it. It was not a pleasant sound; neither was a livid face, new branded on the cheek with a great R, and with a trickle of dark blood from the mutilated ears staining the board in which the head was immovably fixed, a pleasant sight. A little to one side was the whipping post: a woman had been whipped that morning, and her cries had tainted the air even more effectually than had the decayed matter with which certain small devils had pelted the runaway in the pillory. I looked away from the poor rogue below me into the clear, hard brightness of the March day, and was most heartily weary of the bars between me and it. The wind blew keenly; the sky was blue as blue could be, and the river a great ribbon of azure sewn with diamonds. All colors were vivid and all distances near. There was no haze over the forest; brown and bare it struck the cloudless blue. The marsh was emerald, the green of the pines deep and rich, the budding maples redder than coral. The church, with the low green graves around it, appeared not a stone's throw away, and the voices of the children up and down the street sounded clearly, as though they played in the brown square below me. When the drum beat for the nooning the roll was close in my ears. The world looked so bright and keen that it seemed new made, and the brilliant sunshine and the cold wind stirred the blood like wine.

Now and then men and women passed through the square below. Well-nigh all glanced up at the window, and their eyes were friendly. It was known now that Buckingham was paramount at home, and my Lord Carnal's following in Virginia was much decayed. Young Hamor strode by, bravely dressed and whistling cheerily, and doffed a hat with a most noble broken feather. "We're going to bait a bear below the fort!" he called. "Sorry you'll miss the sport! There will be all the world—and my Lord Carnal." He whistled himself away, and presently there came along Master Edward Sharpless. He stopped and stared at the rogue in the pillory,—with no prescience, I suppose, of a day when he was to stand there himself; then looked up at me with as much malevolence as his small soul could write upon his mean features, and passed on. He had a jaded look; moreover, his clothes were swamp-stained and his cloak had been torn by briers. "What did you go to the forest for?" I muttered.

The key grated in the door behind me, and it opened to admit the gaoler and Diccon with my dinner,—which I was not sorry to see. "Sir George sent the venison, sir," said the gaoler, grinning, "and Master Piersey the wild fowl, and Madam West the pasty and the marchpane, and Master Pory the sack. Be there anything you lack, sir?"

"Nothing that you can supply," I answered curtly.

The fellow grinned again, straightened the things upon the table, and started for the door. "You can stay until I come for the platters," he said to Diccon, and went out, locking the door after him with ostentation.

I applied myself to the dinner, and Diccon went to the window, and stood there looking out at the blue sky and at the man in the pillory. He had the freedom of the gaol. I was somewhat more straitly confined, though my friends had easy access to me. As for Jeremy Sparrow, he had spent twenty-four hours in gaol, at the end of which time Madam West had a fit of the spleen, declared she was dying, and insisted upon Master Sparrow's being sent for to administer consolation; Master Bucke, unfortunately, having gone up to Henricus on business connected with the college. From the bedside of that despotic lady Sparrow was called to bury a man on the other side of the river, and from the grave to marry a couple at Mulberry Island. And the next day being Sunday, and no minister at hand, he preached again in Master Bucke's pulpit,—and preached a sermon so powerful and moving that its like had never been heard in Virginia. They marched him not back from the pulpit to gaol. There were but five ministers in Virginia, and there were a many more sick to visit and dead to bury. Master Bucke, still feeble in body, tarried up river discussing with Thorpe the latter's darling project of converting every imp of an Indian this side the South Sea, and Jeremy slipped into his old place. There had been some talk of a public censure, but it died away.

The pasty and sack disposed of, I turned in my seat and spoke to Diccon: "I looked for Master Rolfe to-day. Have you heard aught of him?"

"No," he answered. As he spoke, the door was opened and the gaoler put in his head. "A messenger from Master Rolfe, captain." He drew back, and the Indian Nantauquas entered the room.

Rolfe I had seen twice since the arrival of the George at Jamestown, but the Indian had not been with him. The young chief now came forward and touched the hand I held out to him. "My brother will be here before the sun touches the tallest pine," he announced in his grave, calm voice. "He asks Captain Percy to deny himself to any other that may come. He wishes to see him alone."

"I shall hardly be troubled with company," I said. "There's a bear-baiting toward."

Nantauquas smiled. "My brother asked me to find a bear for to-day. I bought one from the Paspaheghs for a piece of copper, and took him to the ring below the fort."

"Where all the town will presently be gone," I said. "I wonder what Rolfe did that for!"

Filling a cup with sack, I pushed it to the Indian across the table. "You are little in the woods nowadays, Nantauquas."

His fine dark face clouded ever so slightly. "Opechancanough has dreamt that I am Indian no longer. Singing birds have lied to him, telling him that I love the white man, and hate my own color. He calls me no more his brave, his brother Powhatan's dear son. I do not sit by his council fire now, nor do I lead his war bands. When I went last to his lodge and stood before him, his eyes burned me like the coals the Monacans once closed my hands upon. He would not speak to me."

"It would not fret me if he never spoke again," I said. "You have been to the forest to-day?"

"Yes," he replied, glancing at the smear of leaf mould upon his beaded moccasins. "Captain Percy's eyes are quick; he should have been an Indian. I went to the Paspaheghs to take them the piece of copper. I could tell Captain Percy a curious thing"—

"Well?" I demanded, as he paused.

"I went to the lodge of the werowance with the copper, and found him not there. The old men declared that he had gone to the weirs for fish,—he and ten of his braves. The old men lied. I had passed the weirs of the Paspaheghs, and no man was there. I sat and smoked before the lodge, and the maidens brought me chinquapin cakes and pohickory; for Nantauquas is a prince and a welcome guest to all save Opechancanough. The old men smoked, with their eyes upon the ground, each seeing only the days when he was even as Nantauquas. They never knew when a wife of the werowance, turned child by pride, unfolded a doeskin and showed Nantauquas a silver cup carved all over and set with colored stones."

"Humph!"

"The cup was a heavy price to pay," continued the Indian. "I do not know what great thing it bought."

"Humph!" I said again. "Did you happen to meet Master Edward Sharpless in the forest?"

He shook his head. "The forest is wide, and there are many trails through it. Nantauquas looked for that of the werowance of the Paspaheghs, but found it not. He had no time to waste upon a white man."

He gathered his otterskin mantle about him and prepared to depart. I rose and gave him my hand, for I thoroughly liked him, and in the past he had made me his debtor. "Tell Rolfe he will find me alone," I said, "and take my thanks for your pains, Nantauquas. If ever we hunt together again, may I have the chance to serve you! I bear the scars of the wolf's teeth yet; you came in the nick of time, that day."

The Indian smiled. "It was a fierce old wolf. I wish Captain Percy free with all my heart, and then we will hunt more wolves, he and I."

When he was gone, and the gaoler and Diccon with him, I returned to the window. The runaway in the pillory was released, and went away homewards, staggering beside his master's stirrup. Passers-by grew more and more infrequent, and up the street came faint sounds of laughter and hurrahing,— the bear must be making good sport. I could see the half-moon, and the guns, and the flag that streamed in the wind, and on the river a sail or two, white in the sunlight as the gulls that swooped past. Beyond rose the bare masts of the George. The Santa Teresa rode no more forever in the James. The King's ship was gone home to the King without the freight he looked for. Three days, and the George would spread her white wings and go down the wide river, and I with her, and the King's ward, and the King's sometime favorite. I looked down the wind-ruffled stream, and saw the great bay into which it emptied, and beyond the bay the heaving ocean, dark and light, league on league, league on league; then green England, and London, and the Tower. The vision disturbed me less than once it would have done. Men that I knew and trusted were to be passengers on that ship, as well as one I knew and did not trust. And if, at the journey's end, I saw the Tower, I saw also his Grace of Buckingham. Where I hated he hated, and was now powerful enough to strike.

The wind blew from the west, from the unknown. I turned my head, and it beat against my forehead, cold and fragrant with the essence of the forest,— pine and cedar, dead leaves and black mould, fen and hollow and hill,—all the world of woods over which it had passed. The ghost of things long dead, which face or voice could never conjure up, will sometimes start across our path at the beckoning of an odor. A day in the Starving Time came back to me: how I had dragged myself from our broken palisade and crazy huts, and the groans of the famished and the plague-stricken, and the presence of the unburied dead, across the neck and into the woods, and had lain down there to die, being taken with a sick fear and horror of the place of cannibals behind me; and how weak I was!—too weak to care any more. I had been a strong man, and it had come to that, and I was content to let it be. The smell of the woods that day, the chill brown earth beneath me, the blowing wind, the long stretch of the river gleaming between the pines,... and fair in sight the white sails of the Patience and the Deliverance.

I had been too nigh gone then to greatly care that I was saved; now I cared, and thanked God for my life. Come what might in the future, the past was mine. Though I should never see my wife again, I had that hour in the state cabin of the George. I loved, and was loved again.

There was a noise outside the door, and Rolfe's voice speaking to the gaoler. Impatient for his entrance I started toward the door, but when it opened he made no move to cross the threshold. "I am not coming in," he said, with a face that he strove to keep grave. "I only came to bring some one else." With that he stepped back, and a second figure, coming forward out of the dimness behind him, crossed the threshold. It was a woman, cloaked and hooded. The door was drawn to behind her, and we were alone together.

Beside the cloak and hood she wore a riding mask. "Do you know who it is?" she asked, when she had stood, so shrouded, for a long minute, during which I had found no words with which to welcome her.

"Yea," I answered: "the princess in the fairy tale."

She freed her dark hair from its covering, and unclasping her cloak let it drop to the floor. "Shall I unmask?" she asked, with a sigh. "Faith! I should keep the bit of silk between your eyes, sir, and my blushes. Am I ever to be the forward one? Do you not think me too bold a lady?" As she spoke, her white hands were busy about the fastening of her mask. "The knot is too hard," she murmured, with a little tremulous laugh and a catch of her breath.

I untied the ribbons.

"May I not sit down?" she said plaintively, but with soft merriment in her eyes. "I am not quite strong yet. My heart—you do not know what pain I have in my heart sometimes. It makes me weep of nights and when none are by, indeed it does!"

There was a settle beneath the window. I led her to it, and she sat down.

"You must know that I am walking in the Governor's garden, that hath only a lane between it and the gaol." Her eyes were downcast, her cheeks pure rose.

"When did you first love me?" I demanded.

"Lady Wyatt must have guessed why Master Rolfe alone went not to the bear-baiting, but joined us in the garden. She said the air was keen, and fetched me her mask, and then herself went indoors to embroider Samson in the arms of Delilah.'

"Was it here at Jamestown, or was it when we were first wrecked, or on the island with the pink hill when you wrote my name in the sand, or"—

"The George will sail in three days, and we are to be taken back to England after all. It does not scare me now."

"In all my life I have kissed you only once," I said.

The rose deepened, and in her eyes there was laughter, with tears behind. "You are a gentleman of determination," she said. "If you are bent upon having your way, I do not know that I—that I—can help myself. I do not even know that I want to help myself."

Outside the wind blew and the sun shone, and the laughter from below the fort was too far away and elfin to jar upon us. The world forgot us, and we were well content. There seemed not much to say: I suppose we were too happy for words. I knelt beside her, and she laid her hands in mine, and now and then we spoke. In her short and lonely life, and in my longer stern and crowded one, there had been little tenderness, little happiness. In her past, to those about her, she had seemed bright and gay; I had been a comrade whom men liked because I could jest as well as fight. Now we were happy, but we were not gay. Each felt for the other a great compassion; each knew that though we smiled to-day, the groan and the tear might be to-morrow's due; the sunshine around us was pure gold, but that the clouds were mounting we knew full well.

"I must soon be gone," she said at last. "It is a stolen meeting. I do not know when we shall meet again."

She rose from the settle, and I rose with her, and we stood together beside the barred window. There was no danger of her being seen; street and square were left to the wind and the sunshine. My arm was around her, and she leaned her head against my breast. "Perhaps we shall never meet again," she said.

"The winter is over," I answered. "Soon the trees will be green and the flowers in bloom. I will not believe that our spring can have no summer."

She took from her bosom a little flower that had been pinned there. It lay, a purple star, in the hollow of her hand. "It grew in the sun. It is the first flower of spring." She put it to her lips, then laid it upon the window ledge beside my hand. "I have brought you evil gifts,—foes and strife and peril. Will you take this little purple flower—and all my heart beside?"

I bent and kissed first the tiny blossom, and then the lips that had proffered it. "I am very rich," I said.

The sun was now low, and the pines in the square and the upright of the pillory cast long shadows. The wind had fallen and the sounds had died away. It seemed very still. Nothing moved but the creeping shadows until a flight of small white-breasted birds went past the window. "The snow is gone," I said. "The snowbirds are flying north."

"The woods will soon be green," she murmured wistfully. "Ah, if we could ride through them once more, back to Weyanoke"—

"To home," I said.

"Home," she echoed softly.

There was a low knocking at the door behind us. "It is Master Rolfe's signal," she said. "I must not stay. Tell me that you love me, and let me go."

I drew her closer to me and pressed my lips upon her bowed head. "Do you not know that I love you?" I asked.

"Yea," she answered. "I have been taught it. Tell me that you believe that God will be good to us. Tell me that we shall be happy yet; for oh, I have a boding heart this day!"

Her voice broke, and she lay trembling in my arms, her face hidden. "If the summer never comes for us"—she whispered. "Good-by, my lover and my husband. If I have brought you ruin and death, I have brought you, too, a love that is very great. Forgive me and kiss me, and let me go."

"Thou art my dearly loved and honored wife," I said. "My heart forebodes summer, and joy, and peace, and home."

We kissed each other solemnly, as those who part for a journey and a warfare. I spoke no word to Rolfe when the door was opened and she had passed out with her cloak drawn about her face, but we clasped hands, and each knew the other for his friend indeed. They were gone, the gaoler closing and locking the door behind them. As for me, I went back to the settle beneath the window, and, falling on my knees beside it, buried my face in my arms.

CHAPTER XXIX
IN WHICH I KEEP TRYST

THE sun dropped below the forest, blood red, dyeing the river its own color. There were no clouds in the sky,—only a great suffusion of crimson climbing to the zenith; against it the woods were as black as war paint. The color faded and the night set in, a night of no wind and of numberless stars. On the hearth burned a fire. I left the window and sat beside it, and in the hollows between the red embers made pictures, as I used to make them when I was a boy.

I sat there long. It grew late, and all sounds in the town were hushed; only now and then the "All's well!" of the watch came faintly to my ears. Diccon lodged with me; he lay in his clothes upon a pallet in the far corner of the room, but whether he slept or not I did not ask. He and I had never wasted words; since chance had thrown us together again we spoke only when occasion required.

The fire was nigh out, and it must have been ten of the clock when, with somewhat more of caution and less of noise than usual, the key grated in the lock; the door opened, and the gaoler entered, closing it noiselessly behind him. There was no reason why he should intrude himself upon me after nightfall, and I regarded him with a frown and an impatience that presently turned to curiosity.

He began to move about the room, making pretense of seeing that there was water in the pitcher beside my pallet, that the straw beneath the coverlet was fresh, that the bars of the window were firm, and ended by approaching the fire and heaping pine upon it. It flamed up brilliantly, and in the strong red light he half opened a clenched hand and showed me two gold pieces, and beneath them a folded paper. I looked at his furtive eyes and brutal, doltish face, but he kept them blank as a wall. The hand closed again over the treasure within it, and he turned away as if to leave the room. I drew a noble—one of a small store of gold pieces conveyed to me by Rolfe—from my pocket, and stooping made it spin upon the hearth in the red firelight. The gaoler looked at it askance, but continued his progress toward the door. I drew out its fellow, set it too to spinning, then leaned back against the table. "They hunt in couples," I said. "There will be no third one."

He had his foot upon them before they had done spinning. The next moment they had kissed the two pieces already in his possession, and he had transferred all four to his pocket. I held out my hand for the paper, and he gave it to me grudgingly, with a spiteful slowness of movement. He would have stayed beside me as I read it, but I sternly bade him keep his distance;

then kneeling before the fire to get the light, I opened the paper. It was written upon in a delicate, woman's hand, and it ran thus:—

An you hold me dear, come to me at once. Come without tarrying to the deserted hut on the neck of land, nearest to the forest. As you love me, as you are my knight, keep this tryst.

In distress and peril, THY WIFE.

Folded with it was a line in the commander's hand and with his signature: "The bearer may pass without the palisade at his pleasure."

I read the first paper again, refolded it, and rose to my feet. "Who brought this, sirrah?" I demanded.

His answer was glib enough: "One of the governor's servants. He said as how there was no harm in the letter, and the gold was good."

"When was this?"

"Just now. No, I did n't know the man."

I saw no way to discover whether or not he lied. Drawing out another gold piece, I laid it upon the table. He eyed it greedily, edging nearer and nearer.

"For leaving this door unlocked," I said.

His eyes narrowed and he moistened his lips, shifting from one foot to the other.

I put down a second piece. "For opening the outer door," I said.

He wet his lips again, made an inarticulate sound in his throat, and finally broke out with, "The commander will nail my ears to the pillory."

"You can lock the doors after me, and know as little as you choose in the morning. No gain without some risk."

"That's so," he agreed, and made a clutch at the gold.

I swept it out of his reach. "First earn it," I said dryly. "Look at the foot of the pillory an hour from now and you'll find it. I'll not pay you this side of the doors."

He bit his lips and studied the floor. "You're a gentleman," he growled at last. "I suppose I can trust ye."

"I suppose you can."

Taking up his lantern he turned toward the door. "It 's growing late," he said, with a most uncouth attempt to feign a guileless drowsiness. "I'll to bed, captain, when I've locked up. Good-night to ye!"

He was gone, and the door was left unlocked. I could walk out of that gaol as I could have walked out of my house at Weyanoke. I was free, but should I take my freedom? Going back to the light of the fire I unfolded the paper and stared at it, turning its contents this way and that in my mind. The hand—but once had I seen her writing, and then it had been wrought with a shell upon firm sand. I could not judge if this were the same. Had the paper indeed come from her? Had it not? If in truth it was a message from my wife, what had befallen in a few hours since our parting? If it was a forger's lie, what trap was set, what toils were laid? I walked up and down, and tried to think it out. The strangeness of it all, the choice of a lonely and distant hut for trysting place, that pass coming from a sworn officer of the Company, certain things I had heard that day... A trap... and to walk into it with my eyes open.... *An you hold me dear. As you are my knight, keep this tryst. In distress and peril....* Come what might, there was a risk I could not run.

I had no weapons to assume, no preparations to make. Gathering up the gaoler's gold I started toward the door, opened it, and going out would have closed it softly behind me but that a booted leg thrust across the jamb prevented me. "I am going with you," said Diccon in a guarded voice. "If you try to prevent me, I will rouse the house." His head was thrown back in the old way; the old daredevil look was upon his face. "I don't know why you are going," he declared, "but there'll be danger, anyhow."

"To the best of my belief I am walking into a trap," I said.

"Then it will shut on two instead of one," he answered doggedly.

By this he was through the door, and there was no shadow of turning on his dark, determined face. I knew my man, and wasted no more words. Long ago it had grown to seem the thing most in nature that the hour of danger should find us side by side.

When the door of the firelit room was shut, the gaol was in darkness that might be felt. It was very still: the few other inmates were fast asleep; the gaoler was somewhere out of sight, dreaming with open eyes. We groped our way through the passage to the stairs, noiselessly descended them, and found the outer door unchained, unbarred, and slightly ajar.

When I had laid the gold beneath the pillory, we struck swiftly across the square, being in fear lest the watch should come upon us, and took the first lane that led toward the palisade. Beneath the burning stars the town lay stark in sleep. So bright in the wintry air were those far-away lights that the darkness below them was not great. We could see the low houses, the shadowy pines, the naked oaks, the sandy lane glimmering away to the river, star-strewn to match the heavens. The air was cold, but exceedingly clear and still. Now and then a dog barked, or wolves howled in the forest across the river. We kept in the shadow of the houses and the trees, and went with the swiftness, silence, and caution of Indians.

The last house we must pass before reaching the palisade was one that Rolfe owned, and in which he lodged when business brought him to Jamestown. It and some low outbuildings beyond it were as dark as the cedars in which they were set, and as silent as the grave. Rolfe and his Indian brother were sleeping there now, while I stood without. Or did they sleep? Were they there at all? Might it not have been Rolfe who had bribed the gaoler and procured the pass from West? Might I not find him at that strange trysting place? Might not all be well, after all? I was sorely tempted to rouse that silent house and demand if its master were within. I did it not. Servants were there, and noise would be made, and time that might be more precious than life-blood was flying fast. I went on, and Diccon with me.

There was a cabin built almost against the palisade, and here one man was supposed to watch, whilst another slept. To-night we found both asleep. I shook the younger to his feet, and heartily cursed him for his negligence. He listened stupidly, and read as stupidly, by the light of his lantern, the pass which I thrust beneath his nose. Staggering to his feet, and drunk with his unlawful slumber, he fumbled at the fastenings of the gate for full three minutes before the ponderous wood finally swung open and showed the road beyond. "It's all right," he muttered thickly. "The commander's pass. Good-night, the three of ye!"

"Are you drunk or drugged?" I demanded. "There are only two. It's not sleep that is the matter with you. What is it?"

He made no answer, but stood holding the gate open and blinking at us with dull, unseeing eyes. Something ailed him besides sleep; he may have been drugged, for aught I know. When we had gone some yards from the gate, we heard him say again, in precisely the same tone, "Good-night, the three of ye!" Then the gate creaked to, and we heard the bars drawn across it.

Without the palisade was a space of waste land, marsh and thicket, tapering to the narrow strip of sand and scrub joining the peninsula to the forest, and here and there upon this waste ground rose a mean house, dwelt in by the poorer sort. All were dark. We left them behind, and found ourselves upon the neck, with the desolate murmur of the river on either hand, and before us the deep blackness of the forest. Suddenly Diccon stopped in his tracks and turned his head. "I did hear something then," he muttered. "Look, sir!"

The stars faintly lit the road that had been trodden hard and bare by the feet of all who came and went. Down this road something was coming toward us, something low and dark, that moved not fast, and not slow, but with a measured and relentless pace. "A panther!" said Diccon.

We watched the creature with more of curiosity than alarm. Unless brought to bay, or hungry, or wantonly irritated, these great cats were cowardly enough. It would hardly attack the two of us. Nearer and nearer it came, showing no signs of anger and none of fear, and paying no attention to the withered branch with which Diccon tried to scare it off. When it was so close that we could see the white of its breast it stopped, looking at us with large unfaltering eyes, and slightly moving its tail to and fro.

"A tame panther!" ejaculated Diccon. "It must be the one Nantauquas tamed, sir. He would have kept it somewhere near Master Rolfe's house."

"And it heard us, and followed us through the gate," I said. "It was the third the warder talked of."

We walked on, and the beast, addressing itself to motion, followed at our heels. Now and then we looked back at it, but we feared it not.

As for me, I had begun to think that a panther might be the least formidable thing I should meet that night. By this I had scarcely any hope—or fear— that I should find her at our journey's end. The lonesome path that led only to the night-time forest, the deep and dark river with its mournful voice, the hard, bright, pitiless stars, the cold, the loneliness, the distance,—how should she be there? And if not she, who then?

The hut to which I had been directed stood in an angle made by the neck and the main bank of the river. On one side of it was the water, on the other a deep wood. The place had an evil name, and no man had lived there since the planter who had built it hanged himself upon its threshold. The hut was ruinous: in the summer tall weeds grew up around it, and venomous snakes harbored beneath its rotted and broken floor; in the winter the snow whitened it, and the wild fowl flew screaming in and out of the open door and the windows that needed no barring. To-night the door was shut and the windows in some way obscured. But the interstices between the logs showed red; the hut was lighted within, and some one was keeping tryst.

The stillness was deadly. It was not silence, for the river murmured in the stiff reeds, and far off in the midnight forest some beast of the night uttered its cry, but a hush, a holding of the breath, an expectant horror. The door, warped and shrunken, was drawn to, but was not fastened, as I could tell by the unbroken line of red light down one side from top to bottom. Making no sound, I laid my hand upon it, pushed it open a little way, and looked within the hut.

I had thought to find it empty or to find it crowded. It was neither. A torch lit it, and on the hearth burned a fire. Drawn in front of the blaze was an old rude chair, and in it sat a slight figure draped from head to foot in a black cloak. The head was bowed and hidden, the whole attitude one of listlessness and dejection. As I looked, there came a long tremulous sigh, and the head drooped lower and lower, as if in a growing hopelessness.

The revulsion of feeling was so great that for the moment I was dazed as by a sudden blow. There had been time during the walk from the gaol for enough of wild and whirling thoughts as to what should greet me in that hut; and now the slight figure by the fire, the exquisite melancholy of its posture, its bent head, the weeping I could divine,—I had but one thought, to comfort her as quickly as I might. Diccon's hand was upon my arm, but I shook it off, and pushing the door open crossed the uneven and noisy floor to the fire, and bent over the lonely figure beside it. "Jocelyn," I said, "I have kept tryst."

As I spoke, I laid my hand upon the bowed and covered head. It was raised, the cloak was drawn aside, and there looked me in the eyes the Italian.

As if it had been the Gorgon's gaze, I was turned to stone. The filmy eyes, the smile that would have been mocking had it not been so very faint, the pallor, the malignance,—I stared and stared, and my heart grew cold and sick.

It was but for a minute; then a warning cry from Diccon roused me. I sprang backward until the width of the hearth was between me and the Italian, then wheeled and found myself face to face with the King's late favorite. Behind him was an open door, and beyond it a small inner room, dimly lighted. He stood and looked at me with an insolence and a triumph most intolerable. His drawn sword was in his hand, the jeweled hilt blazing in the firelight, and on his dark, superb face a taunting smile. I met it with one as bold, at least, but I said no word, good or bad. In the cabin of the George I had sworn to myself that thenceforward my sword should speak for me to this gentleman.

"You came," he said. "I thought you would."

I glanced around the hut, seeking for a weapon. Seeing nothing more promising than the thick, half-consumed torch, I sprang to it and wrested it from the socket. Diccon caught up a piece of rusted iron from the hearth, and together we faced my lord's drawn sword and a small, sharp, and strangely shaped dagger that the Italian drew from a velvet sheath.

My lord laughed, reading my thoughts. "You are mistaken," he declared coolly. "I am content that Captain Percy knows I do not fear to fight him. This time I play to win." Turning toward the outer door, he raised his hand with a gesture of command.

In an instant the room was filled. The red-brown figures, naked save for the loincloth and the headdress, the impassive faces dashed with black, the ruthless eyes—I knew now why Master Edward Sharpless had gone to the forest, and what service had been bought with that silver cup. The

Paspaheghs and I were old enemies; doubtless they would find their task a pleasant one.

"My own knaves, unfortunately, were out of the way; sent home on the Santa Teresa," said my lord, still smiling. "I am not yet so poor that I cannot hire others. True, Nicolo might have done the work just now, when you bent over him so lovingly and spoke so softly; but the river might give up your body to tell strange tales. I have heard that the Indians are more ingenious, and leave no such witness anywhere."

Before the words were out of his mouth I had sprung upon him, and had caught him by the sword wrist and the throat. He strove to free his hand, to withdraw himself from my grasp. Locked together, we struggled backward and forward in what seemed a blaze of lights and a roaring as of mighty waters. Red hands caught at me, sharp knives panted to drink my blood; but so fast we turned and writhed, now he uppermost, now I, that for very fear of striking the wrong man hands and knives could not be bold. I heard Diccon fighting, and knew that there would be howling tomorrow among the squaws of the Paspaheghs. With all his might my lord strove to bend the sword against me, and at last did cut me across the arm, causing the blood to flow freely. It made a pool upon the floor, and once my foot slipped in it, and I stumbled and almost fell.

Two of the Paspaheghs were silent for evermore. Diccon had the knife of the first to fall, and it ran red. The Italian, quick and sinuous as a serpent, kept beside my lord and me, striving to bring his dagger to his master's aid. We two panted hard; before our eyes blood, within our ears the sea. The noise of the other combatants suddenly fell. The hush could only mean that Diccon was dead or taken. I could not look behind to see. With an access of fury I drove my antagonist toward a corner of the hut,—the corner, so it chanced, in which the panther had taken up its quarters. With his heel he struck the beast out of his way, then made a last desperate effort to throw me. I let him think he was about to succeed, gathered my forces and brought him crashing to the ground. The sword was in my hand and shortened, the point was at his throat, when my arm was jerked backwards. A moment, and half a dozen hands had dragged me from the man beneath me, and a supple savage had passed a thong of deerskin around my arms and pinioned them to my sides. The game was up; there remained only to pay the forfeit without a grimace.

Diccon was not dead; pinioned, like myself, and breathing hard, he leaned sullenly against the wall, they that he had slain at his feet. My lord rose, and stood over against me. His rich doublet was torn and dragged away at the neck, and my blood stained his hand and arm. A smile was upon the face that had made him master of a kingdom's master.

"The game was long," he said, "but I have won at last. A long good-night to you, Captain Percy, and a dreamless sleep!"

There was a swift backward movement of the Indians, and a loud "The panther, sir! Have a care!" from Diccon. I turned. The panther, maddened by the noise and light, the shifting figures, the blocked doors, the sight and smell of blood, the blow that had been dealt it, was crouching for a spring. The red-brown hair was bristling, the eyes were terrible. I was before it, but those glaring eyes had marked me not. It passed me like a bar from a catapult, and the man whose heel it had felt was full in its path. One of its forefeet sank in the velvet of the doublet; the claws of the other entered the flesh below the temple, and tore downwards and across. With a cry as awful as the panther's scream the Italian threw himself upon the beast and buried his poniard in its neck. The panther and the man it had attacked went down together.

When the Indians had unlocked that dread embrace and had thrust aside the dead brute, there emerged from the dimness of the inner room Master Edward Sharpless, gray with fear, trembling in every limb, to take the reins that had fallen from my lord's hands. The King's minion lay in his blood, a ghastly spectacle; unconscious now, but with life before him,—life through which to pass a nightmare vision. The face out of which had looked that sullen, proud, and wicked spirit had been one of great beauty; it had brought him exceeding wealth and power beyond measure; the King had loved to look upon it; and it had come to this. He lived, and I was to die: better my death than his life. In every heart there are dark depths, whence at times ugly things creep into the daylight; but at least I could drive back that unmanly triumph, and bid it never come again. I would have killed him, but I would not have had him thus.

The Italian was upon his knees beside his master: even such a creature could love. From his skeleton throat came a low, prolonged, croaking sound, and his bony hands strove to wipe away the blood. The Paspaheghs drew around us closer and closer, and the werowance clutched me by the shoulder. I shook him off. "Give the word, Sharpless," I said, "or nod, if thou art too frightened to speak. Murder is too stern a stuff for such a base kitchen knave as thou to deal in."

White and shaking, he would not meet my eyes, but beckoned the werowance to him, and began to whisper vehemently; pointing now to the man upon the floor, now to the town, now to the forest. The Indian listened, nodded, and glided back to his fellows.

"The white men upon the Powhatan are many," he said in his own tongue, "but they build not their wigwams upon the banks of the Pamunkey. 1 The singing birds of the Pamunkey tell no tales. The pine splinters will burn as brightly there, and the white men will smell them not. We will build a fire at Uttamussac, between the red hills, before the temple and the graves of the kings." There was a murmur of assent from his braves.

Uttamussac! They would probably make a two days' journey of it. We had that long, then, to live.

Captors and captives, we presently left the hut. On the threshold I looked back, past the poltroon whom I had flung into the river one midsummer day, to that prone and bleeding figure. As I looked, it groaned and moved. The Indians behind me forced me on; a moment, and we were out beneath the stars. They shone so very brightly; there was one—large, steadfast, golden— just over the dark town behind us, over the Governor's house. Did she sleep or did she wake? Sleeping or waking, I prayed God to keep her safe and give her comfort. The stars now shone through naked branches, black tree trunks hemmed us round, and under our feet was the dreary rustling of dead leaves. The leafless trees gave way to pines and cedars, and the closely woven, scented roof hid the heavens, and made a darkness of the world beneath.

1. The modern York.

CHAPTER XXX
IN WHICH WE START UPON A JOURNEY

WHEN the dawn broke, it found us traveling through a narrow valley, beside a stream of some width. Upon its banks grew trees of extraordinary height and girth; cypress and oak and walnut, they towered into the air, their topmost branches stark and black against the roseate heavens. Below that iron tracery glowed the firebrands of the maples, and here and there a willow leaned a pale green cloud above the stream. Mist closed the distances; we could hear, but not see, the deer where they stood to drink in the shallow places, or couched in the gray and dreamlike recesses of the forest.

Spectral, unreal, and hollow seems the world at dawn. Then, if ever, the heart sickens and the will flags, and life becomes a pageant that hath ceased to entertain. As I moved through the mist and the silence, and felt the tug of the thong that bound me to the wrist of the savage who stalked before me, I cared not how soon they made an end, seeing how stale and unprofitable were all things under the sun.

Diccon, walking behind me, stumbled over a root and fell upon his knees, dragging down with him the Indian to whom he was tied. In a sudden access of fury, aggravated by the jeers with which his fellows greeted his mishap, the savage turned upon his prisoner and would have stuck a knife into him, bound and helpless as he was, had not the werowance interfered. The momentary altercation over, and the knife restored to its owner's belt, the Indians relapsed into their usual menacing silence, and the sullen march was resumed. Presently the stream made a sharp bend across our path, and we forded it as best we might. It ran dark and swift, and the water was of icy coldness. Beyond, the woods had been burnt, the trees rising from the red ground like charred and blackened stakes, with the ghostlike mist between. We left this dismal tract behind, and entered a wood of mighty oaks, standing well apart, and with the earth below carpeted with moss and early wild flowers. The sun rose, the mist vanished, and there set in the March day of keen wind and brilliant sunshine.

Farther on, an Indian bent his bow against a bear shambling across a little sunny glade. The arrow did its errand, and where the creature fell, there we sat down and feasted beside a fire kindled by rubbing two sticks together. According to their wont the Indians ate ravenously, and when the meal was ended began to smoke, each warrior first throwing into the air, as thank-offering to Kiwassa, a pinch of tobacco. They all stared at the fire around which we sat, and the silence was unbroken. One by one, as the pipes were smoked, they laid themselves down upon the brown leaves and went to sleep, only our two guardians and a third Indian over against us remaining wide-eyed and watchful.

There was no hope of escape, and we entertained no thought of it. Diccon sat, biting his nails, staring into the fire, and I stretched myself out, and burying my head in my arms tried to sleep, but could not.

With the midday we were afoot again, and we went steadily on through the bright afternoon. We met with no harsh treatment other than our bonds. Instead, when our captors spoke to us, it was with words of amity and smiling lips. Who accounteth for Indian fashions? It is a way they have, to flatter and caress the wretch for whom have been provided the torments of the damned. If, when at sunset we halted for supper and gathered around the fire, the werowance began to tell of a foray I had led against the Paspaheghs years before, and if he and his warriors, for all the world like generous foes, loudly applauded some daring that had accompanied that raid, none the less did the red stake wait for us; none the less would they strive, as for heaven, to wring from us groans and cries.

The sun sank, and the darkness entered the forest. In the distance we heard the wolves, so the fire was kept up through the night. Diccon and I were tied to trees, and all the savages save one lay down and slept. I worked awhile at my bonds; but an Indian had tied them, and after a time I desisted from the useless labor. We two could have no speech together; the fire was between us, and we saw each other but dimly through the flame and wreathing smoke,—as each might see the other to-morrow. What Diccon's thoughts were I know not; mine were not of the morrow.

There had been no rain for a long time, and the multitude of leaves underfoot were crisp and dry. The wind was loud in them and in the swaying trees. Off in the forest was a bog, and the will-o'-the-wisps danced over it,—pale, cold flames, moving aimlessly here and there like ghosts of those lost in the woods. Toward the middle of the night some heavy animal crashed through a thicket to the left of us, and tore away into the darkness over the loud-rustling leaves; and later on wolves' eyes gleamed from out the ring of darkness beyond the firelight. Far on in the night the wind fell and the moon rose, changing the forest into some dim, exquisite, far-off land, seen only in dreams. The Indians awoke silently and all at once, as at an appointed hour. They spoke for a while among themselves; then we were loosed from the trees, and the walk toward death began anew.

On this march the werowance himself stalked beside me, the moonlight whitening his dark limbs and relentless face. He spoke no word, nor did I deign to question or reason or entreat. Alike in the darkness of the deep woods, and in the silver of the glades, and in the long twilight stretches of sassafras and sighing grass, there was for me but one vision. Slender and still and white, she moved before me, with her wide dark eyes upon my face. Jocelyn! Jocelyn!

At sunrise the mist lifted from a low hill before us, and showed an Indian boy, painted white, poised upon the summit, like a spirit about to take its flight. He prayed to the One over All, and his voice came down to us pure and earnest. At sight of us he bounded down the hillside like a ball, and would have rushed away into the forest had not a Paspahegh starting out of line seized him and set him in our midst, where he stood, cool and undismayed, a warrior in miniature. He was of the Pamunkeys, and his tribe and the Paspaheghs were at peace; therefore, when he saw the totem burnt upon the breast of the werowance, he became loquacious enough, and offered to go before us to his village, upon the banks of a stream, some bowshots away. He went, and the Paspaheghs rested under the trees until the old men of the village came forth to lead them through the brown fields and past the ring of leafless mulberries to the strangers' lodge. Here on the green turf mats were laid for the visitors, and water was brought for their hands. Later on, the women spread a great breakfast of fish and turkey and venison, maize bread, tuckahoe and pohickory. When it was eaten, the Paspaheghs ranged themselves in a semicircle upon the grass, the Pamunkeys faced them, and each warrior and old man drew out his pipe and tobacco pouch. They smoked gravely, in a silence broken only by an occasional slow and stately question or compliment. The blue incense from the pipes mingled with the sunshine falling freely through the bare branches; the stream which ran by the lodge rippled and shone, and the wind rose and fell in the pines upon its farther bank.

Diccon and I had been freed for the time from our bonds, and placed in the centre of this ring, and when the Indians raised their eyes from the ground it was to gaze steadfastly at us. I knew their ways, and how they valued pride, indifference, and a bravado disregard of the worst an enemy could do. They should not find the white man less proud than the savage.

They gave us readily enough the pipes I asked for. Diccon lit one and I the other, and sitting side by side we smoked in a contentment as absolute as the Indians' own. With his eyes upon the werowance, Diccon told an old story of a piece of Paspahegh villainy and of the payment which the English exacted, and I laughed as at the most amusing thing in the world. The story ended, we smoked with serenity for a while; then I drew my dice from my pocket, and, beginning to throw, we were at once as much absorbed in the game as if there were no other stake in the world beside the remnant of gold that I piled between us. The strange people in whose power we found ourselves looked on with grim approval, as at brave men who could laugh in Death's face.

The sun was high in the heavens when we bade the Pamunkeys farewell. The cleared ground, the mulberry trees, and the grass beneath, the few rude lodges with the curling smoke above them, the warriors and women and brown naked children,—all vanished, and the forest closed around us. A high wind was blowing, and the branches far above beat at one another furiously, while the pendent, leafless vines swayed against us, and the dead leaves went past in the whirlwind. A monstrous flight of pigeons crossed the heavens, flying from west to east, and darkening the land beneath like a transient cloud. We came to a plain covered with very tall trees that had one and all been ringed by the Indians. Long dead, and partially stripped of the bark, with their branches, great and small, squandered upon the ground, they stood, gaunt and silver gray, ready for their fall. As we passed, the wind brought two crashing to the earth. In the centre of the plain something—deer or wolf or bear or man—lay dead, for to that point the buzzards were sweeping from every quarter of the blue. Beyond was a pine wood, silent and dim, with a high green roof and a smooth and scented floor. We walked through it for an hour, and it led us to the Pamunkey. A tiny village, counting no more than a dozen warriors, stood among the pines that ran to the water's edge, and tied to the trees that shadowed the slow-moving flood were its canoes. When the people came forth to meet us, the Paspaheghs bought from them, for a string of roanoke, two of these boats; and we made no tarrying, but, embarking at once, rowed up river toward Uttamussac and its three temples.

Diccon and I were placed in the same canoe. We were not bound: what need of bonds, when we had no friend nearer than the Powhatan, and when Uttamussac was so near? After a time the paddles were put into our hands, and we were required to row while our captors rested. There was no use in sulkiness; we laughed as at some huge jest, and bent to the task with a will that sent our canoe well in advance of its mate. Diccon burst into an old song that we had sung in the Low Countries, by camp fires, on the march, before the battle. The forest echoed to the loud and warlike tune, and a multitude of birds rose startled from the trees upon the bank. The Indians frowned, and one in the boat behind called out to strike the singer upon the mouth; but the werowance shook his head. There were none upon that river who might not know that the Paspaheghs journeyed to Uttamussac with prisoners in their midst. Diccon sang on, his head thrown back, the old bold laugh in his eyes. When he came to the chorus I joined my voice to his, and the woodland rang to the song. A psalm had better befitted our lips than those rude and vaunting words, seeing that we should never sing again upon this earth; but at least we sang bravely and gayly, with minds that were reasonably quiet.

The sun dropped low in the heavens, and the trees cast shadows across the water. The Paspaheghs now began to recount the entertainment they meant to offer us in the morning. All those tortures that they were wont to practice with hellish ingenuity they told over, slowly and tauntingly, watching to see a lip whiten or an eyelid quiver. They boasted that they would make women of us at the stake. At all events, they made not women of us beforehand. We laughed as we rowed, and Diccon whistled to the leaping fish, and the fish-hawk, and the otter lying along a fallen tree beneath the bank.

The sunset came, and the river lay beneath the colored clouds like molten gold, with the gaunt forest black upon either hand. From the lifted paddles the water showered in golden drops. The wind died away, and with it all noises, and a dank stillness settled upon the flood and upon the endless forest. We were nearing Uttamussac, and the Indians rowed quietly, with bent heads and fearful glances; for Okee brooded over this place, and he might be angry. It grew colder and stiller, but the light dwelt in the heavens, and was reflected in the bosom of the river. The trees upon the southern bank were all pines; as if they had been carved from black stone they stood rigid against the saffron sky. Presently, back from the shore, there rose before us a few small hills, treeless, but covered with some low, dark growth. The one that stood the highest bore upon its crest three black houses shaped like coffins. Behind them was the deep yellow of the sunset.

An Indian rowing in the second canoe commenced a chant or prayer to Okee. The notes were low and broken, unutterably wild and melancholy. One by one his fellows took up the strain; it swelled higher, louder, and sterner, became a deafening cry, then ceased abruptly, making the stillness that followed like death itself. Both canoes swung round from the middle stream and made for the bank. When the boats had slipped from the stripe of gold into the inky shadow of the pines, the Paspaheghs began to divest themselves of this or that which they conceived Okee might desire to possess. One flung into the stream a handful of copper links, another the chaplet of feathers from his head, a third a bracelet of blue beads. The werowance drew out the arrows from a gaudily painted and beaded quiver, stuck them into his belt, and dropped the quiver into the water.

We landed, dragging the canoes into a covert of overhanging bushes and fastening them there; then struck through the pines toward the rising ground, and presently came to a large village, with many long huts, and a great central lodge where dwelt the emperors when they came to Uttamussac. It was vacant now, Opechancanough being no man knew where.

When the usual stately welcome had been extended to the Paspaheghs, and when they had returned as stately thanks, the werowance began a harangue for which I furnished the matter. When he ceased to speak a great acclamation and tumult arose, and I thought they would scarce wait for the morrow. But it was late, and their werowance and conjurer restrained them.

In the end the men drew off, and the yelling of the children and the passionate cries of the women, importunate for vengeance, were stilled. A guard was placed around the vacant lodge, and we two Englishmen were taken within and bound down to great logs, such as the Indians use to roll against their doors when they go from home.

There was revelry in the village; for hours after the night came, everywhere were bright firelight and the rise and fall of laughter and song. The voices of the women were musical, tender, and plaintive, and yet they waited for the morrow as for a gala day. I thought of a woman who used to sing, softly and sweetly, in the twilight at Weyanoke, in the firelight at the minister's house. At last the noises ceased, the light died away, and the village slept beneath a heaven that seemed somewhat deaf and blind.

CHAPTER XXXI
IN WHICH NANTAUQUAS COMES TO OUR RESCUE

A MAN who hath been a soldier and an adventurer into far and strange countries must needs have faced Death many times and in many guises. I had learned to know that grim countenance, and to have no great fear of it. And beneath the ugliness of the mask that now presented itself there was only Death at last. I was no babe to whimper at a sudden darkness, to cry out against a curtain that a Hand chose to drop between me and the life I had lived. Death frighted me not, but when I thought of one whom I should leave behind me I feared lest I should go mad. Had this thing come to me a year before, I could have slept the night through; now—now—I lay, bound to the log, before the open door of the lodge, and, looking through it, saw the pines waving in the night wind and the gleam of the river beneath the stars, and saw her as plainly as though she had stood there under the trees, in a flood of noon sunshine. Now she was the Jocelyn Percy of Weyanoke, now of the minister's house, now of a storm-tossed boat and a pirate ship, now of the gaol at Jamestown. One of my arms was free; I could take from within my doublet the little purple flower, and drop my face upon the hand that held it. The bloom was quite withered, and scalding tears would not give it life again.

The face that was, now gay, now defiant, now pale and suffering, became steadfastly the face that had leaned upon my breast in the Jamestown gaol, and looked at me with a mournful brightness of love and sorrow. Spring was in the land, and the summer would come, but not to us. I stretched forth my hand to the wife who was not there, and my heart lay crushed within me. She had been my wife not a year; it was but the other day that I knew she loved me—

After a while the anguish lessened, and I lay, dull and hopeless, thinking of trifling things, counting the stars between the pines. Another slow hour, and, a braver mood coming upon me, I thought of Diccon, who was in that plight because of me, and spoke to him, asking him how he did. He answered from the other side of the lodge, but the words were scarcely out of his mouth before our guard broke in upon us commanding silence. Diccon cursed them, whereupon a savage struck him across the head with the handle of a tomahawk, stunning him for a time. As soon as I heard him move I spoke again, to know if he were much hurt; when he had answered in the negative we said no more.

It was now moonlight without the lodge and very quiet. The night was far gone; already we could smell the morning, and it would come apace. Knowing the swiftness of that approach, and what the early light would bring, I strove for a courage which should be the steadfastness of the Christian, and not the vainglorious pride of the heathen. If my thoughts wandered, if her face would come athwart the verses I tried to remember, the prayer I tried to frame, perhaps He who made her lovely understood and forgave. I said the prayer I used to say when I was a child, and wished with all my heart for Jeremy.

Suddenly, in the first gray dawn, as at a trumpet's call, the village awoke. From the long, communal houses poured forth men, women, and children; fires sprang up, dispersing the mist, and a commotion arose through the length and breadth of the place. The women made haste with their cooking, and bore maize cakes and broiled fish to the warriors who sat on the ground in front of the royal lodge. Diccon and I were loosed, brought without, and allotted our share of the food. We ate sitting side by side with our captors, and Diccon, with a great cut across his head, seized the Indian girl who brought him his platter of fish, and pulling her down beside him kissed her soundly, whereat the maid seemed not ill pleased and the warriors laughed.

In the usual order of things, the meal over, tobacco should have followed. But now not a pipe was lit, and the women made haste to take away the platters and to get all things in readiness. The werowance of the Paspaheghs rose to his feet, cast aside his mantle, and began to speak. He was a man in the prime of life, of a great figure, strong as a Susquehannock, and a savage cruel and crafty beyond measure. Over his breast, stained with strange figures, hung a chain of small bones, and the scalp locks of his enemies fringed his moccasins. His tribe being the nearest to Jamestown, and in frequent altercation with us, I had heard him speak many times, and knew his power over the passions of his people. No player could be more skillful in gesture and expression, no poet more nice in the choice of words, no general more quick to raise a wild enthusiasm in the soldiers to whom he called. All Indians are eloquent, but this savage was a leader among them.

He spoke now to some effect. Commencing with a day in the moon of blossoms when for the first time winged canoes brought white men into the Powhatan, he came down through year after year to the present hour, ceased, and stood in silence, regarding his triumph. It was complete. In its wild excitement the village was ready then and there to make an end of us who had sprung to our feet and stood with our backs against a great bay tree, facing the maddened throng. So much the best for us would it be if the tomahawks left the hands that were drawn back to throw, if the knives that were flourished in our faces should be buried to the haft in our hearts, that we courted death, striving with word and look to infuriate our executioners to the point of forgetting their former purpose in the lust for instant vengeance. It was not to be. The werowance spoke again, pointing to the hills with the black houses upon them, dimly seen through the mist. A moment, and the hands clenched upon the weapons fell; another, and we were upon the march.

As one man, the village swept through the forest toward the rising ground that was but a few bowshots away. The young men bounded ahead to make preparation; but the approved warriors and the old men went more sedately, and with them walked Diccon and I, as steady of step as they. The women and children for the most part brought up the rear, though a few impatient hags ran past us, calling the men tortoises who would never reach the goal. One of these women bore a great burning torch, the flame and smoke streaming over her shoulder as she ran. Others carried pieces of bark heaped with the slivers of pine of which every wigwam has store.

The sun was yet to rise when we reached a hollow amongst the low red hills. Above us were the three long houses in which they keep the image of Okee and the mummies of their kings. These temples faced the crimson east, and the mist was yet about them. Hideous priests, painted over with strange devices, the stuffed skins of snakes knotted about their heads, in their hands great rattles which they shook vehemently, rushed through the doors and down the bank to meet us, and began to dance around us, contorting their bodies, throwing up their arms, and making a hellish noise. Diccon stared at them, shrugged his shoulders, and with a grunt of contempt sat down upon a fallen tree to watch the enemy's manoeuvres.

The place was a natural amphitheatre, well fitted for a spectacle. Those Indians who could not crowd into the narrow level spread themselves over the rising ground, and looked down with fierce laughter upon the driving of the stakes which the young men brought. The women and children scattered into the woods beyond the cleft between the hills, and returned bearing great armfuls of dry branches. The hollow rang to the exultation of the playgoers. Taunting laughter, cries of savage triumph, the shaking of the rattles, and the furious beating of two great drums combined to make a clamor deafening to stupor. And above the hollow was the angry reddening of the heavens, and the white mist curling up like smoke.

I sat down beside Diccon on the log. Beneath it there were growing tufts of a pale blue, slender-stemmed flower. I plucked a handful of the blossoms, and thought how blue they would look against the whiteness of her hand; then dropped them in a sudden shame that in that hour I was so little steadfast to things which were not of earth. I did not speak to Diccon, nor he to me. There seemed no need of speech. In the pandemonium to which the world had narrowed, the one familiar, matter-of-course thing was that he and I were to die together.

The stakes were in the ground and painted red, the wood properly arranged. The Indian woman who held the torch that was to light the pile ran past us, whirling the wood around her head to make it blaze more fiercely. As she went by she lowered the brand and slowly dragged it across my wrists. The beating of the drums suddenly ceased, and the loud voices died away. To Indians no music is so sweet as the cry of an enemy; if they have wrung it from a brave man who has striven to endure, so much the better. They were very still now, because they would not lose so much as a drawing in of the breath.

Seeing that they were coming for us, Diccon and I rose to await them. When they were nearly upon us I turned to him and held out my hand.

He made no motion to take it. Instead he stood with fixed eyes looking past me and slightly upwards. A sudden pallor had overspread the bronze of his face. "There's a verse somewhere," he said in a quiet voice,—"it's in the Bible, I think,—I heard it once long ago, before I was lost: 'I will look unto the hills from whence cometh my help'—Look, sir!"

I turned and followed with my eyes the pointing of his finger. In front of us the bank rose steeply, bare to the summit,—no trees, only the red earth, with here and there a low growth of leafless bushes. Behind it was the eastern sky. Upon the crest, against the sunrise, stood the figure of a man,—an Indian. From one shoulder hung an otterskin, and a great bow was in his hand. His limbs were bare, and as he stood motionless, bathed in the rosy light, he looked like some bronze god, perfect from the beaded moccasins to the calm, uneager face below the feathered headdress. He had but just risen above the brow of the hill; the Indians in the hollow saw him not.

While Diccon and I stared our tormentors were upon us. They came a dozen or more at once, and we had no weapons. Two hung upon my arms, while a third laid hold of my doublet to rend it from me. An arrow whistled over our heads and stuck into a tree behind us. The hands that clutched me dropped, and with a yell the busy throng turned their faces in the direction whence had come the arrow.

The Indian who had sent that dart before him was descending the bank. An instant's breathless hush while they stared at the solitary figure; then the dark forms bent forward for the rush straightened, and there arose a loud cry of recognition. "The son of Powhatan! The son of Powhatan!"

He came down the hillside to the level of the hollow, the authority of his look and gesture making way for him through the crowd that surged this way and that, and walked up to us where we stood, hemmed round, but no longer in the clutch of our enemies. "It was a very big wolf this time, Captain Percy," he said.

"You were never more welcome, Nantauquas," I answered,—"unless, indeed, the wolf intends making a meal of three instead of two."

He smiled. "The wolf will go hungry to-day." Taking my hand in his he turned to his frowning countrymen. "Men of the Pamunkeys!" he cried. "This is Nantauquas' friend, and so the friend of all the tribes that called Powhatan 'father.' The fire is not for him nor for his servant; keep it for the Monacans and for the dogs of the Long House! The calumet is for the friend of Nantauquas, and the dance of the maidens, the noblest buck and the best of the weirs"—

There was a surging forward of the Indians, and a fierce murmur of dissent. The werowance, standing out from the throng, lifted his voice. "There was a time," he cried, "when Nantauquas was the panther crouched upon the bough above the leader of the herd; now Nantauquas is a tame panther and rolls at the white men's feet! There was a time when the word of the son of Powhatan weighed more than the lives of many dogs such as these, but now I know not why we should put out the fire at his command! He is war chief no longer, for Opechancanough will have no tame panther to lead the tribes. Opechancanough is our head, and Opechancanough kindleth a fire indeed! We will give to this one what fuel we choose, and to-night Nantauquas may look for the bones of the white men!"

He ended, and a great clamor arose. The Paspaheghs would have cast themselves upon us again but for a sudden action of the young chief, who had stood motionless, with raised head and unmoved face, during the werowance's bitter speech. Now he flung up his hand, and in it was a bracelet of gold carved and twisted like a coiled snake and set with a green stone. I had never seen the toy before, but evidently others had done so. The excited voices fell, and the Indians, Pamunkeys and Paspaheghs alike, stood as though turned to stone.

Nantauquas smiled coldly. "This day hath Opechancanough made me war chief again. We have smoked the peace pipe together—my father's brother and I—in the starlight, sitting before his lodge, with the wide marshes and the river dark at our feet. Singing birds in the forest have been many; evil tales have they told; Opechancanough has stopped his ears against their false singing. My friends are his friends, my brother is his brother, my word is his word: witness the armlet that hath no like; that Opechancanough brought with him when he came from no man knows where to the land of the Powhatans, many Huskanawings ago; that no white men but these have ever seen. Opechancanough is at hand; he comes through the forest with his two hundred warriors that are as tall as Susquehannocks, and as brave as the children of Wahunsonacock. He comes to the temples to pray to Kiwassa for a great hunting. Will you, when you lie at his feet, that he ask you, 'Where is the friend of my friend, of my war chief, of the Panther who is one with me again?'"

There came a long, deep breath from the Indians, then a silence, in which they fell back, slowly and sullenly; whipped hounds, but with the will to break that leash of fear.

"Hark!" said Nantauquas, smiling. "I hear Opechancanough and his warriors coming over the leaves."

The noise of many footsteps was indeed audible, coming toward the hollow from the woods beyond. With a burst of cries, the priests and the conjurer whirled away to bear the welcome of Okee to the royal worshiper, and at their heels went the chief men of the Pamunkeys. The werowance of the Paspaheghs was one that sailed with the wind; he listened to the deepening sound, and glanced at the son of Powhatan where he stood, calm and confident, then smoothed his own countenance and made a most pacific speech, in which all the blame of the late proceedings was laid upon the singing birds. When he had done speaking, the young men tore the stakes from the earth and threw them into a thicket, while the women plucked apart the newly kindled fire and flung the brands into a little near-by stream, where they went out in a cloud of hissing steam.

I turned to the Indian who had wrought this miracle. "Art sure it is not a dream, Nantauquas?" I said. "I think that Opechancanough would not lift a finger to save me from all the deaths the tribes could invent."

"Opechancanough is very wise," he answered quietly. "He says that now the English will believe in his love indeed when they see that he holds dear even one who might be called his enemy, who hath spoken against him at the Englishmen's council fire. He says that for five suns Captain Percy shall feast with Opechancanough, and that then he shall be sent back free to Jamestown. He thinks that then Captain Percy will not speak against him any more, calling his love to the white men only words with no good deeds behind."

He spoke simply, out of the nobility of his nature, believing his own speech. I that was older, and had more knowledge of men and the masks that they wear, was but half deceived. My belief in the hatred of the dark Emperor was not shaken, and I looked yet to find the drop of poison within this honey flower. How poisoned was that bloom God knows I could not guess!

"When you were missed, three suns ago," Nantauquas went on, "I and my brother tracked you to the hut beside the forest, where we found only the dead panther. There we struck the trail of the Paspaheghs; but presently we came to running water, and the trail was gone."

"We walked up the bed of the stream for half the night," I said.

The Indian nodded. "I know. My brother went back to Jamestown for men and boats and guns to go to the Paspahegh village and up the Powhatan. He was wise with the wisdom of the white men, but I, who needed no gun, and who would not fight against my own people, I stepped into the stream and walked up it until past the full sun power. Then I found a broken twig and the print of a moccasin, half hidden by a bush, overlooked when the other prints were smoothed away. I left the stream and followed the trail until it was broken again. I looked for it no more then, for I knew that the Paspaheghs had turned their faces toward Uttamussac, and that they would make a fire where many others had been made, in the hollow below the three temples. Instead I went with speed to seek Opechancanough. Yesterday, when the sun was low, I found him, sitting in his lodge above the marshes and the colored river. We smoked the peace pipe together, and I am his war chief again. I asked for the green stone, that I might show it to the Paspaheghs for a sign. He gave it, but he willed to come to Uttamussac with me."

"I owe you my life," I said, with my hand upon his. "I and Diccon"—What I would have said he put aside with a fine gesture. "Captain Percy is my friend. My brother loves him, and he was kind to Matoax when she was brought prisoner to Jamestown. I am glad that I could pull off this wolf."

"Tell me one thing," I asked. "Before you left Jamestown, had you heard aught of my wife or of my enemy?"

He shook his head. "At sunrise, the commander came to rouse my brother, crying out that you had broken gaol and were nowhere to be found, and that the man you hate was lying within the guest house, sorely torn by some beast of the forest. My brother and I followed your trail at once; the town was scarce awake when we left it behind us,—and I did not return."

By this we three were alone in the hollow, for all the savages, men and women, had gone forth to meet the Indian whose word was law from the falls of the far west to the Chesapeake. The sun now rode above the low hills, pouring its gold into the hollow and brightening all the world besides. The little stream flashed diamonds, and the carven devils upon the black houses above us were frightful no longer. There was not a menace anywhere from the cloudless skies to the sweet and plaintive chant to Kiwassa, sung by women and floating to us from the woods beyond the hollow. The singing grew nearer, and the rustling of the leaves beneath many feet more loud and deep; then all noise ceased, and Opechancanough entered the hollow alone. An eagle feather was thrust through his scalp lock; over his naked breast, that was neither painted nor pricked into strange figures, hung a triple row of pearls; his mantle was woven of bluebird feathers, as soft and sleek as satin. The face of this barbarian was dark, cold, and impassive as death. Behind that changeless mask, as in a safe retreat, the supersubtle devil that was the man might plot destruction and plan the laying of dreadful mines. He had dignity and courage,—no man denied him that. I suppose he thought that he and his had wrongs: God knows! perhaps they had. But if ever we were hard or unjust in our dealings with the savages,—I say not that this was the case,— at least we were not treacherous and dealt not in Judas kisses.

I stepped forward, and met him on the spot where the fire had been. For a minute neither spoke. It was true that I had striven against him many a time, and I knew that he knew it. It was also true that without his aid Nantauquas could not have rescued us from that dire peril. And it was again the truth that an Indian neither forgives nor forgets. He was my saviour, and I knew that mercy had been shown for some dark reason which I could not divine. Yet I owed him thanks, and gave them as shortly and simply as I could.

He heard me out with neither liking nor disliking nor any other emotion written upon his face; but when I had finished, as though he suddenly bethought himself, he smiled and held out his hand, white-man fashion. Now, when a man's lips widen I look into his eyes. The eyes of Opechancanough were as fathomless as a pool at midnight, and as devoid of mirth or friendliness as the staring orbs of the carven imps upon the temple corners.

"Singing birds have lied to Captain Percy," he said, and his voice was like his eyes. "Opechancanough thinks that Captain Percy will never listen to them again. The chief of the Powhatans is a lover of the white men, of the English, and of other white men,—if there are others. He would call the Englishmen his brothers, and be taught of them how to rule, and who to pray to"—

"Let Opechancanough go with me to-day to Jamestown," I said. "He hath the wisdom of the woods; let him come and gain that of the town."

The Emperor smiled again. "I will come to Jamestown soon, but not to-day nor to-morrow nor the next day. And Captain Percy must smoke the peace pipe in my lodge above the Pamunkey, and watch my young men and maidens dance, and eat with me five days. Then he may go back to Jamestown with presents for the great white father there, and with a message that Opechancanough is coming soon to learn of the white men."

I could have gnashed my teeth at that delay when she must think me dead, but it would have been the madness of folly to show the impatience which I felt. I too could smile with my lips when occasion drove, and drink a bitter draught as though my soul delighted in it. Blithe enough to all seeming, and with as few inward misgivings as the case called for, Diccon and I went with the subtle Emperor and the young chief he had bound to himself once more, and with their fierce train, back to that village which we had never thought to see again. A day and a night we stayed there; then Opechancanough sent away the Paspaheghs,—where we knew not,—and taking us with him went to his own village above the great marshes of the Pamunkey.

CHAPTER XXXII
IN WHICH WE ARE THE GUESTS OF AN EMPEROR

I HAD before this spent days among the Indians, on voyages of discovery, as conqueror, as negotiator for food, exchanging blue beads for corn and turkeys. Other Englishmen had been with me. Knowing those with whom we dealt for sly and fierce heathen, friends to-day, to-morrow deadly foes, we kept our muskets ready and our eyes and ears open, and, what with the danger and the novelty and the bold wild life, managed to extract some merriment as well as profit from these visits. It was different now.

Day after day I ate my heart out in that cursed village. The feasting and the hunting and the triumph, the wild songs and wilder dances, the fantastic mummeries, the sudden rages, the sudden laughter, the great fires with their rings of painted warriors, the sleepless sentinels, the wide marshes that could not be crossed by night, the leaves that rustled so loudly beneath the lightest footfall, the monotonous days, the endless nights when I thought of her grief, of her peril, maybe,—it was an evil dream, and for my own pleasure I could not wake too soon.

Should we ever wake? Should we not sink from that dream without pause into a deeper sleep whence there would be no waking? It was a question that I asked myself each morning, half looking to find another hollow between the hills before the night should fall. The night fell, and there was no change in the dream.

I will allow that the dark Emperor to whom we were so much beholden gave us courteous keeping. The best of the hunt was ours, the noblest fish, the most delicate roots. The skins beneath which we slept were fine and soft; the women waited upon us, and the old men and warriors held with us much stately converse, sitting beneath the budding trees with the blue tobacco smoke curling above our heads. We were alive and sound of limb, well treated and with the promise of release; we might have waited, seeing that wait we must, in some measure of content. We did not so. There was a horror in the air. From the marshes that were growing green, from the sluggish river, from the rotting leaves and cold black earth and naked forest, it rose like an exhalation. We knew not what it was, but we breathed it in, and it went to the marrow of our bones.

Opechancanough we rarely saw, though we were bestowed so near to him that his sentinels served for ours. Like some god, he kept within his lodge with the winding passage, and the hanging mats between him and the world without. At other times, issuing from that retirement, he would stride away into the forest. Picked men went with him, and they were gone for hours; but when they returned they bore no trophies, brute or human. What they did we could not guess. We might have had much comfort in Nantauquas, but the morning after our arrival in this village the Emperor sent him upon an embassy to the Rappahannocks, and when for the fourth time the forest stood black against the sunset he had not returned. If escape had been possible, we would not have awaited the doubtful fulfillment of that promise made to us below the Uttamussac temples. But the vigilance of the Indians never slept; they watched us like hawks, night and day. And the dry leaves underfoot would not hold their peace, and there were the marshes to cross and the river.

Thus four days dragged themselves by, and in the early morning of the fifth, when we came from our wigwam, it was to find Nantauquas sitting by the fire, magnificent in the paint and trappings of the ambassador, motionless as a piece of bronze, and apparently quite unmindful of the admiring glances of the women who knelt about the fire preparing our breakfast. When he saw us he rose and came to meet us, and I embraced him, I was so glad to see him. "The Rappahannocks feasted me long," he said. "I was afraid that Captain Percy would be gone to Jamestown before I was back upon the Pamunkey."

"Shall I ever see Jamestown again, Nantauquas?" I demanded. "I have my doubts."

He looked me full in the eyes, and there was no doubting the candor of his own. "You go with the next sunrise," he answered. "Opechancanough has given me his word."

"I am glad to hear it," I said. "Why have we been kept at all? Why did he not free us five days agone?"

He shook his head. "I do not know. Opechancanough has many thoughts which he shares with no man. But now he will send you with presents for the Governor, and with messages of his love to the white men. There will be a great feast to-day, and to-night the young men and maidens will dance before you. Then in the morning you will go."

"Will you not come with us?" I asked. "You are ever welcome amongst us, Nantauquas, both for your sister's sake and for your own. Rolfe will rejoice to have you with him again; he ever grudgeth you to the forest."

He shook his head again. "Nantauquas, the son of Powhatan, hath had much talk with himself lately," he said simply. "The white men's ways have seemed very good to him, and the God of the white men he knows to be greater than Okee, and to be good and tender; not like Okee, who sucks the blood of the children. He remembers Matoax, too, and how she loved and cared for the white men and would weep when danger threatened them. And Rolfe is his brother and his teacher. But Opechancanough is his king, and the red men are his people, and the forest is his home. If, because he loved Rolfe, and because the ways of the white men seemed to him better than his own ways, he forgot these things, he did wrong, and the One over All frowns upon him. Now he has come back to his home again, to the forest and the hunting and the warpath, to his king and his people. He will be again the panther crouching upon the bough"—

"Above the white men?"

He gazed at me in silence, a shadow upon his face. "Above the Monacans," he answered slowly. "Why did Captain Percy say 'above the white men'? Opechancanough and the English have buried the hatchet forever, and the smoke of the peace pipe will never fade from the air. Nantauquas meant 'above the Monacans or the Long House dogs.'"

I put my hand upon his shoulder. "I know you did, brother of Rolfe by nature if not by blood! Forget what I said; it was without thought or meaning. If we go indeed to-morrow, I shall be loath to leave you behind; and yet, were I in your place, I should do as you are doing."

The shadow left his face and he drew himself up. "Is it what you call faith and loyalty and like a knight?" he demanded, with a touch of eagerness breaking through the slowness and gravity with which an Indian speaks.

"Yea," I made reply. "I think you good knight and true, Nantauquas, and my friend, moreover, who saved my life."

His smile was like his sister's, quick and very bright, and leaving behind it a most entire gravity. Together we sat down by the fire and ate of the sylvan breakfast, with shy brown maidens to serve us and with the sunshine streaming down upon us through the trees that were growing faintly green. It was a thing to smile at to see how the Indian girls manoeuvred to give the choicest meat, the most delicate maize cakes, to the young war chief, and to see how quietly he turned aside their benevolence. The meal over, he went to divest himself of his red and white paint, of the stuffed hawk and strings of copper that formed his headdress, of his gorgeous belt and quiver and his mantle of raccoon skins, while Diccon and I sat still before our wigwam, smoking, and reckoning the distance to Jamestown and the shortest time in which we could cover it.

When we had sat there for an hour the old men and the warriors came to visit us, and the smoking must commence all over again. The women laid mats in a great half circle, and each savage took his seat with perfect breeding; that is, in absolute silence and with a face like a stone. The peace paint was upon them all,—red, or red and white; they sat and looked at the ground until I had made the speech of welcome. Soon the air was dense with the fragrant smoke; in the thick blue haze the sweep of painted figures had the seeming of some fantastic dream. An old man arose and made a long and touching speech with much reference to calumets and buried hatchets. When he had finished a chief talked of Opechancanough's love for the English, "high as the stars, deep as Popogusso, wide as from the sunrise to the sunset," adding that the death of Nemattanow last year and the troubles over the hunting grounds had kindled in the breasts of the Indians no desire for revenge. With which highly probable statement he made an end, and all sat in silence looking at me and waiting for my contribution of honeyed words. These Pamunkeys, living at a distance from the settlements, had but little English to their credit, and the learning of the Paspaheghs was not much greater. I sat and repeated to them the better part of the seventh canto of the second book of Master Spenser's "Faery Queen." Then I told them the story of the Moor of Venice, and ended by relating Smith's tale of the three Turks' heads. It all answered the purpose to admiration. When at length they went away to change their paint for the coming feast Diccon and I laughed at that foolery as though there were none beside us who could juggle with words. We were as light-hearted as children—God forgive us!

The day wore on, with relay after relay of food which we must taste at least, with endless smoking of pipes and speeches that must be listened to and answered. When evening came and our entertainers drew off to prepare for the dance, they left us as wearied as by a long day's march.

The wind had been high during the day, but with the sunset it sank to a desolate murmur. The sky wore the strange crimson of the past year at Weyanoke. Against that sea of color the pines were drawn in ink, and beneath it the winding, threadlike creeks that pierced the marshes had the look of spilt blood moving slowly and heavily to join the river that was black where the pines shadowed it, red where the light touched it. From the marsh arose the cry of some great bird that made its home there; it had a lonely and a boding sound, like a trumpet blown above the dead. The color died into an ashen gray and the air grew cold, with a heaviness beside that dragged at the very soul. Diccon shivered violently, turned restlessly upon the log that served him as settle, and began to mutter to himself.

"Art cold?" I asked.

He shook his head. "Something walked over my grave," he said. "I would give all the pohickory that was ever brewed by heathen for a toss of aqua vitae!"

In the centre of the village rose a great heap of logs and dry branches, built during the day by the women and children. When the twilight fell and the owls began to hoot this pile was fired, and lit the place from end to end. The scattered wigwams, the scaffolding where the fish were dried, the tall pines and wide-branching mulberries, the trodden grass,—all flashed into sight as the flame roared up to the top-most withered bough. The village glowed like a lamp set in the dead blackness of marsh and forest. Opechancanough came from the forest with a score of warriors behind him, and stopped beside me. I rose to greet him, as was decent; for he was an Emperor, albeit a savage and a pagan. "Tell the English that Opechancanough grows old," he said. "The years that once were as light upon him as the dew upon the maize are now hailstones to beat him back to the earth whence he came. His arm is not swift to strike and strong as it once was. He is old; the warpath and the scalp dance please him no longer. He would die at peace with all men. Tell the English this; tell them also that Opechancanough knows that they are good and just, that they do not treat men whose color is not their own like babes, fooling them with toys, thrusting them out of their path when they grow troublesome. The land is wide and the hunting grounds are many. Let the red men who were here as many moons ago as there are leaves in summer and the white men who came yesterday dwell side by side in peace, sharing the maize fields and the weirs and the hunting grounds together." He waited not for my answer, but passed on, and there was no sign of age in his stately figure and his slow, firm step. I watched him with a frown until the darkness of his lodge had swallowed up him and his warriors, and mistrusted him for a cold and subtle devil.

Suddenly, as we sat staring at the fire we were beset by a band of maidens, coming out of the woods, painted, with antlers upon their heads and pine branches in their hands. They danced about us, now advancing until the green needles met above our heads, now retreating until there was a space of turf between us. Their slender limbs gleamed in the firelight; they moved with grace, keeping time to a plaintive song, now raised by the whole choir, now fallen to a single voice. Pocahontas had danced thus before the English many a time. I thought of the little maid, of her great wondering eyes and her piteous, untimely death, of how loving she was to Rolfe and how happy they had been in their brief wedded life. It had bloomed like a rose, as fair and as early fallen, with only a memory of past sweetness. Death was a coward, passing by men whose trade it was to out-brave him, and striking at the young and lovely and innocent....

We were tired with all the mummery of the day; moreover, every fibre of our souls had been strained to meet the hours that had passed since we left the gaol at Jamestown. The elation we had felt earlier in the day was all gone. Now, the plaintive song, the swaying figures, the red light beating against the trees, the blackness of the enshrouding forest, the low, melancholy wind,— all things seemed strange, and yet deadly old, as though we had seen and heard them since the beginning of the world. All at once a fear fell upon me, causeless and unreasonable, but weighing upon my heart like a stone. She was in a palisaded town, under the Governor's protection, with my friends about her and my enemy lying sick, unable to harm her. It was I, not she, that was in danger. I laughed at myself, but my heart was heavy, and I was in a fever to be gone.

The Indian girls danced more and more swiftly, and their song changed, becoming gay and shrill and sweet. Higher and higher rang the notes, faster and faster moved the dark limbs; then, quite suddenly, song and motion ceased together. They who had danced with the abandonment of wild priestesses to some wild god were again but shy brown Indian maids who went and set them meekly down upon the grass beneath the trees. From the darkness now came a burst of savage cries only less appalling than the war whoop itself. In a moment the men of the village had rushed from the shadow of the trees into the broad, firelit space before us. Now they circled around us, now around the fire; now each man danced and stamped and muttered to himself. For the most part they were painted red, but some were white from head to heel,—statues come to life,—while others had first oiled their bodies, then plastered them over with small bright-colored feathers. The tall headdresses made giants of them all; as they leaped and danced in the glare of the fire they had a fiendish look. They sang, too, but the air was rude, and broken by dreadful cries. Out of a hut behind us burst two or three priests, the conjurer, and a score or more of old men. They had Indian drums upon which they beat furiously, and long pipes made of reeds which gave forth no uncertain sound. Fixed upon a pole and borne high above them was the image of their Okee, a hideous thing of stuffed skins and rattling chains of copper. When they had joined themselves to the throng in the firelight the clamor became deafening. Some one piled on more logs, and the place grew light as day. Opechancanough was not there, nor Nantauquas.

Diccon and I watched that uncouth spectacle, that Virginian masque, as we had watched many another one, with disgust and weariness. It would last, we knew, for the better part of the night. It was in our honor, and for a while we must stay and testify our pleasure; but after a time, when they had sung and danced themselves into oblivion of our presence, we might retire, and leave the very old men, the women, and the children sole spectators. We waited for that relief with impatience, though we showed it not to those who pressed about us.

Time passed, and the noise deepened and the dancing became more frantic. The dancers struck at one another as they leaped and whirled, the sweat rolled from their bodies, and from their lips came hoarse, animal-like cries. The fire, ever freshly fed, roared and crackled, mocking the silent stars. The pines were bronze-red, the woods beyond a dead black. All noises of marsh and forest were lost in the scream of the pipes, the wild yelling, and the beating of the drums.

From the ranks of the women beneath the reddened pines rose shrill laughter and applause as they sat or knelt, bent forward, watching the dancers. One girl alone watched not them, but us. She stood somewhat back of her companions, one slim brown hand touching the trunk of a tree, one brown foot advanced, her attitude that of one who waits but for a signal to be gone. Now and then she glanced impatiently at the wheeling figures, or at the old men and the few warriors who took no part in the masque, but her eyes always came back to us. She had been among the maidens who danced before us earlier in the night; when they rested beneath the trees she had gone away, and the night was much older when I marked her again, coming out of the firelit distance back to the fire and her dusky mates. It was soon after this that I became aware that she must have some reason for her anxious scrutiny, some message to deliver or warning to give. Once when I made a slight motion as if to go to her, she shook her head and laid her finger upon her lips.

A dancer fell from sheer exhaustion, another and another, and warriors from the dozen or more seated at our right began to take the places of the fallen. The priests shook their rattles, and made themselves dizzy with bending and whirling about their Okee; the old men, too, though they sat like statues, thought only of the dance, and of how they themselves had excelled, long ago when they were young.

I rose, and making my way to the werowance of the village where he sat with his eyes fixed upon a young Indian, his son, who bade fair to outlast all others in that wild contest, told him that I was wearied and would go to my hut, I and my servant, to rest for the few hours that yet remained of the night. He listened dreamily, his eyes upon the dancing Indian, but made offer to escort me thither. I pointed out to him that my quarters were not fifty yards away, in the broad firelight, in sight of them all, and that it were a pity to take him or any others from the contemplation of that whirling Indian, so strong and so brave that he would surely one day lead the war parties.

After a moment he acquiesced, and Diccon and I, quietly and yet with some ostentation, so as to avoid all appearance of stealing away, left the press of savages and began to cross the firelit turf between them and our lodge. When we had gone fifty paces I glanced over my shoulder and saw that the Indian maid no longer stood where we had last seen her, beneath the pines. A little farther on we caught a glimpse of her winding in and out among a row of trees to our left. The trees ran past our lodge. When we had reached its entrance we paused and looked back to the throng we had left. Every back seemed turned to us, every eye intent upon the leaping figures around the great fire. Swiftly and quietly we walked across the bit of even ground to the friendly trees, and found ourselves in a thin strip of shadow between the light of the great fire we had left and that of a lesser one burning redly before the Emperor's lodge. Beneath the trees, waiting for us, was the Indian maid, with her light form, and large, shy eyes, and finger upon her lips. She would not speak or tarry, but flitted before us as dusk and noiseless as a moth, and we followed her into the darkness beyond the firelight, well-nigh to the line of sentinels. A wigwam, larger than common and shadowed by trees, rose in our path; the girl, gliding in front of us, held aside the mats that curtained the entrance. We hesitated a moment, then stooped and entered the place.

CHAPTER XXXIII
IN WHICH MY FRIEND BECOMES MY FOE

IN the centre of the wigwam the customary fire burned clear and bright, showing the white mats, the dressed skins, the implements of war hanging upon the bark walls,—all the usual furniture of an Indian dwelling,—and showing also Nantauquas standing against the stripped trunk of a pine that pierced the wigwam from floor to roof. The fire was between us. He stood so rigid, at his full height, with folded arms and head held high, and his features were so blank and still, so forced and frozen, as it were, into composure, that, with the red light beating upon him and the thin smoke curling above his head, he had the look of a warrior tied to the stake.

"Nantauquas!" I exclaimed, and striding past the fire would have touched him but that with a slight and authoritative motion of the hand he kept me back. Otherwise there was no change in his position or in the dead calm of his face.

The Indian maid had dropped the mat at the entrance, and if she waited, waited without in the darkness. Diccon, now staring at the young chief, now eyeing the weapons upon the wall with all a lover's passion, kept near the doorway. Through the thickness of the bark and woven twigs the wild cries and singing came to us somewhat faintly; beneath that distant noise could be heard the wind in the trees and the soft fall of the burning pine.

"Well!" I asked at last. "What is the matter, my friend?"

For a full minute he made no answer, and when he did speak his voice matched his face.

"My friend," he said, "I am going to show myself a friend indeed to the English, to the strangers who were not content with their own hunting grounds beyond the great salt water. When I have done this, I do not know that Captain Percy will call me 'friend' again."

"You were wont to speak plainly, Nantauquas," I answered him. "I am not fond of riddles."

Again he waited, as though he found speech difficult. I stared at him in amazement, he was so changed in so short a time.

He spoke at last: "When the dance is over, and the fires are low, and the sunrise is at hand, then will Opechancanough come to you to bid you farewell. He will give you the pearls that he wears about his neck for a present to the Governor, and a bracelet for yourself. Also he will give you three men for a guard through the forest. He has messages of love to send the white men, and he would send them by you who were his enemy and his captive. So all the white men shall believe in his love."

"Well," I said dryly as he paused. "I will take his messages. What next?"

"Those are the words of Opechancanough. Now listen to the words of Nantauquas, the son of Wahunsonacock, a war chief of the Powhatans. There are two sharp knives there, hanging beneath the bow and the quiver and the shield. Take them and hide them."

The words were scarcely out of his mouth before Diccon had the two keen English blades. I took the one he offered me, and hid it in my doublet.

"So we go armed, Nantauquas," I said. "Love and peace and goodwill consort not with such toys."

"You may want them," he went on, with no change in his low, measured tones. "If you see aught in the forest that you should not see, if they think you know more than you are meant to know, then those three, who have knives and tomahawks, are to kill you, whom they believe unarmed."

"See aught that we should not see, know more than we are meant to know?" I said. "To the point, friend."

"They will go slowly, too, through the forest to Jamestown, stopping to eat and to sleep. For them there is no need to run like the stag with the hunter behind him."

"Then we should make for Jamestown as for life," I said, "not sleeping or eating or making pause?"

"Yea," he replied, "if you would not die, you and all your people."

In the silence of the hut the fire crackled, and the branches of the trees outside, bent by the wind, made a grating sound against the bark roof.

"How die?" I asked at last. "Speak out!"

"Die by the arrow and the tomahawk," he answered,—"yea, and by the guns you have given the red men. To-morrow's sun, and the next, and the next,— three suns,—and the tribes will fall upon the English. At the same hour, when the men are in the fields and the women and children are in the houses, they will strike,—Kecoughtans, Paspaheghs, Chickahominies, Pamunkeys, Arrowhatocks, Chesapeakes, Nansemonds, Accomacs,—as one man will they strike; and from where the Powhatan falls over the rocks to the salt water beyond Accomac, there will not be one white man left alive."

He ceased to speak, and for a minute the fire made the only sound in the hut. Then, "All die?" I asked dully. "There are three thousand Englishmen in Virginia."

"They are scattered and unwarned. The fighting men of the villages of the Powhatan and the Pamunkey and the great bay are many, and they have sharpened their hatchets and filled their quivers with arrows."

"Scattered," I said, "strewn broadcast up and down the river,—here a lonely house, there a cluster of two or three; they at Jamestown and Henricus off guard,—the men in the fields or at the wharves, the women and the children busy within doors, all unwarned—O my God!"

Diccon strode over from the doorway to the fire. "We'd best be going, I reckon, sir," he cried. "Or you wait until morning; then there'll be two chances. Now that I've a knife, I'm thinking I can give account of one of them damned sentries, at least. Once clear of them"—

I shook my head, and the Indian too made a gesture of dissent. "You would only be the first to die."

I leaned against the side of the hut, for my heart beat like a frightened woman's. "Three days!" I exclaimed. "If we go with all our speed we shall be in time. When did you learn this thing?"

"While you watched the dance," he answered, "Opechancanough and I sat within his lodge in the darkness. His heart was moved, and he talked to me of his own youth in a strange country, south of the sunset, where he and his people dwelt in stone houses and worshiped a great and fierce god, giving him blood to drink and flesh to eat. To that country, too, white men had come in ships. Then he spoke to me of Powhatan, my father,—of how wise he was and how great a chief before the English came, and how the English made him kneel in sign that he held his lands from their King, and how he hated them; and then he told me that the tribes had called me 'woman,' 'lover no longer of the warpath and the scalp dance,' but that he, who had no son, loved me as his son, knowing my heart to be Indian still; and then I heard what I have told you."

"How long had this been planned?"

"For many moons. I have been a child, fooled and turned aside from the trail; not wise enough to see it beneath the flowers, through the smoke of the peace pipes."

"Why does Opechancanough send us back to the settlements?" I demanded. "Their faith in him needs no strengthening."

"It is his fancy. Every hunter and trader and learner of our tongues, living in the villages or straying in the woods, has been sent back to Jamestown or to his hundred with presents and with words that are sweeter than honey. He has told the three who go with you the hour in which you are to reach Jamestown; he would have you as singing birds, telling lying tales to the

Governor, with scarce the smoking of a pipe between those words of peace and the war whoop. But if those who go with you see reason to misdoubt you, they will kill you in the forest."

His voice fell, and he stood in silence, straight as an arrow, against the post, the firelight playing over his dark limbs and sternly quiet face. Outside, the night wind, rising, began to howl through the naked branches, and a louder burst of yells came to us from the roisterers in the distance. The mat before the doorway shook, and a slim brown hand, slipped between the wood and the woven grass, beckoned to us.

"Why did you come?" demanded the Indian. "Long ago, when there were none but dark men from the Chesapeake to the hunting grounds beneath the sunset, we were happy. Why did you leave your own land, in the strange black ships with sails like the piled-up clouds of summer? Was it not a good land? Were not your forests broad and green, your fields fruitful, your rivers deep and filled with fish? And the towns I have heard of—were they not fair? You are brave men: had you no enemies there, and no warpaths? It was your home: a man should love the good earth over which he hunts, upon which stands his village. This is the red man's land. He wishes his hunting grounds, his maize fields, and his rivers for himself, his women and children. He has no ships in which to go to another country. When you first came we thought you were gods; but you have not done like the great white God who, you say, loves you so. You are wiser and stronger than we, but your strength and wisdom help us not: they press us down from men to children; they are weights upon the head and shoulders of a babe to keep him under stature. Ill gifts have you brought us, evil have you wrought us"—

"Not to you, Nantauquas!" I cried, stung into speech.

He turned his eyes upon me. "Nantauquas is the war chief of his tribe. Opechancanough is his king, and he lies upon his bed in his lodge and says within himself: 'My war chief, the Panther, the son of Wahunsonacock, who was chief of all the Powhatans, sits now within his wigwam, sharpening flints for his arrows, making his tomahawk bright and keen, thinking of a day three suns hence, when the tribes will shake off forever the hand upon their shoulder,—the hand so heavy and white that strives always to bend them to the earth and keep them there.' Tell me, you Englishman who have led in war, another name for Nantauquas, and ask no more what evil you have done him."

"I will not call you 'traitor,' Nantauquas," I said, after a pause. "There is a difference. You are not the first child of Powhatan who has loved and shielded the white men."

"She was a woman, a child," he answered. "Out of pity she saved your lives, not knowing that it was to the hurt of her people. Then you were few and weak, and could not take your revenge. Now, if you die not, you will drink deep of vengeance,—so deep that your lips may never leave the cup. More ships will come, and more; you will grow ever stronger. There may come a moon when the deep forests and the shining rivers know us, to whom Kiwassa gave them, no more." He paused, with unmoved face, and eyes that seemed to pierce the wall and look out into unfathomable distances. "Go!" he said at last. "If you die not in the woods, if you see again the man whom I called my brother and teacher, tell him. .. tell him nothing! Go!"

"Come with us," urged Diccon gruffly. "We English will make a place for you among us"—and got no further, for I turned upon him with a stern command for silence.

"I ask of you no such thing, Nantauquas," I said. "Come against us, if you will. Nobly warned, fair upon our guard, we will meet you as knightly foe should be met."

He stood for a minute, the quick change that had come into his face at Diccon's blundering words gone, and his features sternly impassive again; then, very slowly, he raised his arm from his side and held out his hand. His eyes met mine in sombre inquiry, half eager, half proudly doubtful.

I went to him at once, and took his hand in mine. No word was spoken. Presently he withdrew his hand from my clasp, and, putting his finger to his lips, whistled low to the Indian girl. She drew aside the hanging mats, and we passed out, Diccon and I, leaving him standing as we had found him, upright against the post, in the red firelight.

Should we ever go through the woods, pass through that gathering storm, reach Jamestown, warn them there of the death that was rushing upon them? Should we ever leave that hated village? Would the morning ever come? When we reached our hut, unseen, and sat down just within the doorway to watch for the dawn, it seemed as though the stars would never pale. Again and again the leaping Indians between us and the fire fed the tall flame; if one figure fell in the wild dancing, another took its place; the yelling never ceased, nor the beating of the drums.

It was an alarum that was sounding, and there were only two to hear; miles away beneath the mute stars English men and women lay asleep, with the hour thundering at their gates, and there was none to cry, "Awake!" When would the dawn come, when should we be gone? I could have cried out in that agony of waiting, with the leagues on leagues to be traveled, and the time so short! If we never reached those sleepers—I saw the dark warriors gathering, tribe on tribe, war party on war party, thick crowding shadows of death, slipping though the silent forest... and the clearings we had made and the houses we had built... the goodly Englishmen, Kent and Thorpe and Yeardley, Maddison, Wynne, Hamor, the men who had striven to win and hold this land so fatal and so fair, West and Rolfe and Jeremy Sparrow... the children about the doorsteps, the women... one woman...

It came to an end, as all things earthly will. The flames of the great bonfire sank lower and lower, and as they sank the gray light faltered into being, grew, and strengthened. At last the dancers were still, the women scattered, the priests with their hideous Okee gone. The wailing of the pipes died away, the drums ceased to beat, and the village lay in the keen wind and the pale light, inert and quiet with the stillness of exhaustion.

The pause and hush did not last. When the ruffled pools amid the marshes were rosy beneath the sunrise, the women brought us food, and the warriors and old men gathered about us. They sat upon mats or billets of wood, and I offered them bread and meat, and told them they must come to Jamestown to taste of the white man's cookery.

Scarcely was the meal over when Opechancanough issued from his lodge, with his picked men behind him, and, coming slowly up to us, took his seat upon the white mat that was spread for him. For a few minutes he sat in a silence that neither we nor his people cared to break. Only the wind sang in the brown branches, and from some forest brake came a stag's hoarse cry. As he sat in the sunshine he glistened all over, like an Ethiop besprent with silver; for his dark limbs and mighty chest had been oiled, and then powdered with antimony. Through his scalp lock was stuck an eagle's feather; across his face, from temple to chin, was a bar of red paint; the eyes above were very bright and watchful, but we upon whom that scrutiny was bent were as little wont as he to let our faces tell our minds.

One of his young men brought a great pipe, carved and painted, stem and bowl; an old man filled it with tobacco, and a warrior lit it and bore it to the Emperor. He put it to his lips and smoked in silence, while the sun climbed higher and higher, and the golden minutes that were more precious than heart's blood went by, at once too slow, too swift.

At last, his part in the solemn mockery played, he held out the pipe to me. "The sky will fall, and the rivers run dry, and the birds cease to sing," he said, "before the smoke of the calumet fades from the land."

I took the symbol of peace, and smoked it as silently and soberly—ay, and as slowly—as he had done before me, then laid it leisurely aside and held out my hand. "My eyes have been holden," I told him, "but now I see plainly the deep graves of the hatchets and the drifting of the peace smoke through the forest. Let Opechancanough come to Jamestown to smoke of the

Englishman's uppowoc, and to receive rich presents,—a red robe like his brother Powhatan's, and a cup from which he shall drink, he and all his people."

He laid his dark fingers in mine for an instant, withdrew them, and, rising to his feet, motioned to three Indians who stood out from the throng of warriors. "These are Captain Percy's guides and friends," he announced. "The sun is high; it is time that he was gone. Here are presents for him and for my brother the Governor." As he spoke, he took from his neck the rope of pearls and from his arm a copper bracelet, and laid both upon my palm.

I thrust the pearls within my doublet, and slipped the bracelet upon my wrist. "Thanks, Opechancanough," I said briefly. "When we meet again I shall not greet you with empty thanks."

By this all the folk of the village had gathered around us; and now the drums beat again, and the maidens raised a wild and plaintive song of farewell. At a sign from the werowance men and women formed a rude procession, and followed us, who were to go upon a journey, to the edge of the village where the marsh began. Only the dark Emperor and the old men stayed behind, sitting and standing in the sunshine, with the peace pipe lying on the grass at their feet, and the wind moving the branches overhead. I looked back and saw them thus, and wondered idly how many minutes they would wait before putting on the black paint. Of Nantauquas we had seen nothing. Either he had gone to the forest, or upon some pretense he kept within his lodge.

We bade farewell to the noisy throng who had brought us upon our way, and went down to the river, where we found a canoe and rowers, crossed the stream, and, bidding the rowers good-by, entered the forest. It was Wednesday morning, and the sun was two hours high. Three suns, Nantauquas had said: on Friday, then, the blow would fall. Three days! Once at Jamestown, it would take three days to warn each lonely scattered settlement, to put the colony into any posture of defense. What of the leagues of danger-haunted forest to be traversed before even a single soul of the three thousand could be warned?

As for the three Indians,—who had their orders to go slowly, who at any suspicious haste or question or anxiety on our part were to kill us whom they deemed unarmed,—when they left their village that morning, they left it forever. There were times when Diccon and I had no need of speech, but knew each other's mind without; so now, though no word had been spoken, we were agreed to set upon and slay our guides the first occasion that offered.

CHAPTER XXXIV
IN WHICH THE RACE IS NOT TO THE SWIFT

THE three Indians of whom we must rid ourselves were approved warriors, fierce as wolves, cunning as foxes, keen-eyed as hawks. They had no reason to doubt us, to dream that we would turn upon them, but from habit they watched us, with tomahawk and knife resting lightly in their belts.

As for us, we walked slowly, smiled freely, and spoke frankly. The sunshine streaming down in the spaces where the trees fell away was not brighter than our mood. Had we not smoked the peace pipe? Were we not on our way home? Diccon, walking behind me, fell into a low-voiced conversation with the savage who strode beside him. It related to the barter for a dozen otterskins of a gun which he had at Jamestown. The savage was to bring the skins to Paspahegh at his earliest convenience, and Diccon would meet him there and give him the gun, provided the pelts were to his liking. As they talked, each, in his mind's eye, saw the other dead before him. The one meant to possess a gun, indeed, but he thought to take it himself from the munition house at Jamestown; the other knew that the otter which died not until this Indian's arrow quivered in its side would live until doomsday. Yet they discussed the matter gravely, hedging themselves about with provisos, and, the bargain clinched, walked on side by side in the silence of a perfect and all-comprehending amity.

The sun rode higher and higher, gilding the misty green of the budding trees, quickening the red maple bloom into fierce scarlet, throwing lances of light down through the pine branches to splinter against the dark earth far below. For an hour it shone; then clouds gathered and shut it from sight. The forest darkened, and the wind arose with a shriek. The young trees cowered before the blast, the strong and vigorous beat their branches together with a groaning sound, the old and worn fell crashing to the earth. Presently the rain rushed down, slant lines of silver tearing through the wood with the sound of the feet of an army; hail followed, a torrent of ice beating and bruising all tender green things to the earth. The wind took the multitudinous sounds,— the cries of frightened birds, the creaking trees, the snap of breaking boughs, the crash of falling giants, the rush of the rain, the drumming of the hail,— enwound them with itself, and made the forest like a great shell held close to the ear.

There was no house to flee to; so long as we could face the hail we staggered on, heads down, buffeting the wind; but at last, the fury of the storm increasing, we were fain to throw ourselves upon the earth, in a little brake, where an overhanging bank somewhat broke the wind. A mighty oak, swaying and groaning above us, might fall and crush us like eggshells; but if we went on, the like fate might meet us in the way. Broken and withered limbs, driven by the wind, went past us like crooked shadows; it grew darker and darker, and the air was deadly cold.

The three Indians pressed their faces against the ground; they dreamed not of harm from us, but Okee was in the merciless hail and the first thunder of the year, now pealing through the wood. Suddenly Diccon raised himself upon his elbow, and looked across at me. Our eyes had no sooner met than his hand was at his bosom. The savage nearest him, feeling the movement, as it were, lifted his head from the earth, of which it was so soon to become a part; but if he saw the knife, he saw it too late. The blade, driven down with all the strength of a desperate man, struck home; when it was drawn from its sheath of flesh, there remained to us but a foe apiece.

In the instant of its descent I had thrown myself upon the Indian nearest me. It was not a time for overniceness. If I could have done so, I would have struck him in the back while he thought no harm; as it was, some subtle instinct warning him, he whirled himself over in time to strike up my hand and to clench with me. He was very strong, and his naked body, wet with rain, slipped like a snake from my hold. Over and over we rolled on the rain-soaked moss and rotted leaves and cold black earth, the hail blinding us, and the wind shrieking like a thousand watching demons. He strove to reach the knife within his belt; I, to prevent him, and to strike deep with the knife I yet held.

At last I did so. Blood gushed over my hand and wrist, the clutch upon my arm relaxed, the head fell back. The dying eyes glared into mine; then the lids shut forever upon that unquenchable hatred. I staggered to my feet and turned, to find that Diccon had given account of the third Indian.

We stood up in the hail and the wind, and looked at the dead men at our feet. Then, without speaking, we went our way through the tossing forest, with the hailstones coming thick against us, and the wind a strong hand to push us back. When we came to a little trickling spring, we knelt and washed our hands.

The hail ceased, but the rain fell and the wind blew throughout the morning. We made what speed we could over the boggy earth against the storm, but we knew that we were measuring miles where we should have measured leagues. There was no breath to waste in words, and thought was a burden quite intolerable; it was enough to stumble on through the partial light, with a mind as gray and blank as the rain-blurred distance.

At noon the clouds broke, and an hour later the sunshine was streaming down from a cloudless heaven, beneath which the forest lay clear before us, naught stirring save shy sylvan creatures to whom it mattered not if red man or white held the land.

Side by side Diccon and I hurried on, not speaking, keeping eye and ear open, proposing with all our will to reach the goal we had set, and to reach it in time, let what might oppose. It was but another forced march; many had we made in our time, through dangers manifold, and had lived to tell the tale.

There was no leisure in which to play the Indian and cover up our footprints as we made them, but when we came to a brook we stepped into the cold, swift-flowing water, and kept it company for a while. The brook flowed between willows, thickly set, already green, and overarching a yard or more of water. Presently it bent sharply, and we turned with it. Ten yards in front of us the growth of willows ceased abruptly, the low, steep banks shelved downwards to a grassy level, and the stream widened into a clear and placid pool, as blue as the sky above. Crouched upon the grass or standing in the shallow water were some fifteen or twenty deer. We had come upon them without noise; the wind blew from them to us, and the willows hid us from their sight. There was no alarm, and we stood a moment watching them before we should throw a stone or branch into their midst and scare them from our path.

Suddenly, as we looked, the leader threw up his head, made a spring, and was off like a dart, across the stream and into the depths of the forest beyond. The herd followed. A moment, and there were only the trodden grass and the troubled waters; no other sign that aught living had passed that way.

"Now what was that for?" muttered Diccon. "I'm thinking we had best not take to the open just yet."

For answer I parted the willows, and forced myself into the covert, pressing as closely as possible against the bank, and motioning him to do the same. He obeyed, and the thick-clustering gold-green twigs swung into place again, shutting us in with the black water and the leafy, crumbling bank. From that green dimness we could look out upon the pool and the grass, with small fear that we ourselves would be seen.

Out of the shadow of the trees into the grassy space stepped an Indian; a second followed, a third, a fourth,—one by one they came from the gloom into the sunlight, until we had counted a score or more. They made no pause, a glance telling them to what were due the trampled grass and the muddied water. As they crossed the stream one stooped and drank from his hand, but they said no word and made no noise. All were painted black; a few had face and chest striped with yellow. Their headdresses were tall and wonderful, their leggings and moccasins fringed with scalp locks; their hatchets glinted in the sunshine, and their quivers were stuck full of arrows. One by one they glided from the stream into the thick woods beyond. We waited until we knew that they were were deep in the forest, then crept from the willows and went our way.

"They were Youghtenunds," I said, in the low tones we used when we spoke at all, "and they went to the southward."

"We may thank our stars that they missed our trail," Diccon answered.

We spoke no more, but, leaving the stream, struck again toward the south. The day wore on, and still we went without pause. Sun and shade and keen wind, long stretches of pine and open glades where we quickened our pace to a run, dense woods, snares of leafless vines, swamp and thicket through which we toiled so slowly that the heart bled at the delay, streams and fallen trees,—on and on we hurried, until the sun sank and the dusk came creeping in upon us.

"We've dined with Duke Humphrey to-day," said Diccon at last; "but if we can keep this pace, and don't meet any more war parties, or fall foul of an Indian village, or have to fight the wolves to-night, we'll dine with the Governor to-morrow. What's that?"

"That" was the report of a musket, and a spent ball had struck me above the knee, bruising the flesh beneath the leather of my boot.

We wheeled, and looked in the direction whence lead come that unwelcome visitor. There was naught to be seen. It was dusk in the distance, and there were thickets too, and fallen logs. Where that ambuscade was planted, if one or twenty Indians lurked in the dusk behind the trees, or lay on the further side of those logs, or crouched within a thicket, no mortal man could tell.

"It was a spent ball," I said. "Our best hope is in our heels."

"There are pines beyond, and smooth going," he answered; "but if ever I thought to run from an Indian!"

Without more ado we started. If we could outstrip that marksman, if we could even hold our distance until night had fallen, all might yet be well. A little longer, and even an Indian must fire at random; moreover, we might reach some stream and manage to break our trail. The ground was smooth before us,—too smooth, and slippery with pine needles; the pines themselves stood in grim brown rows, and we ran between them lightly and easily, husbanding our strength. Now and again one or the other looked behind, but we saw only the pines and the gathering dusk. Hope was strengthening in us, when a second bullet dug into the earth just beyond us.

Diccon swore beneath his breath. "It struck deep," he muttered. "The dark is slow in coming."

A minute later, as I ran with my head over my shoulder, I saw our pursuer, dimly, like a deeper shadow in the shadows far down the arcade behind us. There was but one man,—a tall warrior, strayed aside from his band, perhaps, or bound upon a warpath of his own. The musket that he carried some English fool had sold him for a mess of pottage.

Putting forth all our strength, we ran for our lives, and for the lives of many others. Before us the pine wood sloped down to a deep and wide thicket, and beyond the thicket a line of sycamores promised water. If we could reach the thicket, its close embrace would hide us,—then the darkness and the stream. A third shot, and Diccon staggered slightly.

"For God's sake, not struck, man?" I cried.

"It grazed my arm," he panted. "No harm done. Here's the thicket!"

Into the dense growth we broke, reckless of the blood which the sharp twigs drew from face and hands. The twigs met in a thick roof over our heads; that was all we cared for, and through the network we saw one of the larger stars brighten into being. The thicket was many yards across. When we had gone thirty feet down we crouched and waited for the dark. If our enemy followed us, he must do so at his peril, with only his knife for dependence.

One by one the stars swam into sight, until the square of sky above us was thickly studded. There was no sound, and no living thing could have entered that thicket without noise. For what seemed an eternity, we waited; then we rose and broke our way through the bushes to the sycamores, to find that they indeed shadowed a little sluggish stream.

Down this we waded for some distance before taking to dry earth again. Since entering the thicket we had seen and heard nothing suspicious, and were now fain to conclude that the dark warrior had wearied of the chase, and was gone on his way toward his mates and that larger and surer quarry which two suns would bring. Certain it is that we saw no more of him.

The stream flowing to the south, we went with it, hurrying along its bank, beneath the shadow of great trees, with the stars gleaming down through the branches. It was cold and still, and far in the distance we heard wolves hunting. As for me, I felt no weariness. Every sense was sharpened; my feet were light; the keen air was like wine in the drinking; there was a star low in the south that shone and beckoned. The leagues between my wife and me were few. I saw her standing beneath the star, with a little purple flower in her hand.

Suddenly, a bend in the stream hiding the star, I became aware that Diccon was no longer keeping step with me, but had fallen somewhat to the rear. I turned, and he was leaning heavily, with drooping head, against the trunk of a tree.

"Art so worn as that?" I exclaimed. "Put more heart into thy heels, man!"

He straightened himself and strode on beside me. "I don't know what came over me for a minute," he answered. "The wolves are loud to-night. I hope they'll keep to their side of the water."

A stone's throw farther on, the stream curving to the west, we left it, and found ourselves in a sparsely wooded glade, with a bare and sandy soil beneath our feet, and above, in the western sky, a crescent moon. Again Diccon lagged behind, and presently I heard him groan in the darkness.

I wheeled. "Diccon!" I cried. "What is the matter?"

Before I could reach him he had sunk to his knees. When I put my hand upon his arm and again demanded what ailed him, he tried to laugh, then tried to swear, and ended with another groan. "The ball did graze my arm," he said, "but it went on into my side. I'll just lie here and die, and wish you well at Jamestown. When the red imps come against you there, and you open fire on them, name a bullet for me."

CHAPTER XXXV
IN WHICH I COME TO THE GOVERNOR'S HOUSE

I LAID him down upon the earth, and, cutting away his doublet and the shirt beneath, saw the wound, and knew that there was a journey indeed that he would shortly make. "The world is turning round," he muttered, "and the stars are falling thicker than the hailstones yesterday. Go on, and I will stay behind,—I and the wolves."

I took him in my arms and carried him back to the bank of the stream, for I knew that he would want water until he died. My head was bare, but he had worn his cap from the gaol at Jamestown that night. I filled it with water and gave him to drink; then washed the wound and did what I could to stanch the bleeding. He turned from side to side, and presently his mind began to wander, and he talked of the tobacco in the fields at Weyanoke. Soon he was raving of old things, old camp fires and night-time marches and wild skirmishes, perils by land and by sea; then of dice and wine and women. Once he cried out that Dale had bound him upon the wheel, and that his arms and legs were broken, and the woods rang to his screams. Why, in that wakeful forest, they were unheard, or why, if heard, they went unheeded, God only knows.

The moon went down, and it was very cold. How black were the shadows around us, what foes might steal from that darkness upon us, it was not worth while to consider. I do not know what I thought of on that night, or even that I thought at all. Between my journeys for the water that he called for I sat beside the dying man with my hand upon his breast, for he was quieter so. Now and then I spoke to him, but he answered not.

Hours before we had heard the howling of wolves, and knew that some ravenous pack was abroad. With the setting of the moon the noise had ceased, and I thought that the brutes had pulled down the deer they hunted, or else had gone with their hunger and their dismal voices out of earshot. Suddenly the howling recommenced, at first faint and far away, then nearer and nearer yet. Earlier in the evening the stream had been between us, but now the wolves had crossed and were coming down our side of the water, and were coming fast.

All the ground was strewn with dead wood, and near by was a growth of low and brittle bushes. I gathered the withered branches, and broke fagots from the bushes; then into the press of dark and stealthy forms I threw a great crooked stick, shouting as I did so, and threatening with my arms. They turned and fled, but presently they were back again. Again I frightened them away, and again they returned. I had flint and steel and tinder box; when I had scared them from us a third time, and they had gone only a little way, I lit a splinter of pine, and with it fired my heap of wood; then dragged Diccon into the light and sat down beside him, with no longer any fear of the wolves, but with absolute confidence in the quick appearance of less cowardly foes. There was wood enough and to spare; when the fire sank low and the hungry eyes gleamed nearer, I fed it again, and the flame leaped up and mocked the eyes.

No human enemy came upon us. The fire blazed and roared, and the man who lay in its rosy glare raved on, crying out now and then at the top of his voice; but on that night of all nights, of all years, light and voice drew no savage band to put out the one and silence the other forever.

Hours passed, and as it drew toward midnight Diccon sank into a stupor. I knew that the end was not far away. The wolves were gone at last, and my fire was dying down. He needed my touch upon his breast no longer, and I went to the stream and bathed my hands and forehead, and then threw myself face downward upon the bank. In a little while the desolate murmur of the water became intolerable, and I rose and went back to the fire, and to the man whom, as God lives, I loved as a brother.

He was conscious. Pale and cold and nigh gone as he was, there came a light to his eyes and a smile to his lips when I knelt beside him. "You did not go?" he breathed.

"No," I answered, "I did not go."

For a few minutes he lay with closed eyes; when he again opened them upon my face, there were in their depths a question and an appeal. I bent over him, and asked him what he would have.

"You know," he whispered. "If you can... I would not go without it."

"Is it that?" I asked. "I forgave you long ago."

"I meant to kill you. I was mad because you struck me before the lady, and because I had betrayed my trust. An you had not caught my hand, I should be your murderer." He spoke with long intervals between the words, and the death dew was on his forehead.

"Remember it not, Diccon," I entreated. "I too was to blame. And I see not that night for other nights,—for other nights and days, Diccon."

He smiled, but there was still in his face a shadowy eagerness. "You said you would never strike me again," he went on, "and that I was man of yours no more forever—and you gave me my freedom in the paper which I tore." He spoke in gasps, with his eyes upon mine. "I'll be gone in a few minutes now.

If I might go as your man still, and could tell the Lord Jesus Christ that my master on earth forgave, and took back, it would be a hand in the dark. I have spent my life in gathering darkness for myself at the last."

I bent lower over him, and took his hand in mine. "Diccon, my man," I said.

A brightness came into his face, and he faintly pressed my hand. I slipped my arm beneath him and raised him a little higher to meet his death. He was smiling now, and his mind was not quite clear. "Do you mind, sir," he asked, "how green and strong and sweet smelled the pines that May day, when we found Virginia, so many years ago?"

"Ay, Diccon," I answered. "Before we saw the land, the fragrance told us we were near it."

"I smell it now," he went on, "and the bloom of the grape, and the May-time flowers. And can you not hear, sir, the whistling and the laughter and the sound of the falling trees, that merry time when Smith made axemen of all our fine gentlemen?"

"Ay, Diccon," I said. "And the sound of the water that was dashed down the sleeve of any that were caught in an oath."

He laughed like a little child. "It is well that I was n't a gentleman, and had not those trees to fell, or I should have been as wet as any merman.... And Pocahontas, the little maid... and how blue the sky was, and how glad we were what time the Patience and Deliverance came in!"

His voice failed, and for a minute I thought he was gone; but he had been a strong man, and life slipped not easily from him. When his eyes opened again he knew me not, but thought he was in some tavern, and struck with his hand upon the ground as upon a table, and called for the drawer.

Around him were only the stillness and the shadows of the night, but to his vision men sat and drank with him, diced and swore and told wild tales of this or that. For a time he talked loudly and at random of the vile quality of the drink, and his viler luck at the dice; then he began to tell a story. As he told it, his senses seemed to steady, and he spoke with coherence and like a shadow of himself.

"And you call that a great thing, William Host?" he demanded. "I can tell a true tale worth two such lies, my masters. (Robin tapster, more ale! And move less like a slug, or my tankard and your ear will cry, 'Well met!') It was between Ypres and Courtrai, friends, and it's nigh fifteen years ago. There were fields in which nothing was sowed because they were ploughed with the hoofs of war horses, and ditches in which dead men were thrown, and dismal marshes, and roads that were no roads at all, but only sloughs. And there was a great stone house, old and ruinous, with tall poplars shivering in the rain and mist.

Into this house there threw themselves a band of Dutch and English, and hard on their heels came two hundred Spaniards. All day they besieged that house,—smoke and flame and thunder and shouting and the crash of masonry,—and when eventide was come we, the Dutch and the English, thought that Death was not an hour behind."

He paused, and made a gesture of raising a tankard to his lips. His eyes were bright, his voice was firm. The memory of that old day and its mortal strife had wrought upon him like wine.

"There was one amongst us," he said, "he was our captain, and it's of him I am going to tell the story. Robin tapster, bring me no more ale, but good mulled wine! It's cold and getting dark, and I have to drink to a brave man besides"—

With the old bold laugh in his eyes, he raised himself, for the moment as strong as I that held him. "Drink to that Englishman, all of ye!" he cried, "and not in filthy ale, but in good, gentlemanly sack! I'll pay the score. Here's to him, brave hearts! Here's to my master!"

With his hand at his mouth, and his story untold, he fell back. I held him in my arms until the brief struggle was over, and then laid his body down upon the earth.

It might have been one of the clock. For a little while I sat beside him, with my head bowed in my hands. Then I straightened his limbs and crossed his hands upon his breast, and kissed him upon the brow, and left him lying dead in the forest.

It was hard going through the blackness of the night-time woods. Once I was nigh sucked under in a great swamp, and once I stumbled into some hole or pit in the earth, and for a time thought that I had broken my leg. The night was very dark, and sometimes when I could not see the stars, I lost my way, and went to the right or the left, or even back upon my track. Though I heard the wolves, they did not come nigh me. Just before daybreak, I crouched behind a log, and watched a party of savages file past like shadows of the night.

At last the dawn came, and I could press on more rapidly. For two days and two nights I had not slept; for a day and a night I had not tasted food. As the sun climbed the heavens, a thousand black spots, like summer gnats, danced between his face and my weary eyes. The forest laid stumbling-blocks before me, and drove me back, and made me wind in and out when I would have had my path straighter than an arrow. When the ground allowed I ran; when I must break my way, panting, through undergrowth so dense and stubborn that it seemed some enchanted thicket, where each twig snapped but to be on the instant stiff in place again, I broke it with what patience I might; when

I must turn aside for this or that obstacle I made the detour, though my heart cried out at the necessity. Once I saw reason to believe that two or more Indians were upon my trail, and lost time in outwitting them; and once I must go a mile out of my way to avoid an Indian village.

As the day wore on, I began to go as in a dream. It had come to seem the gigantic wood of some fantastic tale through which I was traveling. The fallen trees ranged themselves into an abatis hard to surmount; the thickets withstood one like iron; the streamlets were like rivers, the marshes leagues wide, the treetops miles away. Little things, twisted roots, trailing vines, dead and rotten wood, made me stumble. A wind was blowing that had blown just so since time began, and the forest was filled with the sound of the sea.

Afternoon came, and the shadows began to lengthen. They were lines of black paint spilt in a thousand places, and stealing swiftly and surely across the brightness of the land. Torn and bleeding and breathless, I hastened on; for it was drawing toward night, and I should have been at Jamestown hours before. My head pained me, and as I ran I saw men and women stealing in and out among the trees before me: Pocahontas with her wistful eyes and braided hair and finger on her lips; Nantauquas; Dale, the knight-marshal, and Argall with his fierce, unscrupulous face; my cousin George Percy, and my mother with her stately figure, her embroidery in her hands. I knew that they were but phantoms of my brain, but their presence confused and troubled me.

The shadows ran together, and the sunshine died out of the forest. Stumbling on, I saw through the thinning trees a long gleam of red, and thought it was blood, but presently knew that it was the river, crimson from the sunset. A minute more and I stood upon the shore of the mighty stream, between the two brightnesses of flood and heavens. There was a silver crescent in the sky with one white star above it, and fair in sight, down the James, with lights springing up through the twilight, was the town,—the English town that we had built and named for our King, and had held in the teeth of Spain, in the teeth of the wilderness and its terrors. It was not a mile away; a little longer,— a little longer and I could rest, with my tidings told.

The dusk had quite fallen when I reached the neck of land. The hut to which I had been enticed that night stood dark and ghastly, with its door swinging in the wind. I ran past it and across the neck, and, arriving at the palisade, beat upon the gate with my hands, and called to the warder to open. When I had told him my name and tidings, he did so, with shaking knees and starting eyes. Cautioning him to raise no alarm in the town, I hurried by him into the street, and down it toward the house that was set aside for the Governor of Virginia. I should find there now, not Yeardley, but Sir Francis Wyatt.

The torches were lighted, and the folk were indoors, for the night was cold. One or two figures that I met or passed would have accosted me, not knowing who I was, but I brushed by them, and hastened on. Only when I passed the guest house I looked up, and saw that mine host's chief rooms were yet in use.

The Governor's door was open, and in the hall servingmen were moving to and fro. When I came in upon them, they cried out as it had been a ghost, and one fellow let a silver dish that he carried fall clattering to the floor. They shook and stood back, as I passed them without a word, and went on to the Governor's great room. The door was ajar, and I pushed it open and stood for a minute upon the threshold, unobserved by the occupants of the room.

After the darkness outside the lights dazzled me; the room, too, seemed crowded with men, though when I counted them there were not so many, after all. Supper had been put upon the table, but they were not eating. Before the fire, his head thoughtfully bent, and his fingers tapping upon the arm of his chair, sat the Governor; over against him, and as serious of aspect, was the Treasurer. West stood by the mantel, tugging at his long mustaches and softly swearing. Clayborne was in the room, Piersey the Cape Merchant, and one or two besides. And Rolfe was there, walking up and down with hasty steps, and a flushed and haggard face. His suit of buff was torn and stained, and his great-boots were spattered with mud.

The Governor let his fingers rest upon the arm of his chair, and raised his head.

"He is dead, Master Rolfe," he said. "There can be no other conclusion,—a brave man lost to you and to the colony. We mourn with you, sir."

"We too have searched, Jack," put in West. "We have not been idle, though well-nigh all men believe that the Indians, who we know had a grudge against him, murdered him and his man that night, then threw their bodies into the river, and themselves made off out of our reach. But we hoped against hope that when your party returned he would be in your midst."

"As for this latest loss," continued the Governor, "within an hour of its discovery this morning search parties were out; yea, if I had allowed it, the whole town would have betaken itself to the woods. The searchers have not returned, and we are gravely anxious. Yet we are not utterly cast down. This trail can hardly be missed, and the Indians are friendly. There were a number in town overnight, and they went with the searchers, volunteering to act as their guides. We cannot but think that of this load, our hearts will soon be eased."

"God grant it!" groaned Rolfe. "I will drink but a cup of wine, sir, and then will be gone upon this new quest."

There was a movement in the room. "You are worn and spent with your fruitless travel, sir," said the Governor kindly. "I give you my word that all that can be done is doing. Wait at least for the morning, and the good news it may bring."

The other shook his head. "I will go now. I could not look my friend in the face else—God in heaven!"

The Governor sprang to his feet; through the Treasurer's lips came a long, sighing breath; West's dark face was ashen. I came forward to the table, and leaned my weight upon it; for all the waves of the sea were roaring in my ears, and the lights were going up and down.

"Are you man or spirit?" cried Rolfe through white lips. "Are you Ralph Percy?"

"Yes, I am Percy," I said. "I have not well understood what quest you would go upon, Rolfe, but you cannot go to-night. And those parties that your Honor talked of, that have gone with Indians to guide them to look for some lost person,—I think that you will never see them again."

With an effort I drew myself erect, and standing so told my tidings, quietly and with circumstance, so as to leave no room for doubt as to their verity, or as to the sanity of him who brought them. They listened, as the warder had listened, with shaking limbs and gasping breath; for this was the fall and wiping out of a people of which I brought warning.

When all was told, and they stood there before me, white and shaken, seeking in their minds the thing to say or do first, I thought to ask a question myself; but before my tongue could frame it, the roaring of the sea became so loud that I could hear naught else, and the lights all ran together into a wheel of fire. Then in a moment all sounds ceased, and to the lights succeeded the blackness of outer darkness.

CHAPTER XXXVI
IN WHICH I HEAR ILL NEWS

WHEN I awoke from the sleep or stupor into which I must have passed from that swoon, it was to find myself lying upon a bed in a room flooded with sunshine. I was alone. For a moment I lay still, staring at the blue sky without the window, and wondering where I was and how I came there. A drum beat, a dog barked, and a man's quick voice gave a command. The sounds stung me into remembrance, and I was at the window while the voice was yet speaking.

It was West in the street below, pointing with his sword now to the fort, now to the palisade, and giving directions to the armed men about him. There were many people in the street. Women hurried by to the fort with white, scared faces, their arms filled with household gear; children ran beside them, sturdily bearing their share of the goods, but pressing close to their elders' skirts; men went to and fro, the most grimly silent, but a few talking loudly. Not all of the faces in the crowd belonged to the town: there were Kingsmell and his wife from the main, and John Ellison from Archer's Hope, and the Italians Vincencio and Bernardo from the Glass House. The nearer plantations, then, had been warned, and their people had come for refuge to the city. A negro passed, but on that morning, alone of many days, no Indian aired his paint and feathers in the white man's village.

I could not see the palisade across the neck, but I knew that it was there that the fight—if fight there were—would be made. Should the Indians take the palisade, there would yet be the houses of the town, and, last of all, the fort in which to make a stand. I believed not that they would take it. Long since we had found out their method of warfare. They used ambuscade, surprise, and massacre; when withstood in force and with determination they withdrew to their stronghold the forest, there to bide their time until, in the blackness of some night, they could again swoop down upon a sleeping foe.

The drum beat again, and a messenger from the palisade came down the street at a run. "They're in the woods over against us, thicker than ants!" he cried to West as he passed. "A boat has just drifted ashore yonder, with two men in it, dead and scalped!"

I turned to leave the room, and ran against Master Pory coming in on tiptoe, with a red and solemn face. He started when he saw me.

"The roll of the drum brought you to your feet, then!" he cried. "You've lain like the dead all night. I came but to see if you were breathing."

"When I have eaten, I shall be myself again," I said. "There's no attack as yet?"

"No," he answered. "They must know that we are prepared. But they have kindled fires along the river bank, and we can hear them yelling. Whether they'll be mad enough to come against us remains to be seen."

"The nearest settlements have been warned?"

"Ay. The Governor offered a thousand pounds of tobacco and the perpetual esteem of the Company to the man or men who would carry the news. Six volunteered, and went off in boats, three up river, three down. How many they reached, or if they still have their scalps, we know not. And awhile ago, just before daybreak, comes with frantic haste Richard Pace, who had rowed up from Pace's Pains to tell the news which you had already brought. Chanco the Christian had betrayed the plot to him, and he managed to give warning at Powel's and one or two other places as he came up the river."

He broke off, but when I would have spoken interrupted me with: "And so you were on the Pamunkey all this while! Then the Paspaheghs fooled us with the simple truth, for they swore so stoutly that their absent chief men were but gone on a hunt toward the Pamunkey that we had no choice but to believe them gone in quite another direction. And one and all of every tribe we questioned swore that Opechancanough was at Orapax. So Master Rolfe puts off up river to find, if not you, then the Emperor, and make him give up your murderers; and the Governor sends a party along the bay, and West another up the Chickahominy. And there you were, all the time, mewed up in the village above the marshes! And Nantauquas, after saving our lives like one of us, is turned Indian again! And your man is killed! Alackaday! there's naught but trouble in the world. 'As the sparks fly upwards,' you know. But a brave man draws his breath and sets his teeth."

In his manner, his rapid talk, his uneasy glances toward the door, I found something forced and strange. "I thought Rolfe was behind me," he said, "but he must have been delayed. There are meat and drink set out in the great room, where the Governor and those of the Council who are safe here with us are advising together. Let's descend; you've not eaten, and the good sack will give you strength. Wilt come?"

"Ay," I answered, "but tell me the news as we go. I have been gone ten days,—faith, it seems ten years! There have no ships sailed, Master Pory? The George is still here?" I looked him full in the eye, for a sudden guess at a possible reason for his confusion had stabbed me like a knife.

"Ay," he said, with a readiness that could scarce be feigned. "She was to have sailed this week, it is true, the Governor fearing to keep her longer. But the Esperance, coming in yesterday, brought news which removed his Honor's scruples. Now she'll wait to see out this hand at the cards, and to take home the names of those who are left alive in Virginia. If the red varlets do swarm in upon us, there are her twelve-pounders; they and the fort guns"—

I let him talk on. The George had not sailed. I saw again a firelit hut, and a man and a panther who went down together. Those claws had dug deep; the man across whose face they had torn their way would keep his room in the guest house at Jamestown until his wounds were somewhat healed. The George would wait for him, would scarcely dare to sail without him, and I should find the lady whom she was to carry away to England in Virginia still. It was this that I had built upon, the grain of comfort, the passionate hope, the sustaining cordial, of those year-long days in the village above the Pamunkey.

My heart was sore because of Diccon; but I could speak of that grief to her, and she would grieve with me. There were awe and dread and stern sorrow in the knowledge that even now in the bright spring morning blood from a hundred homes might be flowing to meet the shining, careless river; but it was the springtime, and she was waiting for me. I strode on toward the stairway so fast that when I asked a question Master Pory, at my side, was too out of breath to answer it. Halfway down the stairs I asked it again, and again received no answer save a "Zooks! you go too fast for my years and having in flesh! Go more slowly, Ralph Percy; there's time enough, there's time enough!"

There was a tone in his voice that I liked not, for it savored of pity. I looked at him with knitted brows; but we were now in the hall, and through the open door of the great room I caught a glimpse of a woman's skirt. There were men in the hall, servants and messengers, who made way for us, staring at me as they did so, and whispering. I knew that my clothing was torn and muddied and stained with blood; as we paused at the door there came to me in a flash that day in the courting meadow when I had tried with my dagger to scrape the dried mud from my boots. I laughed at myself for caring now, and for thinking that she would care that I was not dressed for a lady's bower. The next moment we were in the great room.

She was not there. The silken skirt that I had seen, and—there being but one woman in all the world for me—had taken for hers, belonged to Lady Wyatt, who, pale and terrified, was sitting with clasped hands, mutely following with her eyes her husband as he walked to and fro. West had come in from the street and was making some report. Around the table were gathered two or three of the Council; Master Sandys stood at a window, Rolfe beside Lady Wyatt's chair. The room was filled with sunshine, and a caged bird was singing, singing. It made the only sound there when they saw that I stood amongst them.

When I had made my bow to Lady Wyatt and to the Governor, and had clasped hands with Rolfe, I began to find in the silence, as I had found in Master Pory's loquaciousness, something strange. They looked at me uneasily, and I caught a swift glance from the Treasurer to Master Pory, and an answering shake of the latter's head. Rolfe was very white and his lips were set; West was pulling at his mustaches and staring at the floor.

"With all our hearts we welcome you back to life and to the service of Virginia, Captain Percy," said the Governor, when the silence had become awkward.

A murmur of assent went round the room.

I bowed. "I thank you, sir, and these gentlemen very heartily. You have but to command me now. I find that I have to-day the best will in the world toward fighting. I trust that your Honor does not deem it necessary to send me back to gaol?"

"Virginia has no gaol for Captain Percy," he answered gravely. "She has only grateful thanks and fullest sympathy."

I glanced at him keenly. "Then I hold myself at your command, sir, when I shall have seen and spoken with my wife."

He looked at the floor, and they one and all held their peace.

"Madam," I said to Lady Wyatt, "I have been watching your ladyship's face. Will you tell me why it is so very full of pity, and why there are tears in your eyes?"

She shrank back in her chair with a little cry, and Rolfe stepped toward me, then turned sharply aside. "I cannot!" he cried, "I that know"—

I drew myself up to meet the blow, whatever it might be. "I demand of you my wife, Sir Francis Wyatt," I said. "If there is ill news to be told, be so good as to tell it quickly. If she is sick, or hath been sent away to England"—

The Governor made as if to speak, then turned and flung out his hands to his wife. "'T is woman's work, Margaret!" he cried. "Tell him!"

More merciful than the men, she came to me at once, the tears running down her cheeks, and laid one trembling hand upon my arm. "She was a brave lady, Captain Percy," she said. "Bear it as she would have had you bear it."

"I am bearing it, madam," I answered at length. "'She was a brave lady.' May it please your ladyship to go on?"

"I will tell you all, Captain Percy; I will tell you everything.... She never believed you dead, and she begged upon her knees that we would allow her to go in search of you with Master Rolfe. That could not be; my husband, in duty to the Company, could not let her have her will. Master Rolfe went, and she sat in the window, yonder, day after day, watching for his return. When other parties went out, she besought the men, as they had wives whom they loved, to search as though those loved ones were in captivity and danger; when they grew weary and fainthearted, to think of her face waiting in the window.... Day after day she sat there watching for them to come back; when they were come, then she watched the river for Master Rolfe's boats. Then came word down the river that he had found no trace of you whom he sought, that he was on his way back to Jamestown, that he too believed you dead.... We put a watch upon her after that, for we feared we knew not what, there was such a light and purpose in her eyes. But two nights ago, in the middle of the night, the woman who stayed in her chamber fell asleep. When she awoke before the dawn, it was to find her gone."

"To find her gone?" I said dully. "To find her dead?"

She locked her hands together and the tears came faster. "Oh, Captain Percy, it had been better so!—it had been better so! Then would she have lain to greet you, calm and white, unmarred and beautiful, with the spring flowers upon her.... She believed not that you were dead; she was distraught with grief and watching; she thought that love might find what friendship missed; she went to the forest to seek you. They that were sent to find and bring her back have never returned"—

"Into the forest!" I cried. "Jocelyn, Jocelyn, Jocelyn, come back!"

Some one pushed me into a chair, and I felt the warmth of wine within my lips. In the moment that the world steadied I rose and went toward the door to find my way barred by Rolfe.

"Not you, too, Ralph!" he cried. "I will not let you go. Look for yourself!"

He drew me to the window, Master Sandys gravely making place for us. From the window was visible the neck of land and the forest beyond, and from the forest, up and down the river as far as the eye could reach, rose here and there thin columns of smoke. Suddenly, as we stared, three or four white smoke puffs, like giant flowers, started out of the shadowy woods across the neck. Following the crack of the muskets—fired out of pure bravado by their Indian owners—came the yelling of the savages. The sound was prolonged and deep, as though issuing from many throats.

I looked and listened, and knew that I could not go,—not now.

"She was not alone, Ralph," said Rolfe, with his arm about me. "On the morning that she was missed, they found not Jeremy Sparrow either. They tracked them both to the forest by the footprints upon the sand, though once in the wood the trail was lost. The minister must have been watching, must have seen her leave the house, and must have followed her. How she, and he after her, passed through the gates, none know. So careless and confident had we grown—God forgive us!—that they may have been left open all that night. But he was with her, Ralph; she had not to face it alone"—His voice broke.

For myself, I was glad that the minister had been there, though I knew that for him also I should grieve after a while.

At the firing and the shouting West had rushed from the room, followed by his fellow Councilors, and now the Governor clapped on his headpiece and called to his men to bring his back-and-breast. His wife hung around his neck, and he bade her good-by with great tenderness. I looked dully on at that parting. I too was going to battle. Once I had tasted such a farewell, the pain, the passion, the sweetness, but never again,—never again.

He went, and the Treasurer, after a few words of comfort to Lady Wyatt, was gone also. Both were merciful, and spoke not to me, but only bowed and turned aside, requiring no answering word or motion of mine. When they were away, and there was no sound in the room save the caged bird's singing and Lady Wyatt's low sobs, I begged Rolfe to leave me, telling him that he was needed, as indeed he was, and that I would stay in the window for a while, and then would join him at the palisade. He was loath to go; but he too had loved and lost, and knew that there is nothing to be said, and that it is best to be alone. He went, and only Lady Wyatt and I kept the quiet room with the singing bird and the sunshine on the floor.

I leaned against the window and looked out into the street,—which was not crowded now, for the men were all at their several posts,—and at the budding trees, and at the smoke of many fires going up from the forest to the sky, from a world of hate and pain and woe to the heaven where she dwelt, and then I turned and went to the table, where had been set bread and meat and wine.

At the sound of my footstep Lady Wyatt uncovered her face. "Is there aught that I can do for you, sir?" she asked timidly.

"I have not broken my fast for many hours, madam," I answered. "I would eat and drink, that I may not be found wanting in strength. There is a thing that I have yet to do."

Rising from her chair, she brushed away her tears, and coming to the table with a little housewifely eagerness would not let me wait upon myself, but carved and poured for me, and then sat down opposite me and covered her eyes with her hand.

"I think that the Governor is quite safe, madam," I said. "I do not believe that the Indians will take the palisade. It may even be that, knowing we are prepared, they will not attack at all. Indeed, I think that you may be easy about him."

She thanked me with a smile. "It is all so strange and dreadful to me, sir," she said. "At my home, in England, it was like a Sunday morning all the year round,—all stillness and peace; no terror, no alarm. I fear that I am not yet a good Virginian."

When I had eaten, and had drunk the wine she gave me, I rose, and asked her if I might not see her safe within the fort before I joined her husband at the palisade. She shook her head, and told me that there were with her faithful servants, and that if the savages broke in upon the town she would have warning in time to flee, the fort being so close at hand. When I thereupon begged her leave to depart, she first curtsied to me, and then, again with tears, came to me and took my hand in hers. "I know that there is naught that I can say.... Your wife loved you, sir, with all her heart." She drew something from the bosom of her gown. "Would you like this? It is a knot of ribbon that she wore. They found it caught in a bush at the edge of the forest."

I took the ribbon from her and put it to my lips, then unknotted it and tied it around my arm; and then, wearing my wife's colors, I went softly out into the street, and turned my face toward the guest house and the man whom I meant to kill.

CHAPTER XXXVII
IN WHICH MY LORD AND I PART COMPANY

THE door of the guest house stood wide, and within the lower room were neither men that drank nor men that gave to drink. Host and drawers and chance guests alike had left pipe and tankard for sword and musket, and were gone to fort or palisade or river bank.

I crossed the empty room and went up the creaking stairway. No one met me or withstood me; only a pigeon perched upon the sill of a sunny window whirred off into the blue. I glanced out of the window as I passed it, and saw the silver river and the George and the Esperance, with the gunners at the guns watching for Indian canoes, and saw smoke rising from the forest on the southern shore. There had been three houses there,—John West's and Minifie's and Crashaw's. I wondered if mine were burning, too, at Weyanoke, and cared not if 't was so.

The door of the upper room was shut. When I raised the latch and pushed against it, it gave at the top and middle, but there was some pressure from within at the bottom. I pushed again, more strongly, and the door slowly opened, moving away whatever thing had lain before it. Another moment, and I was in the room, and had closed and barred the door behind me.

The weight that had opposed me was the body of the Italian, lying face downwards, upon the floor. I stooped and turned it over, and saw that the venomous spirit had flown. The face was purple and distorted; the lips were drawn back from the teeth in a dreadful smile. There was in the room a faint, peculiar, not unpleasant odor. It did not seem strange to me to find that serpent, which had coiled in my path, dead and harmless for evermore. Death had been busy of late; if he struck down the flower, why should he spare the thing that I pushed out of my way with my foot?

Ten feet from the door stood a great screen, hiding from view all that might be beyond. It was very quiet in the room, with the sunshine coming through the window, and a breeze that smelt of the sea. I had not cared to walk lightly or to close the door softly, and yet no voice had challenged my entrance. For a minute I feared to find the dead physician the room's only occupant; then I passed the screen and came upon my enemy.

He was sitting beside a table, with his arms outstretched and his head bowed upon them. My footfall did not rouse him; he sat there in the sunshine as still as the figure that lay before the threshold. I thought with a dull fury that maybe he was dead already, and I walked hastily and heavily across the floor to the table. He was a living man, for with the fingers of one hand he was slowly striking against a sheet of paper that lay beneath them. He knew not that I stood above him; he was listening to other footsteps.

The paper was a letter, unfolded and written over with great black characters. The few lines above those moving fingers stared me in the face. They ran thus: "I told you that you had as well cut your throat as go upon that mad Virginia voyage. Now all's gone,—wealth, honors, favor. Buckingham is the sun in heaven, and cold are the shadows in which we walk who hailed another luminary. There's a warrant out for the Black Death; look to it that one meets not you too, when you come at last. But come, in the name of all the fiends, and play your last card. There's your cursed beauty still. Come, and let the King behold your face once more"—The rest was hidden.

I put out my hand and touched him upon the shoulder, and he raised his head and stared at me as at one come from the grave.

Over one side of his face, from temple to chin, was drawn and fastened a black cloth; the unharmed cheek was bloodless and shrunken, the lip twisted. Only the eyes, dark, sinister, and splendid, were as they had been. "I dig not my graves deep enough," he said. "Is she behind you there in the shadow?"

Flung across a chair was a cloak of scarlet cloth. I took it and spread it out upon the floor, then unsheathed a dagger which I had taken from the rack of weapons in the Governor's hall. "Loosen thy poniard, thou murderer," I cried, "and come stand with me upon the cloak."

"Art quick or dead?" he answered. "I will not fight the dead." He had not moved in his seat, and there was a lethargy and a dullness in his voice and eyes. "There is time enough," he said. "I too will soon be of thy world, thou haggard, bloody shape. Wait until I come, and I will fight thee, shadow to shadow."

"I am not dead," I said, "but there is one that is. Stand up, villain and murderer, or I will kill you sitting there, with her blood upon your hands!"

He rose at that, and drew his dagger from the sheath. I laid aside my doublet, and he followed my example, but his hands moved listlessly and his fingers bungled at the fastenings. I waited for him in some wonder, it not being like him to come tardily to such pastime.

He came at length, slowly and with an uncertain step, and we stood together on the scarlet cloak. I raised my left arm and he raised his, and we locked hands. There was no strength in his clasp; his hand lay within mine cold and languid. "Art ready?" I demanded.

"Yea," he answered in a strange voice, "but I would that she did not stand there with her head upon your breast.... I too loved thee, Jocelyn,—Jocelyn lying dead in the forest!"

I struck at him with the dagger in my right hand, and wounded him, but not deeply, in the side. He gave blow for blow, but his poniard scarce drew blood, so nerveless was the arm that would have driven it home. I struck again, and he stabbed weakly at the air, then let his arm drop to his side, as though the light and jeweled blade had weighed it down.

Loosening the clasp of our left hands, I fell back until the narrow scarlet field was between us. "Hast no more strength than that?" I cried. "I cannot murder you!"

He stood looking past me as into a great distance. He was bleeding, but I had as yet been able to strike no mortal blow. "It is as you choose," he said. "I am as one bound before you. I am sick unto death."

Turning, he went back, swaying as he walked, to his chair, and sinking into it sat there a minute with half-closed eyes; then raised his head and looked at me, with a shadow of the old arrogance, pride, and disdain upon his scarred face. "Not yet, captain?" he demanded. "To the heart, man! So I would strike an you sat here and I stood there."

"I know you would," I said, and going to the window I flung the dagger down into the empty street; then stood and watched the smoke across the river, and thought it strange that the sun shone and the birds sang.

When I turned to the room again, he still sat there in the great chair, a tragic, splendid figure, with his ruined face and the sullen woe of his eyes. "I had sworn to kill you," I said. "It is not just that you should live."

He gazed at me with something like a smile upon his bloodless lips. "Fret not thyself, Ralph Percy," he said. "Within a week I shall be gone. Did you see my servant, my Italian doctor, lying dead upon the floor, there beyond the screen? He had poisons, had Nicolo whom men called the Black Death,— poisons swift and strong, or subtle and slow. Day and night, the earth and sunshine have become hateful to me. I will go to the fires of hell, and see if they can make me forget,—can make me forget the face of a woman." He was speaking half to me, half to himself. "Her eyes are dark and large," he said, "and there are shadows beneath them, and the mark of tears. She stands there day and night with her eyes upon me. Her lips are parted, but she never speaks. There was a way that she had with her hands, holding them one within the other, thus"—

I stopped him with a cry for silence, and I leaned trembling against the table. "Thou wretch!" I cried. "Thou art her murderer!"

He raised his head and looked beyond me with that strange, faint smile. "I know," he replied, with the dignity which was his at times. "You may play the headsman, if you choose. I dispute not your right. But it is scarce worth while. I have taken poison."

The sunshine came into the room, and the wind from the river, and the trumpet notes of swans flying to the north. "The George is ready for sailing," he said at last. "To-morrow or the next day she will be going home with the tidings of this massacre. I shall go with her, and within a week they will bury me at sea. There is a stealthy, slow, and secret poison.... I would not die in a land where I have lost every throw of the dice, and I would not die in England for Buckingham to come and look upon my face, and so I took that poison. For the man upon the floor, there,—prison and death awaited him at home. He chose to flee at once."

He ceased to speak, and sat with his head bowed upon his breast. "If you are content that it should be as it is," he said at length, "perhaps you will leave me? I am not good company to-day."

His hand was busy again with the letter upon the table, and his gaze was fixed beyond me. "I have lost," he muttered. "How I came to play my cards so badly I do not know. The stake was heavy,—I have not wherewithal to play again."

His head sank upon his outstretched arm. As for me, I stood a minute with set lips and clenched hands, and then I turned and went out of the room and down the stair and out into the street. In the dust beneath the window lay my dagger. I picked it up, sheathed it, and went my way.

The street was very quiet. All windows and doors were closed and barred; not a soul was there to trouble me with look or speech. The yelling from the forest had ceased; only the keen wind blew, and brought from the Esperance upon the river a sound of singing. The sea was the home of the men upon her decks, and their hearts dwelt not in this port; they could sing while the smoke went up from our homes and the dead lay across the thresholds.

I went on through the sunshine and the stillness to the minister's house. The trees in the garden were bare, the flowers dead. The door was not barred. I entered the house and went into the great room and flung the heavy shutters wide, then stood and looked about me. Naught was changed; it was as we had left it that wild November night. Even the mirror which, one other night, had shown me Diccon still hung upon the wall. Master Bucke had been seldom at home, perhaps, or was feeble and careless of altering matters. All was as though we had been but an hour gone, save that no fire burned upon the hearth.

I went to the table, and the books upon it were Jeremy Sparrow's: the minister's house, then, had been his home once more. Beside the books lay a packet, tied with silk, sealed, and addressed to me. Perhaps the Governor had given it, the day before, into Master Bucke's care,—I do not know; at any rate, there it lay. I looked at the "By the Esperance" upon the cover, and wondered dully who at home would care to write to me; then broke the seal and untied the silk. Within the cover there was a letter with the superscription, "To a Gentleman who has served me well."

I read the letter through to the signature, which was that of his Grace of Buckingham, and then I laughed, who had never thought to laugh again, and threw the paper down. It mattered naught to me now that George Villiers should be grateful, or that James Stewart could deny a favorite nothing. "The King graciously sanctions the marriage of his sometime ward, the Lady Jocelyn Leigh, with Captain Ralph Percy; invites them home"—

She was gone home, and I her husband, I who loved her, was left behind. How many years of pilgrimage... how long, how long, O Lord?

The minister's great armchair was drawn before the cold and blackened hearth. How often she had sat there within its dark clasp, the firelight on her dress, her hands, her face! She had been fair to look upon; the pride, the daring, the willfulness, were but the thorns about the rose; behind those defenses was the flower, pure and lovely, with a heart of gold. I flung myself down beside the chair, and, putting my arms across it, hid my face upon them, and could weep at last.

That passion spent itself, and I lay with my face against the wood and well-nigh slept. The battle was done; the field was lost; the storm and stress of life had sunk into this dull calm, as still as peace, as hopeless as the charred log and white ash upon the hearth, cold, never to be quickened again.

Time passed, and at length I raised my head, roused suddenly to the consciousness that for a while there had been no stillness. The air was full of sound, shouts, savage cries, the beating of a drum, the noise of musketry. I sprang to my feet, and went to the door to meet Rolfe crossing the threshold.

He put his arm within mine and drew me out into the sunshine upon the doorstep. "I thought I should find you here," he said; "but it is only a room with its memories, Ralph. Out here is more breadth, more height. There is country yet, Ralph, and after a while, friends. The Indians are beginning to attack in force. Humphry Boyse is killed, and Morris Chaloner. There is smoke over the plantations up and down the river, as far as we can see, and awhile ago the body of a child drifted down to us."

"I am unarmed," I said. "I will but run to the fort for sword and musket"—

"No need," he answered. "There are the dead whom you may rob." The noise increasing as he spoke, we made no further tarrying, but, leaving behind us house and garden, hurried to the palisade.

CHAPTER XXXVIII
IN WHICH I GO UPON A QUEST

THROUGH a loophole in the gate of the palisade I looked, and saw the sandy neck joining the town to the main, and the deep and dark woods beyond, the fairy mantle giving invisibility to a host. Between us and that refuge dead men lay here and there, stiff and stark, with the black paint upon them, and the colored feathers of their headdresses red or blue against the sand. One warrior, shot through the back, crawled like a wounded beetle to the forest. We let him go, for we cared not to waste ammunition upon him.

I drew back from my loophole, and held out my hand to the women for a freshly loaded musket. A quick murmur like the drawing of a breath came from our line. The Governor, standing near me, cast an anxious glance along the stretch of wooden stakes that were neither so high nor so thick as they should have been. "I am new to this warfare, Captain Percy," he said. "Do they think to use those logs that they carry as battering rams?"

"As scaling ladders, your Honor," I replied. "It is on the cards that we may have some sword play, after all."

"We'll take your advice, the next time we build a palisade, Ralph Percy," muttered West on my other side. Mounting the breastwork that we had thrown up to shelter the women who were to load the muskets, he coolly looked over the pales at the oncoming savages. "Wait until they pass the blasted pine, men!" he cried. "Then give them a hail of lead that will beat them back to the Pamunkey!"

An arrow whistled by his ear; a second struck him on the shoulder, but pierced not his coat of mail. He came down from his dangerous post with a laugh.

"If the leader could be picked off"—I said. "It's a long shot, but there's no harm in trying."

As I spoke I raised my gun to my shoulder; but he leaned across Rolfe, who stood between us, and plucked me by the sleeve. "You've not looked at him closely. Look again."

I did as he told me, and lowered my musket. It was not for me to send that Indian leader to his account. Rolfe's lips tightened and a sudden pallor overspread his face. "Nantauquas?" he muttered in my ear, and I nodded yes.

The volley that we fired full into the ranks of our foe was deadly, and we looked to see them turn and flee, as they had fled before. But this time they were led by one who had been trained in English steadfastness. Broken for the moment, they rallied and came on yelling, bearing logs, thick branches of trees, oars tied together,—anything by whose help they could hope to surmount the palisade. We fired again, but they had planted their ladders. Before we could snatch the loaded muskets from the women a dozen painted figures appeared above the sharpened stakes. A moment, and they and a score behind them had leaped down upon us.

It was no time now to skulk behind a palisade. At all hazards, that tide from the forest must be stemmed. Those that were amongst us we might kill, but more were swarming after them, and from the neck came the exultant yelling of madly hurrying reinforcements.

We flung open the gates. I drove my sword through the heart of an Indian who would have opposed me, and, calling for men to follow me, sprang forward. Perhaps thirty came at my call; together we made for the opening. A party of the savages in our midst interposed. We set upon them with sword and musket butt, and though they fought like very devils drove them before us through the gateway. Behind us were wild clamor, the shrieking of women, the stern shouts of the English, the whooping of the savages; before us a rush that must be met and turned.

It was done. A moment's fierce fighting, then the Indians wavered, broke, and fled. Like sheep we drove them before us, across the neck, to the edge of the forest, into which they plunged. Into that ambush we cared not to follow, but fell back to the palisade and the town, believing, and with reason, that the lesson had been taught. The strip of sand was strewn with the dead and the dying, but they belonged not to us. Our dead numbered but three, and we bore their bodies with us.

Within the palisade we found the English in sufficiently good case. Of the score or more Indians cut off by us from their mates and penned within that death trap, half at least were already dead, run through with sword and pike, shot down with the muskets that there was now time to load. The remainder, hemmed about, pressed against the wall, were fast meeting with a like fate. They stood no chance against us; we cared not to make prisoners of them; it was a slaughter, but they had taken the initiative. They fought with the courage of despair, striving to spring in upon us, striking when they could with hatchet and knife, and through it all talking and laughing, making God knows what savage boasts, what taunts against the English, what references to the hunting grounds to which they were going. They were brave men that we slew that day.

At last there was left but the leader,—unharmed, unwounded, though time and again he had striven to close with some one of us, to strike and to die striking with his fellows. Behind him was the wall: of the half circle which he faced well-nigh all were old soldiers and servants of the colony, gentlemen none of whom had come in later than Dale,—Rolfe, West, Wynne, and others. We were swordsmen all. When in his desperation he would have thrown himself upon us, we contented ourselves with keeping him at sword's length, and at last West sent the knife in the dark hand whirling over the palisade. Some one had shouted to the musketeers to spare him.

When he saw that he stood alone, he stepped back against the wall, drew himself up to his full height, and folded his arms. Perhaps he thought that we would shoot him down then and there; perhaps he saw himself a captive amongst us, a show for the idle and for the strangers that the ships brought in.

The din had ceased, and we the living, the victors, stood and looked at the vanquished dead at our feet, and at the dead beyond the gates, and at the neck upon which was no living foe, and at the blue sky bending over all. Our hearts told us, and told us truly, that the lesson had been taught, that no more forever need we at Jamestown fear an Indian attack. And then we looked at him whose life we had spared.

He opposed our gaze with his folded arms and his head held high and his back against the wall. Many of us could remember him, a proud, shy lad, coming for the first time from the forest with his sister to see the English village and its wonders. For idleness we had set him in our midst that summer day, long ago, on the green by the fort, and had called him "your royal highness," laughing at the quickness of our wit, and admiring the spirit and bearing of the lad and the promise he gave of a splendid manhood. And all knew the tale I had brought the night before.

Slowly, as one man, and with no spoken word, we fell back, the half circle straightening into a line and leaving a clear pathway to the open gates. The wind had ceased to blow, I remember, and a sunny stillness lay upon the sand, and the rough-hewn wooden stakes, and a little patch of tender grass across which stretched a dead man's arm. The church bells began to ring.

The Indian out of whose path to life and freedom we had stepped glanced from the line of lowered steel to the open gates and the forest beyond, and understood. For a full minute he waited, moving not a muscle, still and stately as some noble masterpiece in bronze. Then he stepped from the shadow of the wall and moved past us through the sunshine that turned the eagle feather in his scalp lock to gold. His eyes were fixed upon the forest; there was no change in the superb calm of his face. He went by the huddled dead and the long line of the living that spoke no word, and out of the gates and across the neck, walking slowly that we might yet shoot him down if we saw fit to repent ourselves, and proudly like a king's son. There was no sound save the church bells ringing for our deliverance. He reached the shadow of the trees: a moment, and the forest had back her own.

We sheathed our swords and listened to the Governor's few earnest words of thankfulness and of recognition of this or that man's service, and then we set to work to clear the ground of the dead, to place sentinels, to bring the town into order, to determine what policy we should pursue, to search for ways by which we might reach and aid those who might be yet alive in the plantations above and below us.

We could not go through the forest where every tree might hide a foe, but there was the river. For the most part, the houses of the English had been built, like mine at Weyanoke, very near to the water. I volunteered to lead a party up river, and Wynne to go with another toward the bay. But as the council at the Governor's was breaking up, and as Wynne and I were hurrying off to make our choice of the craft at the landing, there came a great noise from the watchers upon the bank, and a cry that boats were coming down the stream.

It was so, and there were in them white men, nearly all of whom had their wounds to show, and cowering women and children. One boat had come from the plantation at Paspahegh, and two from Martin-Brandon; they held all that were left of the people.... A woman had in her lap the body of a child, and would not let us take it from her; another, with a half-severed arm, crouched above a man who lay in his blood in the bottom of the boat.

Thus began that strange procession that lasted throughout the afternoon and night and into the next day, when a sloop came down from Henricus with the news that the English were in force there to stand their ground, although their loss had been heavy. Hour after hour they came as fast as sail and oar could bring them, the panic-stricken folk, whose homes were burned, whose kindred were slain, who had themselves escaped as by a miracle. Many were sorely wounded, so that they died when we lifted them from the boats; others had slighter hurts. Each boatload had the same tale to tell of treachery, surprise, and fiendish butchery. Wherever it had been possible the English had made a desperate defense, in the face of which the savages gave way and finally retired to the forest. Contrary to their wont, the Indians took few prisoners, but for the most part slew outright those whom they seized, wreaking their spite upon the senseless corpses. A man too good for this world, George Thorpe, who would think no evil, was killed and his body mutilated by those whom he had taught and loved. And Nathaniel Powel was dead, and four others of the Council, besides many more of name and note. There were many women slain and little children.

From the stronger hundreds came tidings of the number lost, and that the survivors would hold the homes that were left, for the time at least. The Indians had withdrawn; it remained to be seen if they were satisfied with the havoc they had wrought. Would his Honor send by boat—there could be no traveling through the woods—news of how others had fared, and also powder and shot?

Before the dawning we had heard from all save the remoter settlements. The blow had been struck, and the hurt was deep. But it was not beyond remedy, thank God! It is known what measures we took for our protection, and how soon the wound to the colony was healed, and what vengeance we meted out to those who had set upon us in the dark, and had failed to reach the heart. These things belong to history, and I am but telling my own story,—mine and another's.

In the chill and darkness of the hour before dawn something like quiet fell upon the distracted, breathless town. There was a pause in the coming of the boats. The wounded and the dying had been cared for, and the noise of the women and the children was stilled at last. All was well at the palisade; the strong party encamped upon the neck reported the forest beyond them as still as death.

In the Governor's house was held a short council, subdued and quiet, for we were all of one mind and our words were few. It was decided that the George should sail at once with the tidings, and with an appeal for arms and powder and a supply of men. The Esperance would still be with us, besides the Hope-in-God and the Tiger; the Margaret and John would shortly come in, being already overdue.

"My Lord Carnal goes upon the George, gentlemen," said Master Pory. "He sent but now to demand if she sailed to-morrow. He is ill, and would be at home."

One or two glanced at me, but I sat with a face like stone, and the Governor, rising, broke up the council.

I left the house, and the street that was lit with torches and noisy with going to and fro, and went down to the river. Rolfe had been detained by the Governor, West commanded the party at the neck. There were great fires burning along the river bank, and men watching for the incoming boats; but I knew of a place where no guard was set, and where one or two canoes were moored. There was no firelight there, and no one saw me when I entered a canoe and cut the rope and pushed off from the land.

Well-nigh a day and a night had passed since Lady Wyatt had told me that which made for my heart a night-time indeed. I believed my wife to be dead,—yea, I trusted that she was dead. I hoped that it had been quickly over,—one blow.... Better that, oh, better that a thousand times, than that she should have been carried off to some village, saved to-day to die a thousand deaths to-morrow.

But I thought that there might have been left, lying on the dead leaves of the forest, that fair shell from which the soul had flown. I knew not where to go,—to the north, to the east, to the west,—but go I must. I had no hope of finding that which I went to seek, and no thought but to take up that quest. I was a soldier, and I had stood to my post; but now the need was past, and I could go. In the hall at the Governor's house, I had written a line of farewell to Rolfe, and had given the paper into the hand of a trusty fellow, charging him not to deliver it for two hours to come.

I rowed two miles downstream through the quiet darkness,—so quiet after the hubbub of the town. When I turned my boat to the shore the day was close at hand. The stars were gone, and a pale, cold light, more desolate than the dark, streamed from the east across which ran, like a faded blood stain, a smear of faint red. Upon the forest the mist lay heavy. When I drove the boat in amongst the sedge and reeds below the bank, I could see only the trunks of the nearest trees, hear only the sullen cry of some river bird that I had disturbed.

Why I was at some pains to fasten the boat to a sycamore that dipped a pallid arm into the stream I do not know. I never thought to come back to the sycamore; I never thought to bend to an oar again, to behold again the river that the trees and the mist hid from me before I had gone twenty yards into the forest.

CHAPTER XXXIX
IN WHICH WE LISTEN TO A SONG

IT was like a May morning, so mild was the air, so gay the sunshine, when the mist had risen. Wild flowers were blooming, and here and there unfolding leaves made a delicate fretwork against a deep blue sky. The wind did not blow; everywhere were stillness soft and sweet, dewy freshness, careless peace.

Hour after hour I walked slowly through the woodland, pausing now and then to look from side to side. It was idle going, wandering in a desert with no guiding star. The place where I would be might lie to the east, to the west. In the wide enshrouding forest I might have passed it by. I believed not that I had done so. Surely, surely I should have known; surely the voice that lived only in my heart would have called to me to stay.

Beside a newly felled tree, in a glade starred with small white flowers, I came upon the bodies of a man and a boy, so hacked, so hewn, so robbed of all comeliness, that at the sight the heart stood still and the brain grew sick. Farther on was a clearing, and in its midst the charred and blackened walls of what had been a home. I crossed the freshly turned earth, and looked in at the cabin door with the stillness and the sunshine. A woman lay dead upon the floor, her outstretched hand clenched upon the foot of a cradle. I entered the room, and, looking within the cradle, found that the babe had not been spared. Taking up the little waxen body with the blood upon its innocent breast, I laid it within the mother's arms, and went my way over the sunny doorstep and the earth that had been made ready for planting. A white butterfly—the first of the year—fluttered before me; then rose through a mist of green and passed from my sight.

The sun climbed higher into the deep blue sky. Save where grew pines or cedars there were no shadowy places in the forest. The slight green of uncurling leaves, the airy scarlet of the maples, the bare branches of the tardier trees, opposed no barrier to the sunlight. It streamed into the world below the treetops, and lay warm upon the dead leaves and the green moss and the fragile wild flowers. There was a noise of birds, and a fox barked. All was lightness, gayety, and warmth; the sap was running, the heyday of the spring at hand. Ah! to be riding with her, to be going home through the fairy forest, the sunshine, and the singing!... The happy miles to Weyanoke, the smell of the sassafras in its woods, the house all lit and trimmed. The fire kindled, the wine upon the table... Diccon's welcoming face, and his hand upon Black Lamoral's bridle; the minister, too, maybe, with his great heart and his kindly eyes; her hand in mine, her head upon my breast—

The vision faded. Never, never, never for me a home-coming such as that, so deep, so dear, so sweet. The men who were my friends, the woman whom I loved, had gone into a far country. This world was not their home. They had crossed the threshold while I lagged behind. The door was shut, and without were the night and I.

With the fading of the vision came a sudden consciousness of a presence in the forest other than my own. I turned sharply, and saw an Indian walking with me, step for step, but with a space between us of earth and brown tree trunks and drooping branches. For a moment I thought that he was a shadow, not substance; then I stood still, waiting for him to speak or to draw nearer. At the first glimpse of the bronze figure I had touched my sword, but when I saw who it was I let my hand fall. He too paused, but he did not offer to speak. With his hand upon a great bow, he waited, motionless in the sunlight. A minute or more thus; then I walked on with my eyes upon him.

At once he addressed himself to motion, not speaking or making any sign or lessening the distance between us, but moving as I moved through the light and shade, the warmth and stillness, of the forest. For a time I kept my eyes upon him, but soon I was back with my dreams again. It seemed not worth while to wonder why he walked with me, who was now the mortal foe of the people to whom he had returned.

From the river bank, the sycamore, and the boat that I had fastened there, I had gone northward toward the Pamunkey; from the clearing and the ruined cabin with the dead within it, I had turned to the eastward. Now, in that hopeless wandering, I would have faced the north again. But the Indian who had made himself my traveling companion stopped short, and pointed to the east. I looked at him, and thought that he knew, maybe, of some war party between us and the Pamunkey, and would save me from it. A listlessness had come upon me, and I obeyed the pointing finger.

So, estranged and silent, with two spears' length of earth between us, we went on until we came to a quiet stream flowing between low, dark banks. Again I would have turned to the northward, but the son of Powhatan, gliding before me, set his face down the stream, toward the river I had left. A minute in which I tried to think and could not, because in my ears was the singing of the birds at Weyanoke; then I followed him.

How long I walked in a dream, hand in hand with the sweetness of the past, I do not know; but when the present and its anguish weighed again upon my heart it was darker, colder, stiller, in the forest. The soundless stream was bright no longer; the golden sunshine that had lain upon the earth was all gathered up; the earth was dark and smooth and bare, with not a flower; the tree trunks were many and straight and tall. Above were no longer brown branch and blue sky, but a deep and sombre green, thick woven, keeping out the sunlight like a pall. I stood still and gazed around me, and knew the place.

To me, whose heart was haunted, the dismal wood, the charmed silence, the withdrawal of the light, were less than nothing. All day I had looked for one sight of horror; yea, had longed to come at last upon it, to fall beside it, to embrace it with my arms. There, there, though it should be some fair and sunny spot, there would be my haunted wood. As for this place of gloom and stillness, it fell in with my mood. More welcome than the mocking sunshine were this cold and solemn light, this deathlike silence, these ranged pines. It was a place in which to think of life as a slight thing and scarcely worth the while, given without the asking, spent in turmoil, strife, suffering, and longings all in vain. Easily laid down, too,—so easily laid down that the wonder was—

I looked at the ghostly wood, and at the dull stream, and at my hand upon the hilt of the sword that I had drawn halfway from the scabbard. The life within that hand I had not asked for. Why should I stand like a soldier left to guard a thing not worth the guarding; seeing his comrades march homeward, hearing a cry to him from his distant hearthstone?

I drew my sword well-nigh from its sheath; and then of a sudden I saw the matter in a truer light; knew that I was indeed the soldier, and willed to be neither coward nor deserter. The blade dropped back into the scabbard with a clang, and, straightening myself, I walked on beside the sluggish stream deep into the haunted wood.

Presently it occurred to me to glance aside at the Indian who had kept pace with me through the forest. He was not there; he walked with me no longer; save for myself there seemed no breathing creature in the dim wood. I looked to right and left, and saw only the tall, straight pines and the needle-strewn ground. How long he had been gone I could not tell. He might have left me when first we came to the pines, for my dreams had held me, and I had not looked his way.

There was that in the twilight place, or in the strangeness, the horror, and the yearning that had kept company with me that day, or in the dull weariness of a mind and body overwrought of late, which made thought impossible. I went on down the stream toward the river, because it chanced that my face was set in that direction.

How dark was the shadow of the pines, how lifeless the earth beneath, how faint and far away the blue that showed here and there through rifts in the heavy roof of foliage! The stream bending to one side I turned with it, and there before me stood the minister!

I do not know what strangled cry burst from me. The earth was rocking, all the wood a glare of light. As for him, at the sight of me and the sound of my voice he had staggered back against a tree; but now, recovering himself, he ran to me and put his great arms about me. "From the power of the dog, from the lion's mouth," he cried brokenly. "And they slew thee not, Ralph, the heathen who took thee away! Yesternight I learned that you lived, but I looked not for you here."

I scarce heard or marked what he was saying, and found no time in which to wonder at his knowledge that I had not perished. I only saw that he was alone, and that in the evening wood there was no sign of other living creature.

"Yea, they slew me not, Jeremy," I said. "I would that they had done so. And you are alone? I am glad that you died not, my friend; yes, faith, I am very glad that one escaped. Tell me about it, and I will sit here upon the bank and listen. Was it done in this wood? A gloomy deathbed, friend, for one so young and fair. She should have died to soft music, in the sunshine, with flowers about her."

With an exclamation he put me from him, but kept his hand upon my arm and his steady eyes upon my face.

"She loved laughter and sunshine and sweet songs," I continued. "She can never know them in this wood. They are outside; they are outside the world, I think. It is sad, is it not? Faith, I think it is the saddest thing I have ever known."

He clapped his other hand upon my shoulder. "Wake, man!" he commanded. "If thou shouldst go mad now—Wake! thy brain is turning. Hold to thyself. Stand fast, as thou art soldier and Christian! Ralph, she is not dead. She will wear flowers,—thy flowers,—sing, laugh, move through the sunshine of earth for many and many a year, please God! Art listening, Ralph? Canst hear what I am saying?"

"I hear," I said at last, "but I do not well understand."

He pushed me back against a pine, and held me there with his hands upon my shoulders. "Listen," he said, speaking rapidly and keeping his eyes upon mine. "All those days that you were gone, when all the world declared you dead, she believed you living. She saw party after party come back without you, and she believed that you were left behind in the forest. Also she knew that the George waited but for the search to be quite given over, and for my Lord Carnal's recovery. She had been told that the King's command might not be defied, that the Governor had no choice but to send her from Virginia. Ralph, I watched her, and I knew that she meant not to go upon that ship. Three nights agone she stole from the Governor's house, and, passing through the gates that the sleeping warder had left unfastened, went toward

- 250 -

the forest. I saw her and followed her, and at the edge of the forest I spoke to her. I stayed her not, I brought her not back, Ralph, because I was convinced that an I did so she would die. I knew of no great danger, and I trusted in the Lord to show me what to do, step by step, and how to guide her gently back when she was weary of wandering,—when, worn out, she was willing to give up the quest for the dead. Art following me, Ralph?"

"Yes," I answered, and took my hand from my eyes. "I was nigh mad, Jeremy, for my faith was not like hers. I have looked on Death too much of late, and yesterday all men believed that he had come to dwell in the forest and had swept clean his house before him. But you escaped, you both escaped"—

"God's hand was over us," he said reverently. "This is the way of it. She had been ill, you know, and of late she had taken no thought of food or sleep. She was so weak, we had to go so slowly, and so winding was our path, who knew not the country, that the evening found us not far upon our way, if way we had. We came to a cabin in a clearing, and they whose home it was gave us shelter for the night. In the morning, when the father and son would go forth to their work we walked with them. When they came to the trees they meant to fell we bade them good-by, and went on alone. We had not gone an hundred paces when, looking back, we saw three Indians start from the dimness of the forest and set upon and slay the man and the boy. That murder done they gave chase to me, who caught up thy wife and ran for both our lives. When I saw that they were light of foot and would overtake me, I set my burden down, and, drawing a sword that I had with me, went back to meet them halfway. Ralph, I slew all three,—may the Lord have mercy on my soul! I knew not what to think of that attack, the peace with the Indians being so profound, and I began to fear for thy wife's safety. She knew not the woods, and I managed to turn our steps back toward Jamestown without her knowledge that I did so. It was about midday when we saw the gleam of the river through the trees before us, and heard the sound of firing and of a great yelling. I made her crouch within a thicket, while I myself went forward to reconnoitre, and well-nigh stumbled into the midst of an army. Yelling, painted, maddened, brandishing their weapons toward the town, human hair dabbled with blood at the belts of many—in the name of God, Ralph, what is the meaning of it all?"

"It means," I said, "that yesterday they rose against us and slew us by the hundred. The town was warned and is safe. Go on."

"I crept back to madam," he continued, "and hurried her away from that dangerous neighborhood. We found a growth of bushes and hid ourselves within it, and just in time, for from the north came a great band of picked warriors, tall and black and wondrously feathered, fresh to the fray, whatever the fray might be. They joined themselves to the imps upon the river bank, and presently we heard another great din with more firing and more yelling. Well, to make a long story short, we crouched there in the bushes until late afternoon, not knowing what was the matter, and not daring to venture forth to find out. The woman of the cabin at which we had slept had given us a packet of bread and meat, so we were not without food, but the time was long. And then of a sudden the wood around us was filled with the heathen, band after band, coming from the river, stealing like serpents this way and that into the depths of the forest. They saw us not in the thick bushes; maybe it was because of the prayers which I said with might and main. At last the distance swallowed them, the forest seemed clear, no sound, no motion. Long we waited, but with the sunset we stole from the bushes and down an aisle of the forest toward the river, rounded a little wood of cedar, and came full upon perhaps fifty of the savages"—He paused to draw a great breath and to raise his brows after a fashion that he had.

"Go on, go on!" I cried. "What did you do? You have said that she is alive and safe!"

"She is," he answered, "but no thanks to me, though I did set lustily upon that painted fry. Who led them, d' ye think, Ralph? Who saved us from those bloody hands?"

A light broke in upon me. "I know," I said. "And he brought you here"—

"Ay, he sent away the devils whose color he is, worse luck! He told us that there were Indians, not of his tribe, between us and the town. If we went on we should fall into their hands. But there was a place that was shunned by the Indian as by the white man: we could bide there until the morrow, when we might find the woods clear. He guided us to this dismal wood that was not altogether strange to us. Ay, he told her that you were alive. He said no more than that; all at once, when we were well within the wood and the twilight was about us, he was gone."

He ceased to speak, and stood regarding me with a smile upon his rugged face. I took his hand and raised it to my lips. "I owe you more than I can ever pay," I said. "Where is she, my friend?"

"Not far away," he answered. "We sought the centre of the wood, and because she was so chilled and weary and shaken I did dare to build a fire there. Not a foe has come against us, and we waited but for the dusk of this evening to try to make the town. I came down to the stream just now to find, if I could, how near we were to the river"—

He broke off, made a gesture with his hand toward one of the long aisles of pine trees, and then, with a muttered "God bless you both," left me, and going a little way down the stream, stood with his back to a great tree and his eyes upon the slow, deep water.

She was coming. I watched the slight figure grow out of the dusk between the trees, and the darkness in which I had walked of late fell away. The wood that had been so gloomy was a place of sunlight and song; had red roses sprung up around me I had felt no wonder. She came softly and slowly, with bent head and hanging arms, not knowing that I was near. I went not to meet her,—it was my fancy to have her come to me still,—but when she raised her eyes and saw me I fell upon my knees.

For a moment she stood still, with her hands at her bosom; then, softly and slowly through the dusky wood, she came to me and touched me upon the shoulder. "Art come to take me home?" she asked. "I have wept and prayed and waited long, but now the spring is here and the woods are growing green."

I took her hands and bowed my head upon them. "I believed thee dead," I said. "I thought that thou hadst gone home, indeed, and I was left in the world alone. I can never tell thee how I love thee."

"I need no telling," she answered. "I am glad that I did so forget my womanhood as to come to Virginia on such an errand; glad that they did laugh at and insult me in the meadow at Jamestown, for else thou mightst have given me no thought; very heartily glad that thou didst buy me with thy handful of tobacco. With all my heart I love thee, my knight, my lover, my lord and husband"—Her voice broke, and I felt the trembling of her frame. "I love not thy tears upon my hands," she murmured. "I have wandered far and am weary. Wilt rise and put thy arm around me and lead me home?"

I stood up, and she came to my arms like a tired bird to its nest. I bent my head, and kissed her upon the brow, the blue-veined eyelids, the perfect lips. "I love thee," I said. "The song is old, but it is sweet. See! I wear thy color, my lady."

The hand that had touched the ribbon upon my arm stole upwards to my lips. "An old song, but a sweet one," she said. "I love thee. I will always love thee. My head may lie upon thy breast, but my heart lies at thy feet."

There was joy in the haunted wood, deep peace, quiet thankfulness, a springtime of the heart,—not riotous like the May, but fair and grave and tender like the young world in the sunshine without the pines. Our lips met again, and then, with my arm around her, we moved to the giant pine beneath which stood the minister. He turned at our approach, and looked at us with a quiet and tender smile, though the water stood in his eyes. "'Heaviness may endure for a night,'" he said, "'but joy cometh in the morning.' I thank God for you both."

"Last summer, in the green meadow, we knelt before you while you blessed us, Jeremy," I answered. "Bless us now again, true friend and man of God."

He laid his hands upon our bowed heads and blessed us, and then we three moved through the dismal wood and beside the sluggish stream down to the great bright river. Ere we reached it the pines had fallen away, the haunted wood was behind us, our steps were set through a fairy world of greening bough and springing bloom. The blue sky laughed above, the late sunshine barred our path with gold. When we came to the river it lay in silver at our feet, making low music amongst its reeds.

I had bethought me of the boat which I had fastened that morning to the sycamore between us and the town, and now we moved along the river bank until we should come to the tree. Though we walked through an enemy's country we saw no foe. Stillness and peace encompassed us; it was like a beautiful dream from which one fears no wakening.

As we went, I told them, speaking low, for we knew not if we were yet in safety, of the slaughter that had been made and of Diccon. My wife shuddered and wept, and the minister drew long breaths while his hands opened and closed. And then, when she asked me, I told of how I had been trapped to the ruined hut that night and of all that had followed. When I had done she turned within my arm and clung to me with her face hidden. I kissed her and comforted her, and presently we came to the sycamore tree reaching out over the clear water, and to the boat that I had fastened there.

The sunset was nigh at hand, and all the west was pink. The wind had died away, and the river lay like tinted glass between the dark borders of the forest. Above the sky was blue, while in the south rose clouds that were like pillars, tall and golden. The air was soft as silk; there was no sound other than the ripple of the water about our keel and the low dash of the oars. The minister rowed, while I sat idle beside my love. He would have it so, and I made slight demur.

We left the bank behind us and glided into the midstream, for it was as well to be out of arrowshot. The shadow of the forest was gone; still and bright around us lay the mighty river. When at length the boat head turned to the west, we saw far up the stream the roofs of Jamestown, dark against the rosy sky.

"There is a ship going home," said the minister.

We to whom he spoke looked with him down the river, and saw a tall ship with her prow to the ocean. All her sails were set; the last rays of the sinking sun struck against her poop windows and made of them a half-moon of fire. She went slowly, for the wind was light, but she went surely, away from the new land back to the old, down the stately river to the bay and the wide ocean, and to the burial at sea of one upon her. With her pearly sails and the line of flame color beneath, she looked a dwindling cloud; a little while, and she would be claimed of the distance and the dusk.

"It is the George," I said.

The lady who sat beside me caught her breath. "Ay, sweetheart," I went on. "She carries one for whom she waited. He has gone from out our life forever."

She uttered a low cry and turned to me, trembling, her lips parted, her eyes eloquent. "We will not speak of him," I said. "As if he were dead let his name rest between us. I have another thing to tell thee, dear heart, dear court lady masking as a waiting damsel, dear ward of the King whom his Majesty hath thundered against for so many weary months. Would it grieve thee to go home, after all?"

"Home?" she asked. "To Weyanoke? That would not grieve me."

"Not to Weyanoke, but to England," I said. "The George is gone, but three days since the Esperance came in. When she sails again I think that we must go."

She gazed at me with a whitening face. "And you?" she whispered. "How will you go? In chains?"

I took her clasped hands, parted them, and drew her arms around my neck. "Ay," I answered, "I will go in chains that I care not to have broken. My dear love, I think that the summer lies fair before us. Listen while I tell thee of news that the Esperance brought."

While I told of new orders from the Company to the Governor and of my letter from Buckingham, the minister rested upon his oars that he might hear the better. When I had ceased to speak he bent to them again, and his tireless strength sent us swiftly over the glassy water toward the town that was no longer distant. "I am more glad than I can tell you, Ralph and Jocelyn," he said, and the smile with which he spoke made his face beautiful.

The light streaming to us from the ruddy west laid roses in the cheeks of the sometime ward of the King, and the low wind lifted the dark hair from her forehead. Her head was on my breast, her hand in mine; we cared not to speak, we were so happy. On her finger was her wedding ring, the ring that was only a link torn from the gold chain Prince Maurice had given me. When she saw my eyes upon it, she raised her hand and kissed the rude circlet.

The hue of the sunset lingered in cloud and water, and in the pale heavens above the rose and purple shone the evening star. The cloudlike ship at which we had gazed was gone into the distance and the twilight; we saw her no more. Broad between its blackening shores stretched the James, mirroring the bloom in the west, the silver star, the lights upon the Esperance that lay between us and the town. Aboard her the mariners were singing, and their song of the sea floated over the water to us, sweetly and like a love song. We passed the ship unhailed, and glided on to the haven where we would be. The singing behind us died away, but the song in our hearts kept on. All things die not: while the soul lives, love lives: the song may be now gay, now plaintive, but it is deathless.

Milton Keynes UK
Ingram Content Group UK Ltd.
UKHW010710240424
441619UK00004B/409